COZUMEL

LATE MAYA SETTLEMENT PATTERNS

Academic Press Rapid Manuscript Reproduction

This is a volume in

Studies in Archaeology

A complete list of titles in this series appears at the end of this volume.

COZUMEL

LATE MAYA SETTLEMENT PATTERNS

David A. Freidel

Department of Anthropology
Southern Methodist University
Dallas, Texas

Jeremy A. Sabloff

Department of Anthropology
University of New Mexico
Albuquerque, New Mexico

1984

ACADEMIC PRESS, INC.
(Harcourt Brace Jovanovich, Publishers)
Orlando   San Diego   San Francisco   New York   London
Toronto   Montreal   Sydney   Tokyo   São Paulo

Cover: the Maya goddess Ix Chel, Lady Rainbow, patroness of Cozumel Island

ACADEMIC PRESS, INC.
Orlando, Florida 32887

United Kingdom Edition published by
ACADEMIC PRESS, INC. (LONDON) LTD.
24/28 Oval Road, London NW1 7DX

Library of Congress Cataloging in Publication Data

Freidel, David A.

  Cozumel, late Maya settlement patterns.

  (Studies in archaeology)
  Bibliography: p.
  Includes index.
  1. Mayas--Antiquities. 2. Cozumel Island (Mexico)--
Antiquities. 3. Indians of Mexico--Cozumel Island--
Antiquities. 4. Mexico--Antiquities. I. Sabloff,
Jeremy A. II. Title. III. Series.
F1435.1.C76F73 1984   972.81'01   83-12222
ISBN 0-12-266980-0

PRINTED IN THE UNITED STATES OF AMERICA

84 85 86 87   9 8 7 6 5 4 3 2 1

to
Alayne
Jennifer
Joshua
Saralinda
with all our love

CONTENTS

8. Cozumel during the Decadent Period: A Functional Synthesis

LIST OF PLATES

LIST OF FIGURES

LIST OF TABLES

PREFACE

Two of the fundamental goals of the Cozumel Archaeological Project, a joint project of the Peabody Museum, Harvard University, and the University of Arizona, with the cooperation and authorization of the Instituto Nacional de Antropología e Historia of Mexico, were to broaden and change traditional conceptions of ancient Maya trade and to increase our understanding of the nature of the Decadent period (Late Postclassic) in Yucatan. In moving from traditonal concerns with traded objects to a focus on the structure of trade and the role it played in the continuing development of Maya civilization, those of us concerned with the settlement survey of Cozumel Island soon realized that many of our assumptions concerning the spatial organization of trade, in general, and of Decadent period settlements, in particular, would have to be scrapped. For example, it soon became clear that our preconceived notion that we would find a single centralized port facility (by analogy, say, with Xicalango) did not hold. In other words, in order even to begin to understand Cozumel's role in the long-distance trading systems of Terminal Classic and Postclassic periods, let alone understand the processes involved in the changing trading systems of the time, we decided that we would have to study the spatial organization of the entire island and attempt to learn what factors helped cause this organization. As Binford (1977:9) has pointed out:

> Human or hominid behavior always takes place in a spatial theater. The way in which this behavior is organized must be conditioned by certain relationships between the properties of alternative spatial organizations and the labor and social pressures operative during periods of organized behavior. If we could isolate even some of the constraints that are operative, within a dynamic system, on the character of spatial usage, we might well be able to analyze at least some aspects of past behavioral systems in structural terms rather than the more commonly emphasized formal or content categories of tool frequencies, types and so on.

In this monograph, we present our hypotheses about the spatial organization of Cozumel based on our interpretation of the functions of the more than 30 sites on the island and their interrelationships. We focus our attention on the Decadent or Late Postclassic period (A.D. 1250–1519), which was the time when Cozumel reached its height in population and importance and to which most of our settlement data pertain.

This monograph is just one of a series of reports on the findings of the Cozumel Archaeological Project (see Sabloff and Rathje [1975b] for the background and history of the project). Other reports are either in press or are being prepared for publication. The senior author's doctoral dissertation at Harvard (Freidel 1976) served as the basis of this volume. The dissertation was edited, updated, and then expanded with the addition of excavated data, many new illustrations, and a reappraisal of our views on Cozumel's late prehispanic settlement.

ACKNOWLEDGMENTS

There are many people and institutions in both Mexico and the United States who made this study possible. A full listing of all the individuals who participated in the Cozumel Archaeological Project and all the people who helped us is given in Sabloff and Rathje (1975b:ix–x). Their help is greatly appreciated. However, we particularly single out three individuals here. First and foremost, William L. Rathje, the codirector of the project, has been a constant source of support and help, both intellectual and material. Second, we thank Judith (Conner) Propper, who directed many of the excavations illustrated in Chapter 6, and whose careful, detailed field notes form the basis of our discussions of the excavations. Her preliminary dating of ceramic materials from the sites discussed in Chapter 6 were quite helpful, too. Third, Richard Leventhal ably assisted Freidel during the 1973 season and has been a great help to us in our analyses of the settlement data.

The support of Mrs. C. Ayling and the National Geographic Society for our publishing program is appreciated. Sabloff additionally acknowledges the aid of a Faculty Research grant at the University of New Mexico that helped in the preparation of illustrations for this volume. The drawings were ably prepared by Robin Robertson, Barbara Westman, Whitney Powell, Charles Steinberg, and Jerry Livingston. The photographs, except where noted, were taken by members of the project's staff. The photographs by Loring Hewen are reproduced by courtesy of E. W. Andrews V and the Middle American Research Institute, Tulane University, whereas the photograph by William T. Sanders is reproduced through the courtesy of the Peabody Museum, Harvard University. We also thank Mrs. K. Andrews for her photograph of Aguada Grande.

Robin Robertson and Paula L. W. Sabloff have given us immense support and aid in the writing and preparation of the volume, and we are deeply grateful for their help. This report would never have been completed without their assistance.

Finally, our research and this monograph were made possible through the following individuals; we thank them all: Suzanne Abel, Anthony Andrews, Aníbal Enríquez Bringas and all the workers on Cozumel, William Davidson, David Gregory, C. C. Lamberg-Karlovsky, Eduardo Matos Moctezuma and all our colleagues in Mexico City and Merida, David Maybury-Lewis, David Phillips, Edwin Snider, George Stuart and the staff of the National Geographic Society, R. H. Thompson, Evon Vogt, Gordon Willey, and Stephen Williams. In addition, we are grateful for the assistance of Mary Kay Day, who typeset the book on the IBM Composer, and all the editorial staff of Academic Press.

CHAPTER 1

INTRODUCTION

And they held Cozumel and the well of Chichen Itza in the same veneration as we have for pilgrimages to Jerusalem and Rome, and so they used to go to visit these places and offer presents there, especially to Cozumel, as we do to holy places. (Landa in Tozzer 1941:109)

Geography

Cozumel is a corralline island, covering approximately 392 km^2 not including the lagoons, situated about 16 km off the northeastern coast of the Yucatan peninsula (Figure 1). The island is virtually a flat slab of limestone that has been exposed for a geologically short period of time. Its maximum elevation above sea level is approximately 15 m (Figure 2) (Davidson 1975:47-48). Slight variations in elevation, resulting in variable soil depth and drainage, seem to have been important to the island's Precolumbian occupants. Although soils are generally thin and lateritic, and vegetation is predominantly low-latitude dry forest, mangrove swamps border the coastal lagoons, and some of the higher parts of the island contain moderate rainforest growth (Davidson 1975:56-57). As is typical of the karstic formations of the peninsula, drainage is predominantly below the surface. This makes water accessible only through natural sinkholes and seasonally innundated basins or wells (although only modern ones are known). Precipitation averages 600 mm annually, falling mostly in early summer and early fall, and temperatures are exceptionally mild, ranging between 21 and 27°C. The natural resources on Cozumel are generally comparable to those found on the mainland coast of Quintana Roo.

History of Exploration

Cozumel's historical fame as a pilgrimage center has made it the subject of exploration by students of the Maya since Stephens and Catherwood first reported some small shrines near San Miguel in 1843. Masonry structures and ancient settlements were observed and published by several professional and amateur archaeologists prior to the Carnegie Institution of Washington's (Lothrop 1924) pathbreaking survey of the East Coast of Quintana Roo between 1916 and 1922 (Holmes 1895-1897; Arnold and Frost 1909; also see Mason 1927). These early reports contain information on extensive fieldwalls on the island, the placement of coastal shrines, and the presence of beveled, Puuc-style vaults at El Cedral. This information and that of later more comprehensive observers (Fernandez 1945; Escalona-Ramos 1946; Sanders 1955, 1960) have done little to rectify Cozumel's reputation among professionals as a cultural backwater characterized by diminutive shrines. Nevertheless, Sanders's (1960) stratified excavations and site descriptions, as well as the plans of numerous standing

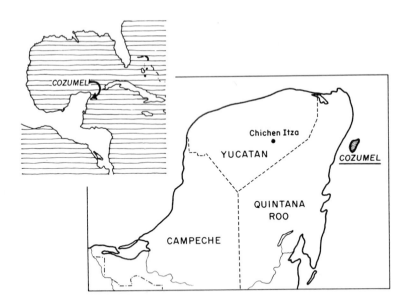

Figure 1. The location of Cozumel.

structures published by Fernandez, Escalona-Ramos, and Sanders, all pointed to a rich source of information on settlement patterns and considerable time depth for occupation on the island (Figures 3 and 4) (also see Sabloff and Rathje 1975b).

Most of the important standing structures and settlements examined in the course of the Harvard-Arizona survey were reported by Escalona-Ramos and Sanders. Important settlements such as Buena Vista (C18) and Chen Cedral (C23), not noted by these investigators, were reported by Davidson in his master's thesis (1967). However, the settlement of Zuuk (C31) and Eleven Mound (C14) as well as several isolated homesteads and shrines were professionally observed for the first time by the Harvard-Arizona Project (see Table 1).

The Harvard-Arizona Survey

The settlement survey and related excavations formed one part of the overall Harvard-Arizona Cozumel Archaeological Project. Although limitations on time and labor precluded a comprehensive and systematic exploration of the entire island and the gathering of information on flora and fauna,

the necessity of concentrating on the details of a select number of settlements turned out to be a serendipitous research strategy. Like those at Mayapan (Pollock *et al.* 1962), the foundations of perishable superstructures are remarkably well preserved on Cozumel. Combined with a relatively large visible sample of masonry superstructures associated with substructures and other features, this preservation encouraged the surveyors to gather as much detailed information as possible on the facilities in the settlements. From the beginning, the preservation of remains and the potentially large sample size encouraged the surveyors to attempt a functional analysis of settlement and community organization similar to that carried out so successfully at Mayapan.

Unfortunately, even the relatively modest goal of gathering as much information as possible on a few of Cozumel's settlements proved to be over-ambitious. When examined in detail, the complexity of settlements turned out to be considerably greater than what was reflected in the literature. As more attention was paid to the disposition of substructures and relatively inconspicuous super-structural foundation walls, the abundance of

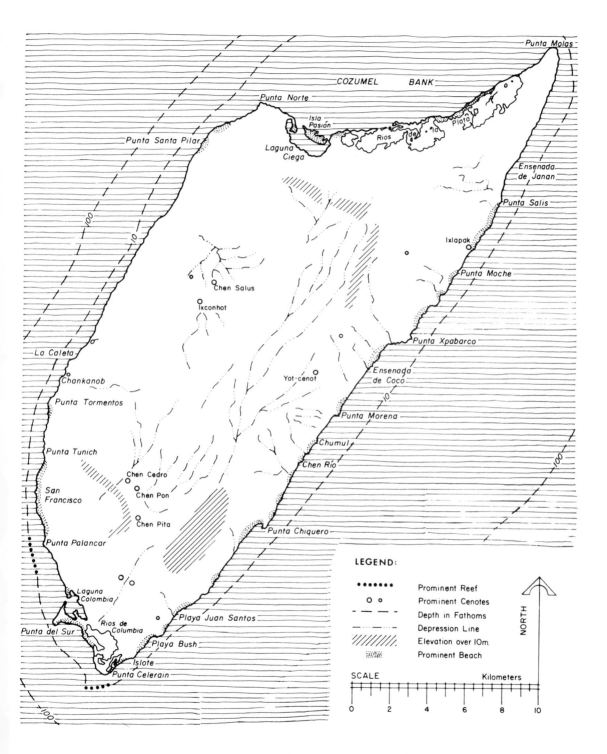

Figure 2. Geography of Cozumel (prepared by W. Davidson).

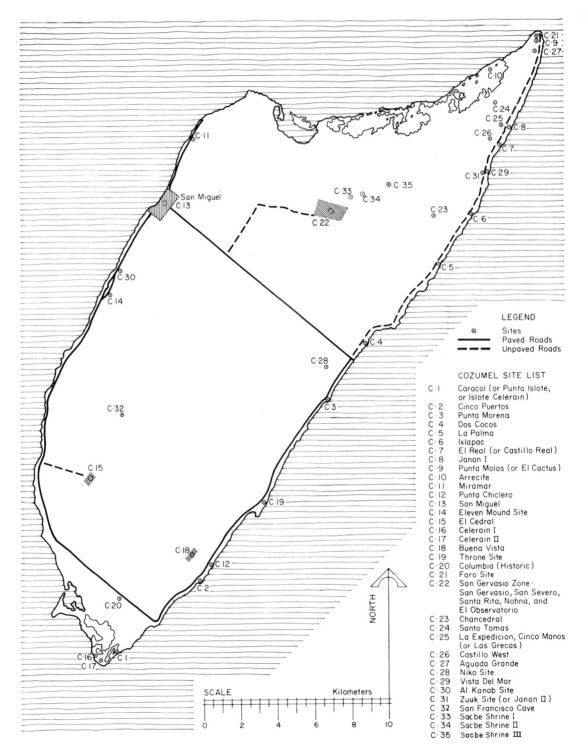

LEGEND

⊙   Sites
——   Paved Roads
– – –   Unpaved Roads

COZUMEL SITE LIST

C·1   Caracol (or Punta Islote, or Islote Celerain)
C·2   Cinco Puertos
C·3   Punta Morena
C·4   Dos Cocos
C·5   La Palma
C·6   Ixlapac
C·7   El Real (or Castillo Real)
C·8   Janan I
C·9   Punta Molas (or El Cactus)
C·10   Arrecife
C·11   Miramar
C·12   Punta Chiclero
C·13   San Miguel
C·14   Eleven Mound Site
C·15   El Cedral
C·16   Celerain I
C·17   Celerain II
C·18   Buena Vista
C·19   Throne Site
C·20   Columbia (Historic)
C·21   Faro Site
C·22   San Gervasio Zone: San Gervasio, San Severo, Santa Rita, Nohna, and El Observatorio
C·23   Chancedral
C·24   Santo Tomas
C·25   La Expedicion, Cinco Manos (or Las Grecas)
C·26   Castillo West
C·27   Aguada Grande
C·28   Niko Site
C·29   Vista Del Mar
C·30   Al Kanab Site
C·31   Zuuk Site (or Janan II)
C·32   San Francisco Cave
C·33   Sacbe Shrine I
C·34   Sacbe Shrine II
C·35   Sacbe Shrine III

SCALE   Kilometers

0   2   4   6   8   10

NORTH

Figure 3. Archaeological Sites of Cozumel.

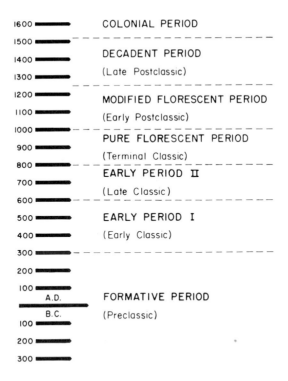

1600 ➤	COLONIAL PERIOD
1500 ➤	– – – – – – – – – – – – – – – – –
1400 ➤	DECADENT PERIOD
1300 ➤	(Late Postclassic)
1200 ➤	– – – – – – – – – – – – – – – –
	MODIFIED FLORESCENT PERIOD
1100 ➤	(Early Postclassic)
1000 ➤	– – – – – – – – – – – – – – – –
900 ➤	PURE FLORESCENT PERIOD
800 ➤	(Terminal Classic) – – – – – – – – –
700 ➤	EARLY PERIOD II
600 ➤	(Late Classic) – – – – – – – – – – –
500 ➤	EARLY PERIOD I
400 ➤	(Early Classic)
300 ➤	– – – – – – – – – – – – – – –
200 ➤	
100 ➤	
A.D.	FORMATIVE PERIOD
B.C.	(Preclassic)
100 ➤	
200 ➤	
300 ➤	

Figure 4. Chronological periods on Cozumel.

these features became increasingly apparent. Even at those sites that were intensively investigated, there is more additional information to be collected on the disposition of facilities. Several of the settlements that were only briefly explored by the surveyors deserve more comprehensive treatment. Hence the information gathered by the survey and presented in this monograph more generally reflects what is preserved on Cozumel than a systematic sample of available remains. It is, in essence, a preliminary exploration of variability in structure and settlement detail analogous to preliminary regional statements on gross size and location of prehistoric sites.

Mapping Techniques

Mapping techniques consisted of a combination of plane table and alidade, chain and compass, and pace and compass procedures. Individual structures were planned with chain and compass or plane table whereas substructures, fieldwalls, and *sacbes* (causeways) were, for the most part, mapped by pace and compass. Large features of particular importance, such as the main complex at Buena Vista, were mapped entirely by plane table and alidade.

Site and Structure Nomenclature

Sites are listed serially as they were encountered in the course of the project (see Figure 3 and Table 1) and designated by the name most commonly used by the local people or established in the literature (Escalona-Ramos 1946; Sanders 1960). Sites with several names are listed in Table 1. A *site* consists of an isolated structure or a concentration of structures that appear to form a settlement zone. In some cases, several sites referred to as discrete entities in the literature have been combined to form a single settlement zone. The sites of San Gervasio, Santa Rita, San Severo, Observatorio, and Nohna, for example, proved to be parts of one extensive settlement called San Gervasio (C22) by the Harvard-Arizona Project. Other sites, such as Ixlapac (C6) consist of single

Table 1
Names used by other observers of sites on Cozumel

Site numbers	Popular designation	Other observers
C1	Caracol	
	Islote de Celerain	Fernandez
	Punta Islote	Sanders
C2	Cinco Puertos	Fernandez
C3	Punta Morena	Hewen
C4	Dos Cocos	
C5	La Palma	Davidson and Hewen (?)
C6	Ixlapac	Davidson
C7	El Real	Sanders
		Escalona-Ramos
		Hewen
		Davidson
C8	Janan I	Sanders
C9	Punta Molas	Escalona-Ramos
		Sanders
C10	Arrecife	Sanders
		Mason and Spinden
C11	Miramar	Holmes
		Lothrop
		Escalona-Ramos
C12	Punta Chiclero	
C13	San Miguel	Stephens and Catherwood
		Holmes
		Escalona-Ramos
		Sanders
		Mason and Spinden
C14	Eleven Mound site	
C15	El Cedral	Holmes
		Fernandez
		Sanders
		Mason and Spinden
C16	Celerain I	Sanders
C17	Celerain II	Sanders
C18	Buena Vista	Davidson
C19	Throne site	
C20	Columbia	(Historic)
C21	Faro site	
C22	San Gervasio	Escalona-Ramos
	San Benito	Sanders
		Arnold and Frost
C23	Chen Cedral (Chancedral)	Davidson
C24	Santo Tomas	(Historic)
C25-38-a	Las Grecas	Escalona-Ramos
		Sanders
C25	La Expedicion	Escalona-Ramos
	Santo Tomas	Mason and Spinden
C26	Castillo West	
C27	Aguada Grande	Escalona-Ramos
		Sanders
C28	Niko site	
C29	Vista del Mar	
C30	Al Kanob site	
C31	Zuuk	
	Janan	Davidson
C32	San Francisco Cave	Davidson
C33	Sacbe Shrine I	
C34	Sacbe Shrine II	
	(Chen Palma)	
C35	Sacbe Shrine III	

(Compiled from Arnold and Frost 1909; Davidson 1967; Escalona-Ramos 1946; Fernandez 1945; Holmes 1895-1897; Lothrop 1924; Mason 1927; Spinden field notes; Sanders 1955).

diminutive structures. In fact, the majority of sites shown in Figure 3 consist of isolated masonry religious structures or groups of such structures. The extent of major settlement zones are shown by hatched areas.

Structures resting on ground level are serially numbered by site. Substructures devoid of superstructural remains have only a second number following the hyphenated site designation. Thus a substructure at San Gervasio might be numbered C22-86. Superstructures resting on ground level are given a lowercase letter designation after their numbers. C25-8a, for example, is a dwelling resting directly on the ground at La Expedicion. If a superstructure rests on a support substructure of any kind, it receives a letter designation separated from its number by a hyphen. C1-1-a, for example, is a masonry structure on a low support substructure at Caracol. Several superstructures resting on a substructure are distinguished by letter designations. Hence C25-1-a through C25-1-e are superstructures on a group plaza at La Expedicion. Composite substructures, consisting of a number of level areas distinguished by variations in height and called *agglutinated substructures* in this monograph, are designated by a single number like simpler ground level structures.

Sacbes are designated by a capital *S* followed by a hyphenated number. They are listed serially by site.

Organization of the Monograph

The monograph is divided into three general parts. First, Chapters 2-5 deal with the functional typology of features on Cozumel. Second, Chapter 6 provides data on the major sites surveyed and discusses the settlement patterns of those sites based on the functional identifications made in Chapters 2 through 5. This discussion draws on general survey and limited excavation information concerning the composition of these settlements as well as analogies from the organization of Maya society at the time of the Spanish Conquest. Emphasis is placed on the manner in which sociocultural institutions express themselves spatially. Chapter 7 offers an overview of the Decadent period settlement patterns on the island. Third, Chapter 8 deals specifically with the functional identification of Cozumel as a whole.

Sabloff and Rathje (1975b) have proposed that Cozumel was a trading center as well as a pilgrimage center in Precolumbian times. That Cozumel was a pilgrimage center is an established fact and there is good reason to believe that additional research into the relationship between modern pilgrimage circuits and long-distance commercial networks in Mesoamerica will provide a very powerful analogical argument for the fact that all major pilgrimage centers were also commercial centers (V. Turner 1974). Indeed, there is reason to believe that this correlation is universally valid. Further discussion of the interpretation of Cozumel as a Decadent period trading center is offered in Chapters 6 through 8.

To end this introduction and begin the study on a personal note, it will be apparent to students of settlement pattern analysis that abstract and mathematically elegant models derived from cultural geography are avoided. Higher-order generalizations about social and spatial processes are, on the whole, superseded by particularistic statements concerning the Conquest period Maya and the organization of society on Cozumel. In other words, this is an attempted ethnography of a specific dead society.

The ideographic approach, as pointed out by Trigger (1973) and Sabloff and Willey (1967), is a necessary complement to higher-order propositions. Particularly when dealing with complex societies, the recognition of patterning in the archaeological record and empirical generalizations about such patterns may sometimes have to be established before a testable theory can be constructed (see Sabloff 1978). Moreover, just as the abstractions of social theory in anthropology are useful only insofar as they relate to specific variability and constancy in real-world cultural phenomena, so the processual generalizations of archaeological theory must be tested against the paleoethnographic detail that can be gleaned from the past.

Arguing for the primacy of higher-order theory over middle-range and low-level propositions is nonsensical. These analytical approaches stand or fall together. It is in the formulation of middle-range theories, particularly concatenations of social, economic, religious, and political processes that the role of analogy becomes crucial. Ultimately it is on this middle ground that archaeology can truly become anthropology, because it is here that we can offer, however, uncertainly, information and test ideas that are comparable to those dealt with by our colleagues in living societies. Although this monograph does not provide new theoretical advances, we hope that it offers the first halting steps toward building a methodology that will enable us to link mercantile behavior and the archaeological record, and ultimately toward the creation of theory that links trade and culture change in general.

CHAPTER 2

PERISHABLE STRUCTURES ON COZUMEL

We begin our analysis with a consideration of the total sample of structures observed in the course of survey. We present the analysis of Precolumbian structures on Cozumel in two parts for the sake of coherence. The first is on buildings with perishable upper portions; the second, on buildings with predominantly masonry upper portions. There is no justification for a functional division along this line. Even in terms of purely formal architectural criteria several structures straddle the two categories. Nevertheless, they reflect a division of the total sample into groups with comparable observed data.

Following our thematic treatment of dwellings as the most intractable type of structure to identify, we focus attention on the isolation of dwellings from nondwellings. We then try to place the residual structures into other functional categories. Frankly, we initially lumped most perishable structures into the functional category of *dwelling* in the field. Even after epistemological soul-searching and typological analysis, we find most of Cozumel's perishable structures conditionally identified as dwellings. This conclusion is as much a reflection of the limited nature of the data as of the various arguments brought to bear.

The Data

We have a total sample of 73 perishable structures for Cozumel. This sample includes only those buildings that were sufficiently well preserved to yield a plan. It excludes a large number of fragmentary walls and substructures without observable remains of superstructures on them.

The former are included in discussions of particular types they may fall into, whereas the latter are treated separately in another section.

In some cases the foundations were only partially preserved and our statistics on them are hence based on extrapolation. Many of the quantitative measurements were taken with relatively coarse techniques, such as pace and compass mapping. The reader should not be gulled by the precise quality of numbers into thinking that the measurements included in the analysis are anything more than a gross descriptive guideline to variability in the sample.

All the data relate to the imperishable residue of primary perishable structures that share the common feature of being observable without excavation. The major categories of information are

1. *Boundary Walls.* These determine the shape and size of the structure. Boundaries can be defined by foundation walls set into the ground, low masonry walls, or bench areas.
2. *Interior Partitions.* These are walls within the identified boundaries of the structure, which in turn allow the identification of multiple rooms.
3. *Interior Stone Roof Supports.* These are columns that are highly correlated with beam and mortar roofing. They allow the definition of large, open spaces combined with this heavy roofing material. However, columns also appear in structures without beam and mortar roofing.
4. *Bench Zones.* These are "interior platforms" (Harrison 1970) above the level of the

floor. They divide the space within structures into distinct units.

5. *Accessways.* Access to the interior of structures or rooms within structures is defined in a variety of ways that may have functional significance.

Minor categories of information relate to wall construction technique; floor covering material; associated features such as *chultuns* (underground storage pits), altars, and interments; location relative to other superstructures and substructures; and approximate cardinal orientation. Location in space is minor only in the sense that it is not one of the formal architectural criteria used in grouping the structures into types. It is crucial, however, in the assignment of function to structures as discussed below.

It should be noted that the kinds of information gathered were determined less by any hypothetical problems formulated prior to the survey than by what was feasible given the general objective of gathering as much data on as many structures as possible.

Method of Analysis

The information available for each structure was abstracted and recorded in terms of the categories given above. The structures were then compared and grouped by the number of shared traits. This approach produced a formal typology. However, there is a great deal of difference between a formal typology and a functional one.

A formal type can act as a functional type only if it can somehow be demonstrated that a correlation exists between the form and a given consistent set of activities. This fortunate situation exists only for a small number of structural types in the Maya area. These are normally shrines, temples, ballcourts, and sweatbaths. Smith (1962), however, used this kind of correlation with success at Mayapan for the identification of dwellings. Similarly, colonnaded structures at Mayapan (Proskouriakoff 1962) have been identified as public buildings. A fair amount of historical documentation can be used to support this latter proposition.

By using this approach, and by relying on previous identifications that fit our formal types, we can remove various kinds of specialized structures from the domain through a process of elimination. However, this still leaves us to deal with the bulk of the structures. Most of these, we intuitively believe, are dwellings. If we accept this conditional identification, we are admitting from the outset that Cozumel has a considerable variety of dwelling forms. Mayapan (Smith 1962:Figure 8) also yielded a variety of forms within the type *dwelling.* In this respect, the major contrast between Mayapan and Cozumel is that Cozumel's dwellings are single rather than two-roomed structures.

Lacking the kind of historical corroboration available for Mayapan's tandem plan two-roomed dwelling, we have no clear grounds for distinguishing the formal characteristics of dwellings on Cozumel from those of other kinds of structures. Hence we must marshal a wide variety of analogical arguments to justify our identifications. These arguments depend on generalizations about structure size, organization of interior space, and organization of buildings in space that are abstracted primarily from modern ethnographic reports. In the final analysis, we have no overall form-function correlation for dwellings on Cozumel. Instead we have a number of formal types that we identify on the basis of these kinds of generalizations as dwellings.

To allow the reader to follow the logic of our identifications, we now offer a brief outline of the generalizations used in the analysis. We begin with structure size.

Despite the normative and fragmentary nature of the data in it, Table 2 clearly demonstrates that no absolute size or size range can be established for modern Maya dwellings. A cutoff below 10 m^2 might be appropriate, as suggested by Haviland (1963), but there is not definite support for this. Useful statements on size-function correlations must be couched in relative terms. An ordinal arrangement of functional types by size as given in Table 3 lends some support to the generalization that Maya dwellings fall more or less in the middle range. Nondwellings are at the extremes. Dwellings, however, tend to cluster at the upper end of the middle range, if the Hispanic style public structures in most modern Maya communities are included. Given historical descriptions of contact period communities, it seems likely that the upper range of aboriginal structures has been truncated

Table 2
Ranges in absolute size of modern dwellings and other structures in the Maya area.

Community or Region	Size Range (m^2)
Tix-Cacal	60
Chontal	20-40
Chol	16-24
Tzotzil	16-42
Tzeltal	9-15
Tojolabal	28
Chorti	12-24
Chankom	47 and 20 (individual houses)
Tzimin	14 and 30 (individual houses)
Piste	28
Telchac pueblo	50
Yucatec apiary	17
Yucatec fowl hut	4.5
San Cristobal	22, 22, and 40 (individual houses)
San Pedro Laguna	17 and 32 (individual houses)
Coban	40
Santiago Atitlan	13 (average room size)
San Sebastian	46
Panajachel kitchen	10

[a]Compiled from Handbook of Middle American Indians, Vol. 7, Part 1; Wisdom 1940; Thompson 1938; Wauchope 1940.

[b]Average size for dwellings from ethnographic sources in 28 m^2.

along with the prehispanic institutions that used them.

The lower range, on the other hand, compares well with historical descriptions. This is in keeping with the general proposition that domestic activi-

ties have been subjected to less radical change than were community-wide activities.

We can go beyond the simple generalization that nondwellings tend to occur at the extremes of the size range only by combining size with relative location. Outbuilding types, such as apiaries, fowl huts, storage huts and pigpens consistently occur within household compounds. As a general rule they are smaller than the main dwelling. Notable exceptions to this rule are kitchens and shrines that may be the same size as the main dwelling(s). Although isolated temporary structures, such as milpa sleeping huts, do occur, isolated kitchens, fowl huts, storage huts, and so forth are not reported for the Maya area.

Modern public buildings occur in centralized locations and in the context of formal plaza areas. On the whole they are larger than dwellings and differ in construction materials. The argument that this situation reflects only postcontact hispanic notions of community layout can be countered with the observations of contact period towns by area (the best known being Landa's description [Tozzer 1941:62]).

The above are all probabilistic statements based on normative generalizations, but they are consistent with the available information.

The strongest ethnohistoric and ethnographic information on dwellings that we have relates to construction materials. The vast majority of dwellings, both modern and historical, are observed to be of perishable materials (Wauchope 1938). The accounts of the *Relaciones de Yucatan* (D.1., 1898:Vol. 11) consistently state that the dwellings of the common folk are perishable, whereas some of the caciques have stone houses,

Table 3
Ordinal arrangement by size of structures in modern Maya communities.

Community or Region	Size		
	Small ⟶	Medium ⟶	Large
Tix-Cacal	Fowl huts, pig pens, shrines, apiaries, houses, churches, barracks		
Chorti	Privy, storage huts, storehouses, shrines, kitchens, houses, cofradias		
Yucatan	Ovens, fowl huts, shrines, apiaries, storehouses, kitchens, houses		
Nekchi	Fowl huts, pig pens, shrines, kitchens, hermitages, houses, churches		
Lacandon	Fowl huts, kitchens, granaries, houses, ceremonial huts		
Zinacantan	Sweatbaths, granaries, houses, shrines (chapels), churches		
Tzeltal	Fowl huts, pig pens, sweatbaths, kitchens, houses, churches		

after the fashion of the Spaniards. For Cozumel in particular, Roys says: "There were many stone houses in the Cozumel towns; some had stone and mud masonry halfway up the walls, but all seem to have been thatched with straw" (1943:18). This observation is presumably based partly upon the *Itinerario* of Juan Diaz, chaplain to Grijalva. An alternative reading for the passage Roys draws on is given by Wagner: "All along it (the street) the citizens have many houses with foundations of stone. Halfway up the walls are of mud, and then they are covered with straw" (1942a:71). Although structures with partial masonry walls occur on Cozumel, most of the perishable structures would fit the second observation better. It is sometimes difficult to evaluate these early descriptions, however, for directly preceding the above quotation Juan Diaz says, "We went into the town, the houses of which were all of stone. Among others were five with towers on top, very elegantly built. . . The bases on which they are built cover much ground and are massive, but the tops occupy but small space. They looked like old buildings although there are also some new ones" (Wagner 1942a:71). His contradiction may be interpreted in two ways. In the first place, perhaps Diaz is describing the center of town in the second quotation and the outskirts in the first. This would be consistent with other descriptions of settlement layout for the period. Secondly (and alternately), Diaz may be using *house* as a gloss for any structure including temples or shrines. In this case, he would be describing the pyramidal substructures supporting temples or shrines as "towers." In either case, the statements are not necessarily contradictory.

Oviedo's account of this first encounter with the natives closely parallels Juan Diaz's second statement: "The captain and his men entered the town nearby which had stone houses with straw roofs" (Wagner 1942a:94). This would seem to support our first interpretation.

All the early accounts agree that the buildings used primarily to house idols—temples and shrines—were built of masonry. Nevertheless, we have reason to believe that some of these types of structures were built of perishable materials. Our reasoning is given below in discussion of the structures in question.

The only type of outbuilding that can be definitely inferred for Cozumel is the apiary. The accounts (Wagner 1942a) consistently point to the vast quantitites of honey and wax produced on Cozumel, both for home consumption and export. Bees are kept in hollow logs stacked in piles under thatched roofed open-sided structures in modern Yucatecan communities. The ground plans of modern apiaries vary little from those of dwellings except that they usually lack foundation walls. Although we believe that the method of housing bees has changed little since the contact period, it is possible that the apiaries of that time were considerably larger because their products played such an important role in Cozumel's economy.

Landa also mentions granaries and *chultuns* for storing and agricultural products, principally maize (Tozzer 1941:98, 195). Although *chultuns* are easily recognized archaeologically, we have no formal material concomitants for other storage facilities. Modern granaries found in domestic contexts are generally smaller than dwellings, and the granary that Wauchope illustrates (1938:Figure 49g) is distinctively square. The major characteristics of granaries on the whole seems to be either that they are raised off the ground or are furnished with a protective sill. In the latter case they could be expected to leave a distinctive foundation plan.

At a more general level, it seems reasonable to suppose that foundation walls are an accurate reflection of structure boundaries. Based upon the observation of recently burned and abandoned structures, Wauchope (1938:154) believes this to be the case. Foundation walls of stone generally help to prevent rot in wooden walls and flaking on wattle ones. Haviland (1963:278), however, argues for the presence of entirely perishable verandahs and this possibility cannot be precluded.

Interior space is more difficult to deal with analogically. It is clear that the contemporary Maya do divide interior space into culturally significant areas, the shrine and the hearth being particularly distinguished in dwellings. Most Maya furniture and interior facilities are perishable, however. This fact makes correlation with archaeological contexts impossible in most cases. On Cozumel we have several kinds of features that define interior space in our structures. These include interior partitions, columns, bench areas, altars, and stepped areas. The first three variables occur in enough structures to be useful in defining formal types. The problem lies in correlating these variables with functional configurations.

Where columns appear in long rows, forming colonnades, they define a formal type that correlates with a variety of historical observations. All these descriptions indicate use as a public building. Landa says, "they were accustomed to have in each town a large, white house, whitened with lime, open on all sides, where the young men came together for their amusements. . . . Almost always they all slept together here also until they married" (Tozzer 1941:124). Tozzer, quoting Roman y Zamora, notes of Guatemala, "No one sleeps in his house in all this time (of sacrifice) but in certain porticos (*portales*) and houses which are near the temple (and) made for this purpose" (1941:124). Oviedo's description of Grijalva's first landing on Cozumel includes the following description:

> When the divine worship had been celebrated at the temple . . . the indians brought to the captain some chickens of that island . . . and vessels of honey and presented them to him. He accepted them and with the present went aside underneath a portico near the tower raised on some stone pillars [Grijalva then proceeds to discuss terms of trade with the cacique]. (Wagner 1941a:94)

That Oviedo's informants were distinguishing between dwellings and other kinds of structures is indicated in the following description: "The captain and his men entered the town nearby which had stone houses with straw roofs, and other buildings of different kinds of stone, some modern and lately built and others which showed antiquity, very beautiful in appearance" (Wagner 1942a:94). Juan Diaz in his *Itinerio* describes the scene Oviedo described above in the following words:

> Then the same Indian who served as their priest came back and in his company were eight Indians who brought chickens, honey and certain roots which they call *maiz* . . . The captain said he only wanted gold . . . and gave them to understand that in exchange for it he would give them such merchandise

as he brought with him for that purpose. These Indians took the captain and some ten or twelve others and gave them dinner in a hall, all surrounded by stone and covered with straw. In front of this was a well where all people drank. (Wagner 1942a:71)

Although there is a difference in the description of formal attributes, both make it clear they are dealing with some public structure. Wagner (1942a: 12) believes that much of Oviedo's account was based on information from the pilot of Grijalva's expedition, Aliminos, which would mean that the discrepancy is probably attributable to two different eyewitnesses selecting different observations to report.

Landa may well be referring to public buildings in this description, "Or else it may be that the (large) towns changed their location for some reason, and so wherever they settled they always built anew their temples, sanctuaries and houses for their lords, according to their custom, and they have always used for themselves wooden houses covered with thatch" (Tozzer 1941:171). These sanctuaries may refer as well to the public buildings used by participants in ceremonies related by Roman y Zamora to private oratories also known to exist at the time.

Cortes, in his fifth letter to Charles V, makes several allusions to large public buildings in the centers of towns he passed through in southern Yucatan. Most of them are too vague to be useful. In addition to calling them *temples* most of the time, and referring to the idols inside them (Pagden 1971:353, 363, 398), he also noted their typical central location in communities (1971:397-398). That all these buildings were not simply temples alone is made clear by Cortes in this description:

> [in preparation for an assault on a town somewhere in the Peten] I had given orders that no one should enter a house or utter a sound, but that we should surround the main house, especially the one belonging to the chieftain, and a large hall in which our guides had told us all the warriors slept . . .
>
> God and our good fortune so willed it that the first house we came upon was indeed that of the warriors; and as it was not light and everything was plainly visible, one of my company, seeing so many men in

arms and seeing how few we were to attack . . . thought it expedient to call for help . . . which woke up the Indians. Some of them took up their weapons, others did not; and, *as the house had no walls on any side, the roof being supported only by posts,* they leapt out anywhere they wished, for we were unable to surround the place completely. (Pagden 1971:396; emphasis ours)

There is corroborative evidence for the existence of such warrior houses given by Villagutierre in his account of Cortes's *entrada*: "and they were puzzled to know the plans of the Indians of that (deserted) town, as much because of the novelty of the situation as because they found in the middle of the village a house full of lances, bows, arrows, *macanas*, and other arms used by those Indians in their wars" (Villagutierre quoted in Means 1917:28).

At a more general level of description, there is evidence that the interior space of public buildings in centralized locations was used for other purposes. Roys states:

At the former [Conil] . . . there was a market-court at one corner of the square, where disputes were settled by certain officials. In the latter town [Chauacha] a part of the market was housed in stone buildings with thatched roofs. It would seem probably that they were open in front like the houses of certain chiefs. (Roys 1943:51)

Roys's interpretation is possibly based in part upon a *Relación de Valladolid* that states:

The people [of Chauaca] were in a town established in a somewhat permanent and organized manner, with their buildings of worked stone and roofs of thatch, in which (town) they came together and held their markets, although the streets were not paved. The citizens . . . had large houses of strong wood covered with the leaves of a palmlike tree. (Chamberlain 1948:51)

Like Roys, we would tend to delete the bracketed "town" in this description.

The significance of interior partitions, which create several rooms within the boundaries of a structure, is more difficult to detail analogically than are colonnades. Aside from Landa's famous

description of the typical two-roomed dwelling in Yucatan (Tozzer 1941:85-86), there are few references to multiroomed structures in historical documents. There are vague allusions in Landa to servants' quarters (Tozzer 1941:26, 86), and to shrine rooms or oratories inside the dwellings of nobles (Tozzer 1941:108). Peter Martyr, in describing the town of Potonchan, says, "Astonishing things are told of the magnificence, the size and the beauty of the country houses built by the natives round about, for their pleasure. They are constructed like ours, with courtyards shaded from the sun and with sumptuous apartments" (in MacNutt 1912:35). Thompson mentions that the chief's house at Dolores had a verandah, suggestive of the tandem plan described by Landa (Thompson 1938:599). Avendano similarly mentions a hall that functions as a vestibule for the chief Ah Canek's house at Tayasal (in Means 1917:19) but it is not clear if this was connected to the house or not. It is interesting to note that these few observations have one thing in common: they refer to dwellings, and particularly to the dwellings of chiefs. (There is good reason to believe that structures used primarily for religious purposes— temples and shrines—also often had interior partitions, but this is dealt with in Chapter 3 on masonry structures.) The tandem plan and its association with the elite (outside of Mayapan) seems reasonable because it reflects a division of the dwelling into relatively public and private areas. This would be a particularly appropriate division in the dwellings of chiefs, which we know often served as public meeting places (Means 1917; Tozzer 1941).

The vast majority of modern Maya dwellings have a single room. When this space is partitioned, the two resulting plans are tandem and transverse in arrangement. The tandem plan consists of a dwelling and verandah. The transverse plan, on the other hand, divides the interior space up into a family end, containing stored possessions, beds, and other personal effects, and a kitchen end, which acts as the center of social activity and food preparation (Wauchope 1938:122). In each case the result is a generally more public and another more private space.

Bench areas are the only form of imperishable furniture found on Cozumel. This is generally the case for the Maya area archaeologically. Masonry benches are rarely referred to in the historical literature. One explicit description is given by Avedano in the context of a public building—in this case, called a *temple*.

> In order to worship the . . . idols there are nine very large buildings, made in the form of the churches of this Province. . . . All such buildings have a wall about a yard and a half high and of the thickness of six quarters; the bench or seat all around, which stands out from the middle inwards, is three quarters thick and the rest, which stands above, is three quarters thick; so that both together form two rows of seats around said churches. (Means 1917:18)

The impression given here is that, in addition to having bench areas, this building was open at the sides. There is good reason to believe that such buildings at Tayasal functioned as men's houses as well as temples. Thompson notes this duality of function for public buildings among the historical Chol (1938:603), and Cortes gives the impression of similar structures encountered in towns north of Acalan (Pagden 1971:353, 363).

We know of no such explicit references to benches in dwellings. Smith (1962:228) regards the bench areas in dwellings at Mayapan as probably sleeping places (among other things), given Landa's description of activities in the front room. The one positively identified kitchen at Mayapan was associated with bench areas (Proskouriakoff and Temple 1955). Given the ubiquitous occurrence of bench areas in structues of various types at Mayapan, on Cozumel, and at other sites in the Maya area, it seems likely that benches were a standard, multipurpose form of furniture. Thus, the presence of bench areas does little, in itself, to further functional identification.

We presume, nevertheless, that the forms benches take in structures, the size relative to overall floor space, and their disposition within structures are functionally significant. Granting a considerable range of size and shape builders could choose from, we believe that builders selected benches that served particular purposes. The construction of masonry benches is an investment in time and energy. Once placed, benches are not easily moved or removed. They constitute a long-term commitment to a given spatial arrangement on the part of the builders. Even though

bench areas, wherever they occur, served a variety of functions, we believe they were designed to fit particular activities carried out in structures, even if these activities were only carried out sporadically.

To give a modern illustration of this hypothesis there are bench areas beside the main doorway at the Church of San Lorenzo in Zinacantan (Vogt 1969:351, Figure 110). Most of the time these benches are used casually as a sitting place for worshipers or minor religious officials. During fiestas, however, the bench areas became a major focus for ceremonial activities carried out by the *cargo* holders. The officials are arranged on the bench areas in a specific rank order, and they spend the better part of their time during fiestas sitting "in state," watching the ceremonies or participating in them. Although the benches serve their primary function only sporadically, their shape and location are nonetheless determined by that function.

A similar situation exists at the *cabildo* in Zinacantan (Vogt 1969:Chapter 12). The *cabildo* is basically a two-roomed tandem structure with a small transverse "jail" at one end. Most of the activities at the *cabildo* are carried out in the front room, which is an open, colonnaded verandah. There are two long, sturdy wooden benches along the back wall of the front room (medial wall) on either side of the doorway. These benches are occupied (apparently exclusively) by members of the political hierarchy. These officials spend the better part of their time sitting on these benches, listening to local disputes or "holding court," as described by Landa in the context of a lord's dwelling (Tozzer 1941:123). Again, officials are arranged on these benches in a precise order. In fact, according to Vogt (1969:573-574) spatial order is an important aspect of many ritual contexts, including the home, and is replicated throughout the cultural system.

Spatial order is manifest throughout the Maya area. Usually it is most strongly expressed in ritual contexts, more informally at other times. If we can assume that spatial order was equally important in preconquest times, we can assume that on certain occasions the arrangement of furniture within structures was very significant. As permanent furniture, benches impose a certain definition of interior space that must be appropriate on given occasions, whether the benches are in public buildings or private dwellings. We cannot detail the variation of benches in Cozumel's structures in terms of specific functions, but we can consider it in terms of the degree of flexibility or rigidity imposed on structure types.

We know, according to Peter Martyr, that the natives of Cozumel used hammocks (in MacNutt 1912:27), and it seems likely that they also had wooden beds (Tozzer 1941:86) along with other kinds of perishable furniture. Permanent benches, then, were not necessary to any specific function. We believe that Cozumel's inhabitants had a choice whether or not to have benches in their dwellings and that this choice is reflected in the variety of formal structure types we identify as dwellings. From this argument it follows that the variation in bench form and disposition reflects part of the acceptable range in spatial organization of dwelling interiors. In constructing permanent benches, we feel that Cozumeleños had to strike a balance between a flexibility required by ordinary use and a formality required by ritual use. This means that, if benches were not going to play an important role in ritual activity, they had to be as unobtrusive as possible. On the other hand, where benches strongly controlled and defined the interior space, it seems likely that they were designed with ritual contexts in mind.

As with benches, altars occur in a variety of structures that are presumably functionally distinct. Smith (1962) found this to be the case at Mayapan and, because the structures on Cozumel date for the most part to the same period, this situation is not surprising. On Cozumel, altars occur in structures we identify as dwellings, shrines, temples, and public buildings. As a rare feature in perishable structures, altars have little typological value. Where they occur in conditionally identified dwellings on Cozumel, they tend to corroborate the wide range of ritual contexts observed at Mayapan.

Clavigero, quoted in Smith (1962:183), notes that the houses of lords consisted of two floors. This may relate to our observation of two-level structures on Cozumel (Structure C15-12-a). This, however, is a very rare feature and is confined to one formal type: tandem plan structures.

The size and number of accessways into structures may have some functional significance.

Leventhal (1974) has emphasized this feature in particular in his analysis of Cozumel's shrines. Aside from colonnades, in which access was presumably defined by columns, access in structures on Cozumel is defined by bench areas, foundation walls and monolithic jambs. In many instances, no foundation of a defined doorway exists on a structure side that presumably had, on the basis of other evidence, a doorway. This is an important problem because the difference between an open verandah arrangement and a small doorway clearly reflects a difference in the private or public nature of the interior space. Although concepts of privacy vary from culture to culture, the concepts are reflected in domestic architecture (Rapoport 1969:66).

Modern Maya dwellings generally have constricted accessways unless they have verandahs, in which case the back room has narrow doorways. That narrow doorways existed during the colonial period is demonstrated by Wauchope (1938:94). His evidence comes from Yucatan. In the *Relación de los Pueblos de Tetzal y Temax*, quoted by Wauchope (1938:115) and again by Smith (1962:183), a doorway is mentioned in the typical dwelling. From the verbal description it would be difficult to say what this doorway looked like. However, the author of this *relación*, Alonso Jullian, has conveniently left us a drawing of a house to go with the verbal description. In the drawing the doorway is clearly small and constricted (D. I. Rel. Yuc. [vol.] 11, 1898). On the other hand, Thompson, in his discussion of the historical Chol, notes, "Villagutierre says that the houses at Dolores had open fronts, but sides and backs were closed with pole work. Roofs were of straw. In each room was a wooden bed of barbecue type sufficiently large to hold four persons" (1938: 599). Presumably these were single-room structures, as they are contrasted with the house of the chief, which had a verandah.

Hence, although the weight of modern ethnographic evidence and some historical data support narrow access for single-roomed structures, wide access single-roomed dwellings are within the realm of possibility. This is unfortunate for us as we are unable to identify access type in many cases. Furthermore, even in cases where open fronts seem more likely, we cannot preclude the possibility of perishable partitions.

The above discussion provides the background observations and generalizations employed in the following type descriptions. The types are arranged in terms of the clustering of formal architectural attributes, which is to say, in terms of the empirical data for Cozumel. A summary provides a functional overview once conditional identification for the types has been established.

STRUCTURE TYPES

TYPE 1

MAJOR CRITERIA

Perishable, rectangular shape, partial masonry walls, no interior partitions, no bench zones, no defined accessways (Figure 5).

STRUCTURES

C25-17a, C25-5a.

DISCUSSION

The first two criteria are so common as to not be functionally significant beyond the observation that in many modern Maya communities the same shape is shared by several functional types in a household compound (Wauchope 1938).

According to Roys (1943:18), partial masonry walls are reported for dwellings on Cozumel by Peter Martyr. The walls are observably dry laid, which would fit Roys's opinion that walls were set in mud mortar. Such walls fall into the modern range of dwelling construction for Yucatan (Wauchope 1938). However, Wauchope (1938:Figures 47, 49) notes that some outbuildings have low masonry walls. The blocks used in the walls are very roughly shaped, hardly distinguishable from the surrounding field walls. It is possible that, in this rocky country, such walls would be easier and cheaper to construct than wooden walls.

C25-17a is isolated and faces away from nearby groups; vague cardinal orientation is to the east. The size (about $43m^2$) is in the middle range for perishable structures on Cozumel.

C25-5a is clearly associated with a group formed around C25-6. It faces south and its size $(26m^2)$ is in the lower range for perishable structures.

CONDITIONAL IDENTIFICATION

On the basis of cheap construction materials,

we would identify these structures as relatively casual, indicating either dwellings of the poor or outbuildings. C25-17a is large enough to be a dwelling, and is isolated, which reduces the possibility of its being an outbuilding. We identify it, therefore, as a dwelling, probably of a poor family. C25-5a, on the other hand, is associated with a group. It is the second smallest in a group of five structures. We conditionally identify it as an outbuilding.

TYPE 2

MAJOR CRITERIA

Perishable, rectangular shape, foundation walls, no partitions, benches, columns or defined accessways (Figure 5).

STRUCTURES

C25-24-a, C25-27-a, C25-3a, C22-40-a, C18-5a, C18-17a, C18-6a.

DISCUSSION

These structures cluster more on what they lack than what they have. The size ranges (about 15 to $109m^2$) and locations are the variables that indicate differences among structures in the type. Although the structures also vary as to orientation, none face west, the direction associated with religious structures (Tozzer 1941:86). In terms of sporadic criteria, two of the structures have *chultuns* in them and plaster floors (C25-24-a and C25-27-a). The lack of interior space definition in these structures makes their functional identification impossible except on the basis of locational evidence.

CONDITIONAL IDENTIFICATION

C-25-24-a is located in a group that includes fragments of a structure facing it, situated to the east. Possibly a second structure stood on a rectangular masonry support substructure at the northern edge of the group platform. Fragments of a third small structure were observed on a secondary substructure attached to the northwestern corner of the main group platform. C25-24-a is the largest of these structures. It is conditionally identified as a dwelling with associated outbuildings.

C25-27-a is situated on a large L-shaped platform. Its size $(109m^2)$ is estimated on the

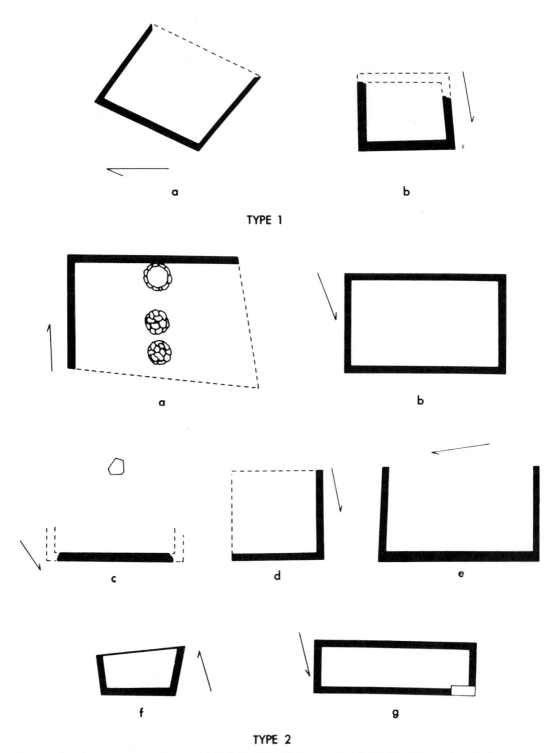

TYPE 1

TYPE 2

Figure 5. Perishable structures. Type 1: (a) C25-17a; (b) C25-5a. Type 2: (a) C18-17a; (b) C25-3a; (c) C25-27-a; (d) C18-6a; (e) C25-24a; (f) C18-5a; (g) C22-40-a. (Scale 1:200).

presumption that the *chultun* was inside rather than in front of the building, which may not be the case. The L-shape of the platform results from the joining of two rectangular platforms; the platform behind the structure is at a different level and is further delineated by a low rubble wall. There is a crude two-step stairway in front of the structure that extends the length of the front platform. The structure faces a large, ground-level plaza defined on its eastern side by a field wall and by a masonry structure C25-28-a on its southern side. To the north of C25-27-a, in the walled lot behind it, fragments of three small structures, including a possible stone circle, were observed. These may be outbuildings associated with C-25-27-a. C25-27-a is conditionally identified as a dwelling on the basis of this association, its association with C25-28-a, and its size. It is the largest structure in a noncentralized group.

C25-3a, at $60m^2$ is in the middle size range for perishable structures. It is located in an enclosure defined by a stone wall. The enclosure lacked evidence of other structures. The size is appropriate for a dwelling and the isolated location precludes its function as an outbuilding. This structure is conditionally identified as a dwelling.

C22-40-a is very fragmentary. Its estimated size of $32m^2$ is probably on the low side. The structure is situated on a large rectangular platform that has fragments of other structures on it. It is further situated on a secondary support substructure. As the most prominent structure in a noncentralized group, it is conditionally identified as a dwelling.

C18-5a, a small ($15m^2$), fragmentary structure, is located on one of the many levels of the massive complex of agglutinated rubble platforms at Buena Vista. The level on which it is situated is not well defined by retaining walls. The structure is apparently isolated. Size would indicate that this is an outbuilding, but its location would indicate a dwelling. As with many of the Buena Vista structures, this one is problematical. No identification can be offered that is consistent with our generalizations.

C18-6a is another fragmentary structure on the main complex of platforms at Buena Vista. Its size ($31m^2$) and apparently isolated location conditionally identify it as a dwelling.

C18-17a is a large ($71m^2$) structure at the southern edge of the main complex of rubble platforms at Buena Vista. In the interior of the structure there are three small circles of piled stone in a line parallel to the short sides of the structure. This unique feature may be the remains of perishable post foundations. C18-17a is situated on a roughly rectangular defined platform, and may be associated with C18-15a, a benched structure nearby on the same platform. This size is appropriate for a dwelling, although it is on the upper end of the middle range. The location may be interpreted as either isolated or loosely associated with C18-15a. The conditional identification is a dwelling.

TYPE 3
MAJOR CRITERIA
Perishable, rectangular structures, with no interior partitions, columns, or bench zones, but with single constricted (0.6-0.8m) accessways (Figure 6).

STRUCTURES
C22-3a, C22-12-a, C18-20-c, C22-35-a.

DISCUSSION
All these structures occur in groups in which they are relatively the smallest buildings. They are at the small end of the size range for Cozumel ($8-18m^2$). These two variables characterize non-dwellings. However, the additional variables of small single doorways, vague cardinal orientation, and location relative to other structures allow us to go further. Constricted access, for example, was found to be characteristic of the small masonry structures traditionally called *shrines* on Cozumel (Leventhal 1974). Doorways defined by walls are generally rare for Cozumel's perishable structures; in other examples where they are present more than one accessway can be inferred.

CONDITIONAL IDENTIFICATION
C22-3-a faces C22-1-a, which is presumed to be a dwelling because it fits the basic plan for dwellings at Mayapan quite well. Between these two structures is a plaza area in which there is a small square masonry platform of the kind identified as a group altar at Mayapan (Smith 1962:221).

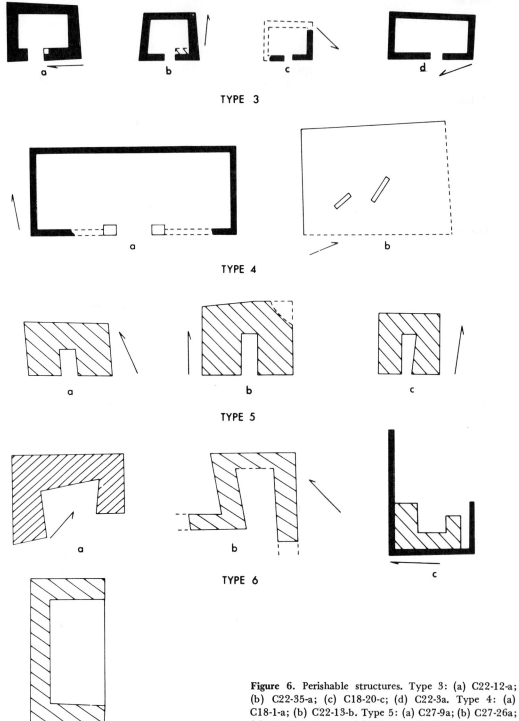

Figure 6. Perishable structures. Type 3: (a) C22-12-a; (b) C22-35-a; (c) C18-20-c; (d) C22-3a. Type 4: (a) C18-1-a; (b) C22-13-b. Type 5: (a) C27-9a; (b) C27-26a; (c) C27-25a. Type 6: (a) C25-1-d; (b) C25-13-a; (c) C18-15a; (d) C22-36-a. (Scale 1:200).

Although the location of C22-3-a is appropriate for a secondary dwelling, it is also appropriate for an oratory or shrine. Furthermore, the structure faces west, the direction strongly associated (though by no means uniformly) with structures having a ritual function. Although none of the arguments alone is strong enough to identify the function of this structure, we believe the combination is sufficiently strong to permit its conditional identification as a ritual structure; it is either a simple oratory or large shrine.

C22-12-a, like C22-3-a, faces west to a large, low well-constructed rectangular platform. Only fragments of walls could be found on this platform, but we believe it supports a large perishable structure. The foundation walls are made of particularly well-cut blocks and are usually thick (0.8m). The floor is paved with flagstones. This is in contrast to the relatively perishable foundations of C22-12-b itself. Generally in the Maya area the only structures constructed with more care and investment of labor than the main dwellings are shrines. This and the combination of other attributes encourages us to conditionally identify this structure as ritual in function, probably an oratory.

C18-20-c is the smallest structure in the type (8.5m^2) and therefore is most likely a nondwelling. The structure is located on a large isolated platform with a long single-roomed masonry structure, the remains of a small masonry structure with a single doorway (identified as a shrine), and the remains of two other small masonry structures almost entirely destroyed by looting (there is a very high correlation between shrines and lootholes on Cozumel). The probable presence of two or more masonry shrines in this group makes it highly unlikely that it functioned as a normal household compound. Under these circumstances, it becomes less likely that C18-20-c is simply an outbuilding, and more likely that it is another shrine, albeit a perishable one. Landa notes that wooden idols were manufactured in small perishable huts (Tozzer 1941:160). This structure seems appropriately located for such a purpose.

C22-35-a is a small (13m^2) structure that falls in the nebulous area between masonry and perishable construction. It has standing walls about 50 cm high of roughly dressed flat slabs. No evidence of beam-and-mortar or vaulted roofing was found on the plastered floor. Additionally, there was little fall around the walls, which might indicate that they once stood substantially higher. We infer that the upper walls and roof were both perishable. In size and plan (access width in the one doorway is 60 cm) this structure compares well with small masonry structures identified as religious in function. Its association with a *sacbe* that connects it with a group of masonry religious structures, and its otherwise isolated location further confirm the assignment of a religious function to this building. A badly ruined feature set against the back wall opposite the doorway may have been an altar. Altars are sporadically associated with religious structures as well as dwellings, but are more strongly associated with the former. We conditionally identify C22-35-a as a religious building, probably a shrine.

TYPE 4
MAJOR CRITERIA
Perishable, rectangular structures with no colonnades or benches, but with single accessways defined by monolithic doorjambs (Figure 6).

STRUCTURES
C18-1-a, C22-13-b

DISCUSSION
These two structures are characterized by large floor space combined with narrow, limited access. In both cases the monolithic jambs are no longer in place. Their position as jambs is the most reasonable inference from their number, matched size, and, in the case of C18-1-a, their location on a narrow staircase. The combination of formal features allows the inference of relative privacy in the context of important structures. Peter Martyr mentions that the houses had doorways of marble (MacNutt 1912:13).

CONDITIONAL IDENTIFICATION
C18-1-a, 132m^2 and centrally located in the main formal plaza complex at Buena Vista, is a good candidate for a public building. However, it has the interior flexibility of space associated with simpler dwellings and limited access. Our conditional identification is a private residence in the public domain.

C22-13-b is situated in an ostensible household group of some importance in San Gervasio.

Its size ($80m^2$) and location are reasonable for an upper-class dwelling. The apparent simplicity of interior arrangement is probably a function of the poor preservation of the structure. It is conditionally identified as a dwelling.

TYPE 5
MAJOR CRITERIA
Perishable, rectangular structures with boundaries defined by bench areas; no interior partitions, columns, or defined accessways, but one straight C-shaped bench area for each structure (Figure 6).

STRUCTURES
C27-9a, C27-25a, C27-26a, C22-88-a.

DISCUSSION
C27-25a and C27-26a are both situated well outside the main zone of settlement at Aguada Grande. Although they appear to be in a single large field-wall enclosure, they are widely separated and both face south. C27-9a occurs in the settlement zone, but appears to be isolated and also faces south. A fourth structure of this type, C27-24, which also faced south, was noted but not planned. All these structures are are on ground level. They are generally at the small end of the size range 18-29m^2). The most notable thing about these structures is the strong dominance of their interior space by bench areas. Floor space is just large enough to allow access to the bench areas. The benches are well built with upright slab retainers, but are not plastered. The floors are of earth. This strong definition of interior space indicates that the activities carried out in these structures were probably specialized around bench use. Assuming no evidence to the contrary it is probable that sitting or lying were the activities carried out inside. Several individuals could have sat in these structures at one time, or even slept in them. Yet the small size and isolated location of these structures argues against their use as everyday dwellings. Our belief is that they were a form of hermitage in the literal sense of the term (an idea suggested by R. Robertson, personal communication, 1975). Ritual isolation is reported by Landa for many occasions. The degree of isolation required cannot be easily determined. The well-built permanent furniture argues against their being simply temporary milpa huts. Sporadic use

by various members of the community and community responsibility for up-keep would be concomitant with the permanence of the bench areas.

C22-88-a fits into this type in having a straight C-shaped bench area defining its boundary. It varies from the type, however, in two significant respects. First, it is located on a large agglutinated platform. Thus, although no other structures were observed in the immediate vicinity, it is likely that this structure was less isolated than those at Aguada Grande. Second, the floor area in this structure is substantially larger than those in the other structures of this type. Hence, the bench areas do not dominate the structure to the same extent. However, in terms of size ($18m^2$) it fits the range of this formal type. Finally, unlike the others, its orientation is to the east.

CONDITIONAL IDENTIFICATION
In light of the above criteria, C27-9-a, C27-25-a, C27-26-a, and C27-24(?) have all been identified as ritual dwellings or hermitages for individuals required to isolate themselves from the community. C22-88-a may be a small dwelling; its identification is very problematic.

TYPE 6
MAJOR CRITERIA
Perishable, rectangular structures with boundaries defined by bench areas and foundation walls; no columns or interior partitions, but with straight C-shaped bench areas (Figure 6).

STRUCTURES
C25-1-d, C25-13-a, C18-15a, C22-36-a.

DISCUSSION
The formal criterion distinguishing this type from the previous one is the presence of a floor area sufficiently large to be the focus of activities distinct from those carried out on the bench areas. The floor area is generally larger with either (1) benches along the side walls or (2) a larger floor area or floor space extending beyond the bench areas. The structures (range 40-55m^2) are generally larger than Type 5 and are oriented to the east. Conditional identifications are based primarily on size and location.

CONDITIONAL IDENTIFICATION

C25-1-d, 40m^2, is the smallest and simplest building in the main group at La Expedicion (C25-1). It is situated in the southeast corner of the plaza, facing north, and is next to C25-1-e, the other perishable structure in the group. As the smallest structure in the group, this structure can be viewed as a substantial outbuilding, perhaps a kitchen (see Plate 1b). If we presume, as Smith does (1962:220), that each group needed a kitchen, this structure might fit the bill. There are no other small platforms in this group like those Smith described for Mayapan and identified as possible kitchens. On the other hand, the structure is well into the middle size range for the island overall. From Smith and Proskouriakoff's findings at Mayapan, and from ethnographic material (Wauchope 1938:134), the potential for separate kitchens on Cozumel is good. Yet the houses in one town Cortes describes in his journey from Acalan across the Peten had fires in them and "all kinds of provisions" (Pagden 1971:398). We believe that C25-1-d is large enough to be a kitchen-sleeping house such as those described by Wisdom (1940:119) among the modern Chorti. In this capacity, all the food for the group would be prepared here, but the building would also serve as a sleeping and storage facility.

C25-13-a is located on a large and otherwise apparently empty platform. However, it seems to be associated with C25-14a, a small structure on ground level behind it to the east. Formally, it is unusual that there is a small rectangular extension of the bench area off one of the arms of the C. On the basis of its relatively larger size and its apparent association with a small outbuilding, C24-13-a is conditionally identified as a dwelling.

C25-36-a is a large structure (55m^2) located on a roughly rectangular platform. Fragments of a second smaller structure were observed in the southeastern corner of the platform. The bench zone is relatively narrow and floor space dominates the interior of the structure. On the basis of both its apparent location in a group, in which it is the largest structure, and its middle range size, C25-36-a is identified as a dwelling.

C18-15a varies from the others in that the bench area is clearly situated at one end, with the rest of the boundary defined by foundation walls.

(Note that David Gregory mapped this as a large block C-benched structure [1975:Map 1]. As we planned the structure ourselves on another occasion, we will follow our own observations.) The structure is located on the aggulutinated main complex at Buena Vista. Fragments of another small structure were observed directly east of this one. Otherwise, the only other possible association is C18-17a. On the basis of size (51m^2), which is in the middle range, and possible association with a small structure (or alternatively its isolation), the structure is conditionally identified as a dwelling.

TYPE 7
MAJOR CRITERIA

Perishable, rectangular structures with no interior partitions or columns, but with block C-shaped bench areas and constricted accessways defined by benches (Figure 7).

STRUCTURES

C22-90-b, C18-3a, C22-6-b (distinguished by presence of colonnade).

DISCUSSION

This is a formal type in which the bench areas strongly define the interior space. As in Type 6, the floor space, however, is large enough to serve puposes other than access to the bench areas. Of the types on Cozumel, this one best fits Avendano's description of "temples" at Tayasal (Means 1917:18). However, in this case, although extending around the entire interior wall, the benches lack rests. Nevertheless, we believe that this form of bench is very well designed for ranging people around the walls, as Avendano ranged the people of Tayasal in the "temple" while preaching to them. We have personally observed this kind of ranging in several modern Maya contexts. At the modern village of El Cedral on Cozumel, people were so arranged inside the church during the fiesta of Santa Cruz in 1973, and again at christening ceremonies on Cozumel and in the vicinity of Corozal town, Belize, in private homes. Although the benches could have been used for any number of purposes, we believe they are designed to maximize this ranging facility and the ritual contexts requiring it in interior space. Although there is a substantial size range (28-98m^2), all these structures are centrally located.

Plate 1 (a) C25-6-a; (b) C25-1-d; (c) C25-1-c; (d) C25-31, showing looted tomb.

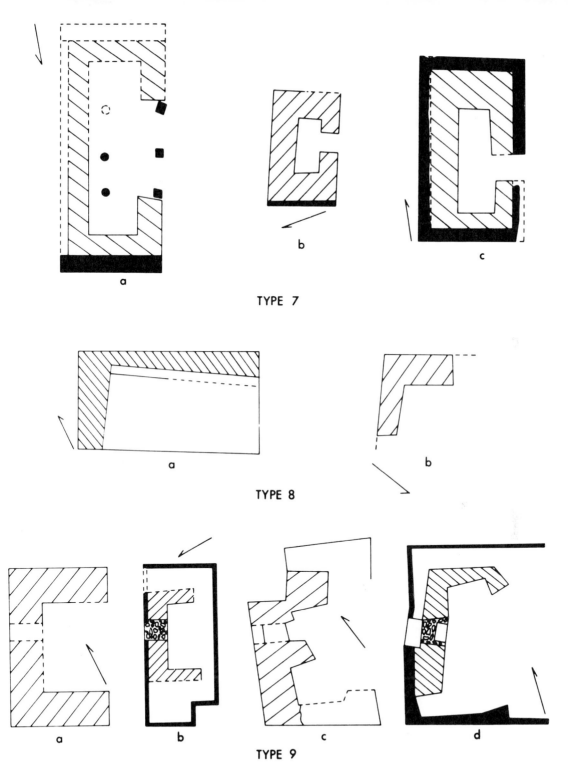

Figure 7. Perishable structures. Type 7: (a) C22-6-b; (b) C18-3a; (c) C22-90-b. Type 8: (a) C25-1-e; (b) C25-36-a. Type 9: (a) C22-87-b; (b) C31-4-a; (c) C25-11a; (d) C25-8a. (Scale 1:200).

25

CONDITIONAL IDENTIFICATION

C18-3a is just south of the major formal plaza group at Buena Vista, where this plaza group connects with the complex of agglutinated platforms. It faces south toward this complex and away from the plaza group. Thus it is not focused on activities in the plaza group, but on those related to the main complex. At the same time, it is situated at the juncture of these two primary features of Buena Vista, which we interpret as a mediating location between them. This interpretation supports the identification of C18-3a as a ritual meeting house. An alternative argument based on location would consider C18-3a as an integral part of the plaza group, and as such the smallest structure in it. This would make it a likely candidate for a separate kitchen or similar outbuilding. The structure's orientation away from the plaza group controverts this argument. Thus, we conditionally identify C18-3a as a ritual meeting house.

C22-90-b is substantially larger than C18-3a (72 as opposed to $28m^2$). It is on a relatively high secondary substructure on the group plaza of C22-90, San Gervasio. It has a well-constructed staircase in front of its single door. It is associated with C22-90-a, which is identified as a dwelling, and C22-90-c, a group altar. The location of C22-90-b and its exalted situation suggest it may be an oratory, following the typology at Mayapan (Smith 1962:220), but it lacks an altar. However, only one of the possible oratories found on Cozumel has an altar, so this may not be a necessary attribute here. On the other hand, because only one of the other structures that might be oratories has benches, it is possible that the benches in this structure functioned in a manner similar to altars in the other oratories. On the basis of centralized location in a formal group, placement on a raised substructure, and the bench areas, we identify this as primarily a ritual meeting house.

C22-6-b could be placed in this type, or in another defined by the presence of a colonnade, depending on which attribute is weighed. In this case the functional arguments tied to the attributes fortunately complement rather than contradict each other. As outlined in the section on method, we believe colonnades to be strongly associated with public functions. This plus the formal arrangement of benches and the centralized location combine to give us a conditional identification of public meeting house for C22-6-b.

TYPE 8

MAJOR CRITERIA

Perishable, rectangular structures with no partitions or columns but with a single L-shaped bench area (Figure 7).

STRUCTURES

C25-1-e, C25-36-a.

DISCUSSION

Aside from the L-shaped bench, these structures have little in common. Although C25-36-a consists exclusively of a bench, given its shape, this feature probably does not define the boundaries of the structure. C25-1-e has clearly defined foundation-wall boundaries. C25-36-a is located on an agglutinated platform whereas C25-1-e is in the main formal plaza group at Expedicion. These two structures share a definition of interior space in which the bench area plays a lesser role than in types previously discussed. They are in this respect less-specialized structures. Identification is based on this inference and locational arguments.

CONDITIONAL IDENTIFICATION

C25-1-e (Plate 1c), roughly $60m^2$, is the largest perishable structure in the main plaza group at La Expedicion. However, it shares this plaza with three masonry two-roomed structures. Hence, it is not the most elaborate structure in the group. This is only the first of many occasions when we have to consider the relationship between masonry and perishable structures in the same group. For now, suffice it to say that these masonry structures at La Expedicion are conditionally identified as nondwellings. In order to explicate the identification of C25-1-e, we must take a broader perspective on settlement pattern on Cozumel than heretofore offered. There are five centralized formal plaza groups on Cozumel. One or more rectangular, single-roomed, benched structures are found in all but one of these. The other structures in these groups can be identified as nondwellings. Aside from their location, these benched structures formally compare well with structures that are found in contexts indicating dwelling as a function. Location, on the other hand, would imply a public function. These lines of reasoning can be combined to support an identification of these structures as a dwelling in the public domain. However, in contrast to colonnaded structures, some of which we believe were public semiresidences, we think these noncolonnaded structures were private residences. As such they would be the homes of the local elite families in the various settlements. C25-1-e is such a home.

C25-36-a occurs on an agglutinated platform that has fragmentary remains of other, smaller structures. Conditional identification: dwelling.

TYPE 9

MAJOR CRITERA

Perishable, rectangular structures with no interior partitions or columns but with two L-shaped bench areas and a rear accessway defined by bench areas (Figure 7).

STRUCTURES

C22-87-b, C31-4-a, C25-8a, C25-11a.

DISCUSSION

The bench zones are accompanied by foundation walls that define the boundaries of the structure. Presumably, all these structures had entrances in the wall opposite the defined doorway. Despite the obvious differences in described plan, Landa's mention of a back door for the "necessary service" may be pertinent here (Tozzer 1941:86). Unlike the situation at Mayapan (Smith 1962:Figure 8b) and at Tulum (Sanders 1960:Figure 2, Structure 49) there is no evidence here for a back room. As with larger structures having straight C-shaped bench areas, the floor space is large enough to act as a focus for activities other than access to the benches. The size range for these structures $(55-94m^2)$ is in the upper middle range for the island as a whole.

CONDITIONAL IDENTIFICATION

C31-4-a is located on an agglutinated platform complex. Fragments of small structures, including a partial circle, were on the platform area in front of it. These were not mapped. There was no evidence of another structure on the platform area behind C31-4-a. On the basis of its probable association with outbuildings and its appropriate

size, this structure is conditionally identified as a dwelling.

C22-87-b is in a centralized formal plaza group at San Gervasio. As with C31-4-a, the bench areas are large enough to serve the purpose of formal ritual gatherings, yet do not dominate the interior space entirely. The "back" door of the structure opens onto a lower plaza level that had remains of an L-shaped benched structure in one corner. As with C25-1-e, we identify this structure as a private residence in the public domain. The L-shaped structure behind it and fragmentary walls of other structures may well be the outbuildings associated with C22-87-b. Due to an oversight on our part this important second plaza area was not mapped.

C25-11a and C25-8a vary from the first two in that their bench areas are not precisely L-shaped. In fact, although they are recognizable as benches, they do not have any specific form. They do, however, define the back doorway and are set against the back wall. C25-11-a is situated in a house lot defined by stone field walls and is associated with a small shrine and a small raised platform that may have supported another outbuilding. C25-8a is in another house lot and is associated with some small, possible outbuildings (C25-7a) and a large structure, C25-9a, toward which its back door may be oriented. Both are located on ground level and are conditionally identified as dwellings.

TYPE 10

MAJOR CRITERIA

Perishable, rectangular structures with two L-shaped bench areas that define a "front" doorway (Figure 8).

STRUCTURES

C18-1-c, C22-95-c.

DISCUSSION

These are clearly single-access structures. Both are located in centralized goups and are thus in the public domain. Both are in the middle size range $(44-49m^2)$. Furthermore, the location of the bench zones in the front part of the structures might also point to a relatively "public" function. If the area at the front of structures' interiors, particularly next to the doorways, is considered more accessible than the space at the rear, then the arrangement of benches in these structures can be considered oriented to more public use.

CONDITIONAL IDENTIFICATION

C18-1-c is conditionally identified as a dwelling, following our argument concerning private residences in the public domain.

C22-95-b is uniquely located on a small plaza area in front of a pyramidal substructure. The factors of location and orientation to the west override the formal characteristics that indicate a dwelling function. It is conditionally identified as a public building, but with more specific functions undetermined.

TYPE 11

MAJOR CRITERIA

Perishable, rectangular structures with no interior partitions or columns but with two side benches (Figure 8).

STRUCTURES

C31-1-c, C31-1-e, C25-4a, C25-31-a (also see Plate 10a), C19-1-e.

DISCUSSION

These structures show that their builders opted for flexibility in that the benches are off to the side, do not dominate the interior, and allow greater latitude for perishable furniture. This does not necessarily mean that the buildings were not used for ceremonial purposes or gatherings, only that the inhabitants opted for more perishable, possibly more portable furniture. We would expect to find this to be the case in structures such as dwellings that served a wide variety of functions.

CONDITIONAL IDENTIFICATION

C31-1-c, located on the southern edge of the main plaza group at Zuuk, is unusual in that one of the benches is not set against the wall but rather defines a separate space at the eastern end. Otherwise it fits our general argument for perishable structures in main plaza goups. We identify it conditionally as a dwelling.

C31-1-e is located on the western edge of the main plaza group at Zuuk. It is conditionally identified as a dwelling.

C25-4a is located in a house lot at Expedicion. It has no associated structures. Its size ($49m^2$) precludes an outbuilding function. Therefore, it is conditionally identified as a dwelling.

C25-31-a (see Plate 10a), located on a large complex of agglutinated platforms, is associated with a group altar. Conditionally, we identify it as a dwelling.

C18-1-e, located in the main plaza group at Buena Vista, is identified as a private residence in the public domain. The presence of a staircase in front of it running the length of the structure implies that it was open in the front.

TYPE 12

MAJOR CRITERIA

Colonnaded structures without benches but with beam-and-mortar roofing (Figure 9).

STRUCTURES

C18-1-b, C22-5-a.

DISCUSSION

Both of these structures are in central plaza groups. C22-5-a is L-shaped, and has a partial masonry wall along the back. C18-1-b has a defined accessway on the back side that probably opened up on a staircase off the plaza to ground level.

CONDITIONAL IDENTIFICATION

Both these structures are identified as public facilities on the basis of arguments given at the beginning of this chapter. The significance of variability in colonnaded structures is difficult to ascertain. The lack of bench areas may indicate that these structures were not specifically designed as halls for formal or ritual meetings that involved ranging people along the walls.

TYPE 13

MAJOR CRITERIA

Colonnaded structures with bench areas (Figure 9).

STRUCTURES

C22-7-a, C22-87-a, C22-90-a, C18-1-d.

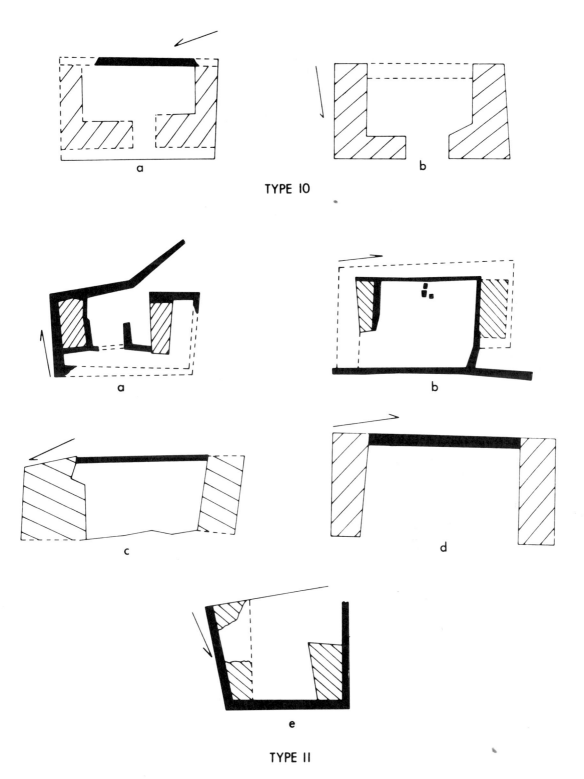

TYPE 10

TYPE 11

Figure 8. Perishable structures. Type 10: (a) C22-95-c; (b) C18-1-c. Type 11: (a) C31-1-c; (b) C31-1-e; (c) C25-31-a; (d) C18-1-e; (e) C25-4a. (Scale 1:200).

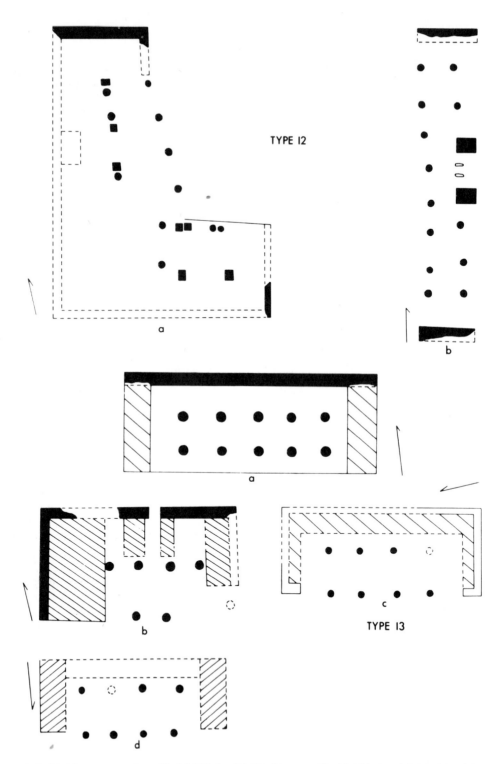

Figure 9. Perishable structures. Type 12: (a) C22-5-a; (b) C18-1-b. Type 13: (a) C22-87-a; (b) C22-90-a; (c) C22-7-a; (d) C18-1-d. (Scale 1:200).

DISCUSSION

All these structures are in centralized plaza groups. As a type they achieve the maximum variety of interior definition in a single room. With the exception of C22-90-a, all are conditionally identified as public facilities. C22-87-a has benches set against the end walls that probably acted as separate foci for activities. C22-7-a has a bench along the back and side walls. It is possible that C18-1-d has a similar arrangement. These last two structures could well have served for formal or ritual meetings as well as public residences. Their interior space seems more specifically designed with these purposes in mind.

CONDITIONAL IDENTIFICATION

C22-90-a is unusual. It has a colonnade but it is greatly foreshortened. The benches that are at the two ends are quite large, and there is a back door. This structure is sufficiently different in these formal respects for us to identify it conditionally as an elaborate private dwelling.

TYPE 14

MAJOR CRITERIA

Perishable, rectangular structures with interior partitions but no bench areas or columns (Figure 10).

STRUCTURES

C22-13-a, C22-29a, C18-10a, C22-34-e.

DISCUSSION

C22-13-a is two-roomed with a transverse arrangement; the other three structures have a tandem arrangement. The tandem arrangement bears some relationship to the Mayapan-type dwelling. However, at Mayapan, the presence of benches in the front room is continuous across the type.

CONDITIONAL IDENTIFICATION

C22-13-a is the largest and best-defined structure in the structure plaza group to which it belongs. It is identified as a dwelling. The end room has a separate doorway opening on to a *sacbe* connecting this group to the main one at San Gervasio.

C22-29a is associated with the large group of C22-30. The flooring in it was of plaster and pavement, carefully prepared. The lack of defined accessways makes it difficult to determine interior arrangements. The location indicates either a large outbuilding or the dwelling of a man who married into the family occupying C30, as described by Landa. Support for this second argument might come from the fact that C22-30-c is the best example of the Mayapan type of dwelling on Cozumel (see also Sabloff and Rathje 1975a:80). C22-29a might be seen as a poor imitation of this impressive dwelling.

C18-10a is a fragmentary structure on the main complex of agglutinated platforms at Buena Vista. The isolated location and size make it a candidate for dwelling.

C22-34-e is not like any of the other perishable structures in plan. It actually compares best with tandem two-roomed masonry structures. Given its location in a group dominated by shrines and a temple, a prominent altar against the back wall in the back room, and a large urn censer found *in situ* we identify this structure as a perishable temple or shrine.

TYPE 15

MAJOR CRITERIA

Perishable, rectangular structures with interior partitions and benches in the front room (Figure 10).

STRUCTURES

C22-1-a, C22-30-c, C15-12-a.

DISCUSSION

The first two structures fit the Mayapan type, and we accept the functional identification as dwellings established there. By comparison with other benched structures on Cozumel, we add only that the benches in these two structures seem to focus attention on a central rectangular bench or dais. This definition of interior space seems well suited for public audiences by an important personage. This relates well to the observation by Landa and others that the lords held court in their houses. Possible further support for this additional function is the presence of a large monolithic stone column in the plaza area in front of C22-1-a. Early explorers mention that criminals to be punished or executed were in some cases tied to such

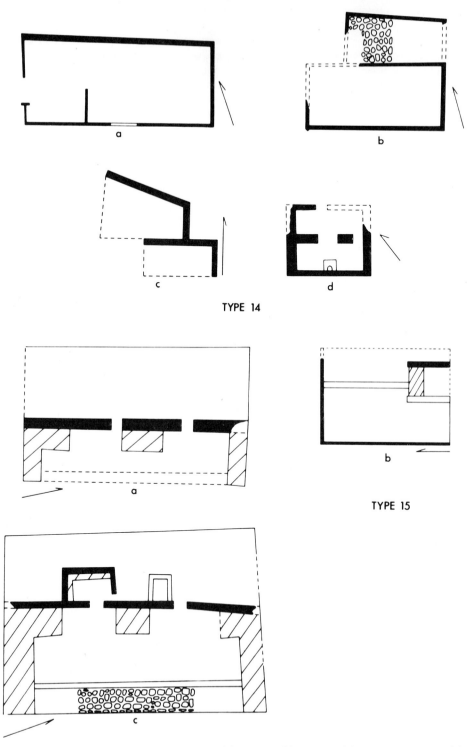

Figure 10. Perishable structures. Type 14: (a) C22-13-a; (b) C22-29a; (c) C18-10a; (d) C22-34-a. Type 15: (a) C22-1-a; (b) C15-12-a; (c) C22-30-c. (Scale 1:200).

columns placed near the courthouses. C15-12-a varies from the others in having only one bench in the front room.

CONDITIONAL IDENTIFICATION

All the Type 15 structures are identified as dwellings.

TYPE 16
MAJOR CRITERIA

Perishable round structures, with no columns, bench areas, or interior partitions (Figure 11).

STRUCTURES

C18-2a, C18-8a, C18-9a, C18-11a, C18-13a, C18-14a, C18-16a, C25-28-b, C25-31-b.

DISCUSSION

Round, as distinct from apsidal, structures are generally rare in the Maya area. They are most common in northern Yucatan during the Postclassic period. Pollock (1936) has associated them with the cult of Kukulcan and the foreign incursions into the area during this period. The unusual thing about these particular round structures is that they have no demonstrable religious function. The Buena Vista structures, for example, form a consistent architectural type. They are located throughout the main agglutinated complex of platforms and other examples, which were not mapped, occur on platforms in the vicinity. Although there are no ethnohistorical references to round dwellings in the Maya area, nor are there modern round dwellings, this function is most easily identified with these structures. They are large enough (range $27-55m^2$), are all essentially isolated, and have well-defined, substantial foundation walls. The only evidence for round dwellings in the Maya area comes from a fresco at Chichen Itza referred to by Pollock (1936:22). This fresco depicts small, thatched round dwellings with individuals who are wearing non-Maya apparel sitting in front of them. These dwellings are in contrast to rectangular structures depicted in another frescoed mural in the same structure at Chichen Itza. The mural dates to the Early Postclassic and ceramic evidence now available indicates occupation at Buena Vista throughout the Postclassic (Rathje and Phillips 1975). The fact that no large round shrines or substructures

were found at Buena Vista, as well as the lack of other evidence indicating that Buena Vista might be a cult center for Kukulcan, would seem to argue against such a function. Furthermore, the location of Buena Vista deep in the interior of the island would seem an unlikely base of operation for an enclave of foreigners. The lack of a substantial number of rectangular structures on the complex (which might allow the argument of specialized outbuilding for the round structure) and the large number of these structures at this site could argue for a dwelling function.

The round structures at La Expedicion, on the other hand, are both located at the western end of agglutinated platforms. Both are attached to rather than resting on the platform proper. A similar arrangement of round structures occurs at San Gervasio C22-103 and at outlying platforms near Buena Vista. These structures seem to be serving some more specialized function than as dwellings. Therefore, it is possible that the round structures on both Buena Vista and La Expedicion are storage facilities.

There is also a type of round structure found throughout the island to which we have not been able to assign a function. Although few of these features were mapped (C27-16, C27-18, C27-19), several were sketch planned. They are large, well-built masonry walled structures. Maximum observed height of walls was 2m. They characteristically have inner and outer retaining walls of roughly shaped blocks and a hearting of rubble and gravel. In several instances, they were observed to have a low parapet running around the outside wall about 0.5 meters above ground level. They are found isolated and in groups of two or three; sometimes they are accompanied by rectangular platforms, sometimes by half-circles and straight walls. The walled features appear to have some correlation with *cenotes* because they were found near most all-year large *cenotes*. Furthermore, a sizable sample of Late Postclassic censerware was collected near one of these features that had been grazed by a large bulldozer, and altarlike platforms and niches were observed in some of them. These associations might indicate that these structures served some kind of ritual function. However, a recent study by Wallace (1978) makes a strong argument that they were apiaries that provided the important marketable commodity, honey. In his re-

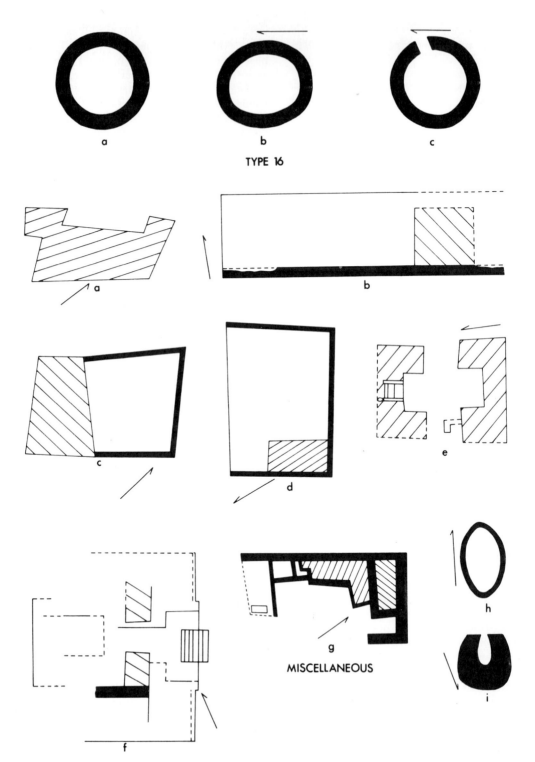

Figure 11. Perishable structures. Type 16: (a) C18-11a; (b) C18-8a; (c) C18-14a. Miscellaneous: (a) C25-6-b; (b) C22-87-d; (c) C25-6-c; (d) C25-9a; (e) C22-27-a; (f) C22-95-a; (g) C25-23-a; (h) C25-14a; (i) C27-4a. (Scale 1:200).

search on the stone disk artifacts fround on Cozumel, Wallace (1978:30) discovered a "well supported" relationship between the stone disks and the stone disks served as plugs for hollow-log beehives, Wallace contends that the association between stone disks and round structures supports the hypothesis that the latter functioned as apiaries. Finally, Hamblin, who studied the fauna of Cozumel, has argued that the round structures may have served as animal pens (William L. Rathje, personal communication, 1980). Further work clearly is needed to test these hypotheses.

MISCELLANEOUS STRUCTURES

Miscellaneous strucutres do not fit into any of the types above; each is discussed individually (Figure 11).

C25-6-a was partially excavated, but did not yield a ground plan. It is clearly a large perishable structure with plaster flooring and bench areas. A column drum was found embedded in the floor (Plate 1a). This may have been an altar or, alternatively, a support for a perishable house column. On the basis of location in a group in which it is the most substantial structure, C25-6-a is conditionally identified as a dwelling.

C25-6-c is attached to the western side of the large support platform of C25-6. It apparently consists of a single, large bench area and a juxtaposed floor area. The unusual plan and western orientation make this structure functionally problematic.

C25-6-b consists of a large, irregular bench zone. No foundation walls could be found around it. It may be part of the same structure as C25-6-c, except that the foundation wall of the latter structure excludes it. For the same reasons as C25-6-c, this structure is functionally problematic.

C25-23-a has an unusual bench shape but the location in a group associated with another, smaller structure supports its conditional identification as a dwelling.

C25-9a is a large rectangular structure with a single bench zone. Sharing a lot with C25-8a, it is conditionally identified as a dwelling.

C25-14a is the only small ellipsoid structure found on Cozumel. Its location as a lot behind C25-13-a gives ground for identifying it as an outbuilding, possibly a kitchen.

C22-87-d is in a formal plaza group (87) at San Gervasio. It yielded an incomplete plan, which hampers interpretation. Our personal observations gave the impression of a long rectangular structure with a small masonry shrine in the center of it. This arrangement accompanied by colonnades, is typical of public buildings at Mayapan. The structure is problematic but may be a public building.

C22-27-a has two straight C-shaped bench areas that define two accessways facing east and west. There are stairways in front of each of the doors. One of the stairways leads off the group in which this structure is located, whereas the other leads on to the group plaza. The structure is situated on a large and elaborate substructure with a simple *talud-tablero* facade. The interior space is strongly defined by the presence of benches and a floor area adequate just for access to benches. There is a stepped niche in the northern bench and a tomb under the southern bench. The structure's location on a particularly elevated substructure, the specialized definition of interior space, and the presence of a possible altar niche such as those found at Mayapan in oratories (Smith 1962: 221) indicate a primarily ritual function for C22-27-a. This structure seems to combine attributes of oratories with attributes associated with structures that face in two directions at Mayapan. It is conditionally identified as an oratory.

C27-4a is a small, roughly rounded structure in front of the shrine group at Aguada Grande. Excavation revealed the walls to be very thick and the interior to be oval with a single small accessway facing south. The shape and the presence of large quantities of burned rock and ash inside the structure indicate that it may have been an oven or kiln. What was prepared in it cannot be ascertained from the excavated remains. Possibilities include sacred foods, ritual drinks such as *chicha*, or ceramic *incensarios*.

SUMMARY OF FUNCTIONAL TYPES OF PERISHABLE STRUCTURES

In the above typology we have split along formal architectural lines and then lumped along functional ones (see Table 4). Born of pragmatic necessity, this approach reflects the basic disposition of the data. We believe that no matter how the empirical pie is cut up, any attempt to consider

Table 4
Correlation of functional and formal types of perishable structures on Cozumel.

Functional types	Formal types
Dwelling	1, 2, 4, 6, 8, 9, 10, 11, 13?, 14, 15
Outbuilding	1, 14?
Hermitage	5
Ritual Meeting House	7
Oratory-shrine	3
Public buildings	10?, 12, 13
Storage structures	16
Temple	14
Oven	One structure, no type

the pieces in functional terms will result in considerable latitude in formal characteristics. This is neither surprising nor peculiar to Cozumel: It is to be expected when attempting to assign function to complex composite artifacts.

Even in those fortunate cases in which function involves a very limited range of activities (e.g., sweatbaths), there are still many material ways to achieve the desired result. Where function glosses a wide range of activities, as in dwellings, only the broad constraints of environment, available construction materials, and cultural models limit the possibilites. The first two factors can be presumed constant across the domain. Therefore, in our functional lumping, we have attempted to deal with the factor of cultural models. Thus, we have tried to design our weighted attributes in terms of the material and locational correlates of cultural models for functional types of structure among the Maya.

The identifications are essentially based upon positive configurations of formal and locational attributes that have some analogic justification. The quality of such justification varies according to the specificity of the formal-functional correlations. We now summarize the functional types.

Dwellings are identified primarily on the basis of locational criteria in combination with a size range above $20m^2$. The locational criteria are: (1) largest structure in a group not containing identified public buildings; (2) relatively smaller size and/or simpler construction in a group containing identified public buildings; and (3) large isolated structure. With the exception of the sec-

ond, these criteria are justified on the basis of generalizations given in Tables 2 and 3. It should be noted that although materials given in the first part of this chapter are appropriate to dwellings, they do not serve to distinguish dwellings from other structure types associated with households.

The Cozumel dwelling is generally rectangular and single roomed. Accessways are usually set in the long sides. Interior definition is supplied by bench areas, whose location, shape, and size vary considerably. We believe that the degree of interior formality or rigidity is a factor attributable to the importance and frequency of ritual activities in dwellings. This belief is in concert with the general observation that the best-constructed, most formally laid out interiors occur in the context of plaza groups containing identified public buildings, whereas the most casual permanent furniture occurs in noncentralized dwellings. Dwellings entirely devoid of permanent furniture do occur in centralized contexts, but these have other attributes that indicate a special function, such as monolithic jambs defining narrow access.

We have defined several structures fitting this general description as private residences in the public domain. The public domain is defined by the presence of identified public buildings in the context of formal plaza groups. The identification of these structures as dwellings is analogically justified by the ethnohistorical descriptions of settlement patterns that state that the dwellings of the elite were built near public buildings, and by the continuity in formal characteristics of these structures with others that are more easily identified as dwellings. Structures with colonnades, which we identify as public buildings, do not occur in the same variety of locational contexts.

Outbuildings are identified as relatively small, simple structures located in association with relatively larger, more substantial structures. Many possible outbuildings were observed but only a few were planned. In hindsight, this field research procedure is regretted.

Hermitages, as a functional type, are highly correlated with formal Type 5. The identification of hermitages is based upon the isolation of these structures in combination with strongly defined interior space. The first attribute would suggest a dwelling, the second a ritual function. Their occurrence outside both the public domain and the household leads to the identification as ritual dwellings used during ceremonial isolation. Although it is known that ritual isolation was observed in a variety of occasions, this specific type has no historical analogs.

Ritual meeting houses are identified by the presence of block C-shaped bench areas that strongly define the interior space. This arrangement is appropriate to the ranging of individuals within the structure, a practice in concert with Maya expression of strong spatial definition in ritual contexts. Secondary positive arguments for such a function include exalted location, central location, and/or mediating location. All three are generally associated with ritual activities.

Oratory-Shrines are small, perishable, single-roomed structures identified primarily by their location, orientation (facing west across a plaza to a substantially larger structure), and narrow access to interior space. Because oratories have been identified as a major component of household groups at Mayapan, more particular arguments for the identification of oratories on Cozumel include associations with Mayapan-type dwellings.

Public buildings are identified primarily by the presence of long, open colonnades. The association of colonnaded structures with public activities are well documented in the historical literature. Although a number of more specific public functions might be assigned to variations within this theme, it is difficult to identify material correlates of the specific functions. We believe that structures with pronounced bench areas within this functional type most likely served for public council meetings and other ritual or formal activities. All the structures identified with this function occur within formal, relatively central plaza groups.

Storage structures might include the round structures found at Buena Vista and at other sites on the island. Because no historical description of storage building exists, the justification for such an identification is based upon Pollock's argument (1936) that round structures in the Maya area are generally associated with the cult of Kukulcan. Thus, the particular shape has ritual significance. These structures, however, are located in a context suggesting dwellings. This combination of factors suggests their identification as storehouses for the elite that are ritually sanctified by their shape. However, the possibility that the round structures were apiaries, as argued by Wallace (1978), must be considered, too.

One perishable structure is identified as a *temple* on the basis of its formal plan, its location in a group of shrines and temples, and the presence of an altar and a large censer *in situ*. Another structure, C22-95-a, was so fragmentary that it did not yield a plan. However, its location on top of a pyramidical substructure ornamented with a stucco facade indicates that it should be included in this general category.

One *oven* was identified at Aguada Grande on the basis of similarity in plan to modern ovens and the presence of ash and fire-burned rocks in its interior.

This concludes the summary of functional types. Before dealing with the resulting conclusions, it is necessary to discuss briefly the distribution of sporadic features associated with perishable structures. These include *chultuns*, altars, tombs, burials, and caches.

SPORADIC FEATURES ASSOCIATED WITH PERISHABLE STRUCTURES

Four *chultuns* were found in association with perishable structures, which were identified as dwellings on other grounds.

Altars are found attached to the support platforms of two dwellings (C25-1-3, C31-4-a) in front of them and inside a dwelling against the back wall (31-1-e). Two possible column-drum altars occur in dwellings (C25-6-a, C25-23-2). Sanders reports an altar against the back wall in C22-5-a, which is a colonnaded hall (Sanders 1960: 195). An altar occurred in C22-34-e, which we identify as a perishable temple. Finally, an altar in the form of a stepped niche was found in C22-27-a, which was identified as an oratory. This range of location, based on very similar findings at Mayapan and the historical descriptions of ritual activity in the context of the home, appears to be quite reasonable for the late Postclassic.

Our information on *tombs, burials, and caches* is quite sparse because the majority of structures were not tested by excavation. Tombs were noted under the south bench in C22-27-a (an oratory) and in an identified dwelling, C22-30-c, against the medial wall in the back room. A looted tomb was found in C25-31 (see Plate 1d). Burials were located in front of C22-36-a (a dwelling) and C22-95-a, a problematic structure tentatively assigned a ritual function. A cache was found in front of the first stair of C22-4-6, an empty cache box was found under the threshold of C25-8a, and a cache of notched sherds in the fill under C25-23-a. A double burial appeared under the threshold of C31-4-a that included a rather rich offering of gold, shell, and jade beads. Their occurrence in dwellings corroborates the findings at Mayapan, where such features are associated with a variety of functional types including dwellings.

CONCLUSIONS

The functional types identified on Cozumel parallel those found at the Decadent period city of Mayapan. This is not surprising because Smith's monograph was an important source of inspiration for us and we had access to the same general literature for analogical arguments. Nevertheless, there are some important points of contrast worth noting. Whereas the Mayapan type of dwelling is consistently multiroomed and tandem in plan, the vast majority of dwellings on Cozumel are single roomed. The presence of Mayapan-type dwellings and groups on Cozumel indicates some definite cultural affinities between the two places. Therefore, this contrast must be attributed to culture preferences. Further, Mayapan dwellings consistently have benches in the front rooms, whereas on Cozumel there are numerous nonbenched dwellings and considerable variety in bench form and location among benched dwellings. In general, Cozumel's dwellings are less elaborate and less complex than those at Mayapan. The Mayapan-style dwellings that do occur on Cozumel are without question the most imposing on the island.

We believe that the Mayapan type of dwelling is the expression of a local cultural model in northwestern Yucatan (although its import from elsewhere cannot be ruled out). We believe further that it was adopted as the "official" dwelling plan of Mayapan and subsequently became associated with that capital and its cosmopolitan elite.

The impression given by our data is that only a few members of Cozumel's elite were closely enough associated with Mayapan to adopt its dwelling type. The minor elite families on the island were content to have larger or more substantial versions of the local dwelling types. That those families using the Mayapan-style dwelling were probably the most important on the island is inferred from the location of these structures around the major public plaza group in the largest settlement on the island. Our conclusion is that the relationships between Mayapan and Cozumel were strongest and most active at the level of the elites, and that there was not strong cultural affinity between the local populations. In this respect, it is probably no accident that the few oratories we identify on Cozumel are also found in the vicinity of the main plaza group at San Gervasio. A much more common local ritual structure found in the context of the household on Cozumel is the shrine. These small structures are discussed in the next chapter.

Additional cultural affinity is reflected in the colonnaded structures on Cozumel. Although simpler than those found at Mayapan, these structures seem to be generally characteristic of the Late Postclassic in Yucatan. Their appearance in large numbers on the peninsula has been attributed to foreign incursions (e.g., Lothrop 1924: 169) and we agree with this ascription. Because, as we have argued, these structures served public community—or supracommunity—level functions, it is possible that their popularity on the peninsula reflects the introduction of foreign institutions operating at that level. Prior to the Postclassic, the Maya of Yucatan certainly had public buildings; the introduction of colonnades may therefore represent a formal disjunction unaccompanied by a functional one.

Similarly the prevalence of round structures on Cozumel certainly reflects foreign influence. Our analysis of these structures suffers from a paucity of comparable Yucatecan data and a lack of historical or modern analogs. In the Late Postclassic, Mayapan and subsequently Mani (Roys 1962:63) were the centers of the Kukulcan cult. Nevertheless, we have descriptions of a round temple near the coast on Cozumel (Wagner 1942a: 28-29), and at San Gervasio we have evidence of a round shrine and a round support substructure for a rectangular shrine. Our two alternative interpretations of these structures see them as (1) the material expression of a foreign cultural model for dwellings, or (2) the material expression of a ritually specialized structure associated in some way with the cult of Kukulcan. There is no corroborating evidence for a foreign enclave at Buena Vista, or at least none that is manifest in the other architectural forms at the site. Nor is there any evidence that the site was a particularly important ritual center associated with Kukulcan. On the basis of this primarily negative evidence, and on the positive evidence that is considered in the chapter on settlement pattern, we are inclined to view these structures as special storage facilities under the protection of Kukulcan and belonging to his elite worshipers.

CHAPTER 3

MASONRY STRUCTURES ON COZUMEL

Introduction

Ancient masonry structures in the Maya area have enjoyed a long and substantial history of analysis, beginning with the intelligent speculations and descriptions of ruined centers provided by Landa (Tozzer 1941:170-180). Although much of this research has focused on the description and comparison of formal architectural features, students of the subject have persistently addressed the problem of identifying the activities associated with these structures. Pollock (1965) and Harrison (1970) provide useful summaries of these attempts at functional identification. Generally as our models of Maya society have become more complex, the trend has been toward the assignment of more complex functions to the masonry structures that occur primarily in centralized locations. As always, the anticipated range of functional possibilities has a great deal to do with the analytical outcome (see Harrison's 1970 notion of *prior suspicion*).

The thrust of more recent functional analyses, particularly those pertaining to Classic period construction (Adams 1974; Harrison 1970; Kurjack 1974a) has been toward the assignment of a residential function to features known as palaces or range structures. These constitute the relatively complex masonry buildings. Relatively simple masonry structures, especially those found in "exalted" locations, have been termed *temples* or *shrines*. At many Classic period sites the dividing line between these two general categories is not easily drawn (Pollock 1965:409).

Ethnohistorical accounts note that the major type of masonry structure on the peninsula were elite dwellings and buildings housing religious ritual. In principle, the problem of overlapping form-functional ranges within masonry structures should be just as apparent in the Late Postclassic remains. In actuality, however, the problem is not so severe because the ground plans, relative locations, and size ranges associated with Decadent period masonry dwellings differ little from those of more elaborate perishable dwellings (as documented at Mayapan by Smith 1962:218-219). Furthermore, such characteristics are in discernible contrast to the smaller and simpler buildings described in early accounts as chapels, oratories, temples, *cues* (small religious structures), and idol houses.

This convenient disjunction apparently results from the introduction of an intervening community structure type following the Classic collapse—the colonnade. Although the colonnade is part of the Classic period Maya repertoire (Andrews 1943; Smith 1950), it plays a significantly different role in the Postclassic. Hence it might be more accurate to say that the colonnade is promoted to a position of significance that it did not enjoy during the Classic period. This general structure form, consistently found in formal plazas on Cozumel and seemingly located in centralized, public places elsewhere on the East Coast and at Mayapan, may have taken over some of the functions associated with range structures in earlier periods. It should be noted, however, that the function of elite palace is notably absent from the long list of possible associations given for colonnades in the previous chapter.

Known palatial masonry dwellings dating to

the Decadent, such as those identified by Smith at Mayapan (1962:218), are generally elaborations on the tandem plan dwelling found in perishable materials there. These buildings are found in household groups that vary only in elaborateness from lesser groups containing perishable homes. The Mayapan elite residences also correspond generally with a description of palaces given by the government of Villa Rica de Veracruz (Cortes's first letter):

> There are houses belonging to certain men of rank which are very cool and have many rooms, for we have seen as many as five courtyards in a single house, and the rooms around them very well laid out, each man having a private room. Inside there are also wells and water tanks and rooms for slaves and servants of which they have many. Each of these chieftains has a front of the entrance to his house a very large courtyard and some two or three or four of them raised very high with steps up to them and all very well built. (Pagden 1971: 30-35).

Such building complexes could hardly be mistaken for the shrines and temples housing religious ritual, although shrines are often found within such complexes.

Similarly Lothrop (1924:Figures 77, 80, 87, and 95) illustrates several masonry buildings he terms *palaces*. These too are basically large versions of the tandem plan dwelling. Smith considers the Tulum palaces to be very close to the Mayapan style, lacking only the bench areas in the front rooms typical of Mayapan. Such bench areas are reported, however, in plans of structures at Tulum given by Fernandez (1945:121). Additionally one of the Tulum palaces, Structure 21, has an interior colonnade not featured in Mayapan elite residences. This suggests that if there is formal overlap between functional classes, it is between colonnades and elite dwellings rather than between elite dwellings and religious structures as in Classic contexts.

There is only one structure, C22-25-a (see Plate 2b and Figure 16b), on Cozumel that might fall into the category of *palace* as defined in formal architectural terms at Mayapan, Tulum, and elsewhere (e.g., Ichpaatun in southern Quintana Roo, reported by Escalona-Ramos [1946]). In terms of size, ground plan, and relative location,

all the other structures on Cozumel that might be considered palacial dwellings are of perishable materials. The other masonry buildings on Cozumel correlate well both with the historical decriptions of religious buildings and with the empirical characteristics attributed to buildings of this function elsewhere on the East Coast and on the peninsula in general.

Thus the great bulk of Cozumel's masonry structures are identified in the following pages as having been primarily religious in function. Although the lack of masonry elite dwellings may come as a surprise to some (but not to others; i.e., Rathje and Sabloff 1975a, 1975b), the presence of masonry religious structures in large numbers is certainly in keeping with Cozumel's reputation as a pilgrimage center of regional importance (Roys *et al.* 1940:5).

The substantial internal variability found in Cozumel's masonry structures must still be dealt with and accommodated in functional terms. Despite the relative wealth of description of masonry religious buildings left by early explorers, justifications for finer identifications within the realm of religious structures (and consequently explanations of observed variability) are hampered by an uncertain understanding of the native equivalents of temple, shrine, oratory, and other similar terms. Hence analogies must be drawn largely from ethnocentric observations by foreigners or members of the native elite of ritual practices associated with religious structures. The religion was subtle and complex. Undoubtedly the native elites' perception of religious and sacred space was likewise complex and different from that of the conquistadors and the common people. The vague explanations that are offered for variability within masonry religious structures are a different reflection of the paucity of detailed behavioral and conceptual associations.

The Data

We have a sample of 55 masonry structures for Cozumel. Many of these have been systematically looted in places one might expect to find an altar on the basis of intact buildings. Additionally a large number of masonry structures have been dynamited into oblivion in the past 10 years. Of the 35 masonry edifices reported by Davidson at the site of Buena Vista in 1967, for example, not one was entirely intact in 1972 and fewer than 10 were sufficiently preserved to yield a plan. Other masonry structures have been reported in the literature that were not observed by the survey crew. Several more were destroyed when the airport and army base were built at San Miguel. The sample, then, is a meagre reflection of what must have been standing at the time of contact. Because of the prevalence of looting on the island, a great deal of detailed architectural observation was recorded on the assumption that the buildings would be destroyed in the next several years. Much of this information concerns variation in construction technique that is of minor importance to the identification of function but is potentially vital to chronological analysis. In this chapter, only that information considered most pertinent to the assignment of function is discussed in detail.

It should be noted that a few masonry structures on Cozumel can be identified as pre-Decadent. The fact that these structures are distinctive in ways that relate them to pre-Decadent styles and distinguish them from the bulk of structures lends some credibility to the presumption that the majority of edifices were raised and used during the Decadent Period. Evidence gathered by the project that firmly dates a portion of features indicates that the basic patterns were established by Florescent time. Thus the ambiguity in dating effects the specific but not the general picture.

Method of Analysis

The masonry structures on Cozumel, particularly those termed *shrines* in the literature, have already been analyzed in functional terms by Leventhal (1974), assistant surveyor for the Cozumel Project in 1973. With respect to the systematic use of analogy, the formulation of architectural types on the basis of uniformly applicable criteria, and the justification of functional identifications, the methods used here and in Leventhal's report are in concert. However, in certain important respects we follow different approaches to the data. Leventhal chose to weigh a particular criterion—visual access width per structure side— in the creation of functional types. The value of this criterion, according to Leventhal, lies in its

utility as a means of both empirically dividing up the Cozumel sample and giving the resulting types functional significance.

Visual access width shows two empirical breaks in Leventhal's sample (1974:50), thus dividing the sample into three classes. However, the third class, that with largest access width, comprises colonnaded structures and the Mayapan-style dwellings we considered in the previous chapter. Thus within the general domain of masonry structures as we perceive it, Leventhal has two classes. On the basis of ground plan he further subdivides these two classes into a total of four types.

If access width does determine function, as Leventhal proposes, these subdivisions based on ground plan should reflect finer divisions within a given functional class. However, although Type IIA (two-roomed tandem plan structures with colonnaded doorways) and Type IIB (long rectangular single-room strucutres with or without columns) belong to the same functional class based on visual access width, Leventhal respectively assigns them a religious and a civic function. This dependence on ground plan would seem to indicate that in reality ground plan provides a more appropriate basis for functionally classifying structures. Furthermore, ground plan incorporates not only the criterion of exterior visual access utilized by Leventhal, but also the interior definition of space and interior access.

It should also be noted that Leventhal offers no means of justifying limited visual access as a functionally significant criterion derived from historical or modern observation of Maya communities. Instead he proposes a very general theory of architectural design in which limited visual access into a structure is supposed to represent symbolically the private and/or sacred nature of the space within.

Thus, in contrast to Leventhal's analysis, we choose to weigh ground plan more heavily, since this seemed to serve our purposes better. This criterion is further qualified by considerations of relative location, vague cardinal orientation, size, and associated features.

The Criteria

Of all structure types described by the early Spanish explorers, those employed primarily for religious ritual are by far the best documented.

a

b

Plate 2 (a) C22-32-a (Nohna) (photograph by Loring Hewen). (b) C25-25-a (photograph by Loring Hewen); these and subsequent Hewen photographs were provided through the courtesy of the Middle American Research Institute, Tulane University.

These descritpions are considered here in terms of the criteria used in creating our typology.

Ground Plan

In the archaeological literature on religious structures, small single-roomed structures have traditionally been interpreted as *shrines*, whereas large multiple-roomed structures have been termed *temples* (Lothrop 1924, Thompson *et al.* 1932). Similar distinctions were made by the early Spanish observers. Las Casas, for example, described a shrine in the following way:

> Near to this (place of sacrifice) they saw a house of masonry like a room with a door, in front of which they had placed a cotton cloth of many colors. Inside the house or *room* were seven or eight statues of men made of baked clay and near them aromatics and perfume things like incense or storax. (In Wagner 1942a:49; emphasis ours)

Diaz, however, described a temple that, although large, appears to have been single-roomed: "They led us to some large houses very well built of masonry, which were the Temples of their Idols, and on the walls were figured bodies of many great serpents and other pictures of evil-looking idols. These walls surrounded a sort of Altar covered with clotted blood" (in Maudslay 1908:19). Thus the distinctions between *temple* and *shrine* based on ground plan gloss variability within the two categories. It should also be noted that in most instances the Spanish observers were more interested in what the structure contained than in specific architectural details, as the following quotation illustrates: "Within the house [cue or shrine] were some little wooden chests. In these were other idols and some small medallions of half-gold, mostly copper, some pendants and three diadems and other small pieces of little fish and ducks of the country all of low grade gold" (Diaz del Castillo in Wagner 1942a:60).

An important exception to this generalization is Lopez de Gomara's description of a major temple on Cozumel:

> Their temple resembles a square tower, wide at the base with steps on all sides, it rises vertically from the middle up and at its top there is a hut with a straw roof and four doors or windows, each with

its sill or gallery. In this hut which seems to be a chapel, they house their gods or paint them on the walls. Such, at least, was the one on the shore, where they kept a very strange idol, very distinct from the others, which are many and differ widely among themselves. The body of this great idol was hollow, made of baked clay and fastened to the wall with mortar, in back of which was something like a sacristy, where the priests had a small secret door cut in the side of the idol, into which one of them would enter, and from it speak to and answer those who came to worship and beg for favors. With this trickery, simple men were made to believe whatever their god told them. (Simpson 1966:24-35)

From other accounts (Roys *et al.* 1940:5) we know that this temple was dedicated to the goddess Ix Chel. Elsewhere we have identified a structure on Cozumel (C22-41-a) as similar to the one described by Lopez de Gomara (Freidel 1975:Figure 25).

But more important, this description indicates not only that relatively elaborate ground plans, interior partitions, and multiple access-ways were found in association with religious structures, but also that such complexity may have reflected specific functional or symbolic attributes. Therefore, not only does complexity of ground plan define the use of space in concrete terms, as indicated by the categories of shrine and temple, but it may also allow us to make inferences as to the kinds of ceremonial movement that took place in and around the structures. Such inferences are crucial in assigning functional significance to ground plan.

Relative Location

Relative location has played an important role in several attempts to organize ancient Maya religious buildings into types. Pollock (1965:409) and Proskouriakoff (1962:89-91) both emphasize location on top of pyramidal substructures in distinguishing temples from shrines. Smith (1962:220-222) used location within the context of household groups to identify certain structures as oratories and group shrines at Mayapan. Although location undoubtedly does have something to do with the particular function of religious buildings, several of the descriptions of location and association available to us simply corroborate what we know to be the case archaeologically and do not provide much insight into the functional significance of these factors.

Isolated small masonry structures are noted in several accounts:

> On shore [at Boca de Terminos] we found some houses built of masonry, used as oratories of their Idols, but we found that the place was altogether uninhabited, and that the oratories were merely those belonging to traders and hunters who put into the port when passing in their canoes and made sacrifices there. (Diaz del Castillo in Maudslay 1908: 44-45)

> Along the coast there were some stone towers, not very high. These are the *mezquitas* or places of worship of these idolatrous people and are built over certain steps and covered with straw. On top of some of them was the foliage of small fruit trees, like guavas, and other trees. (Oviedo in Wagner 1942a: 37)

> Between this [cape] and the point of Cozumel where we were was a gulf which we entered and came close to the shore of the Isla de Cozumel, along which we coasted. From the first tower we saw fourteen others of the same form as the first one mentioned. (Juan Diaz in Wagner 1942a:69)

Such coastal shrines are still observable along the east coast of Cozumel and the coast of Quintana Roo. That they occur in groups at some distance from the settlements is made clear in Bernal Diaz del Castillo's quotation above and in others:

> A short distance ahead of the place where they attacked us [at Cape Catoche], was a small *plaza* with three houses built of masonry, which served as *Cues* and oratories. These houses contained many pottery Idols, some with the faces of demons and others with women's faces. (Diaz del Castillo in Maudslay 1908:16-17)

> We stayed in that bay [at Isla Mugeres] for a day and we lowered two boats and went on shore and found farms and maize plantations, and there were four *Cues* which are the houses of their Idols, and there were many Idols in them, nearly all

of them figures of tall women so that we called that place the *Punta de las Mugeres*. (Diaz del Castillo in Maudslay 1908:104-105)

Small religious structures also occur in association with other kinds of buildings:

> Monday afternoon a point hove into sight on which there were two buildings like towers, one very wide and the other like a small chapel along the roadside, on four pillars and very white. There were also other buildings. (Oviedo in Wagner 1942a:98)

> Thence beginning the voyage, on Monday of the aforesaid May, we beheld a new land and approaching it we saw on a certain headland a stone house and huts which the inhabitants call *Buhia* (thatched houses) and a large stone arch. And since the well-known discovery of the cross was on that day we gave to the island the name of Santa Cruz (Cozumel). (The Provinciae in Wagner 1942a:58)

Apparently shrines, shrine groups, or pyramidal temples were located by the sea in front of several of the coastal towns such as San Juan Porta Latina (San Miguel) on Cozumel, the town at Cape Catoche in northeastern Quintana Roo, and Champoton in Campeche.

Religious structures were also located in centralized plaza groups in settlements. In addition to Juan Diaz's descriptions of this association on Cozumel discussed in Chapter 2 on perishable structures, we have Bernal Diaz del Castillo's description of the center of Cotouchan:

> Now we all joined together to drive the enemy out of their strongholds, and we compelled them to retreat, but like brave warriors they kept on shooting. . . . and never turned their backs on us until [we gained] a great court with chambers and large halls, and three Idol houses, where they had already carried all the goods they possessed. (in Maudslay 1908:112)

The following description by Las Casas indicates public religious structures were distributed around the town. Although this description is supposed to describe Cozumel, it is garbled by an account of events known to have taken place at it contains much interesting and pertinent information:

> Leaving these (idols) they went to see and ponder on the town by a street where they saw a stone-paved highway. Here the Indians placed themselves in front of the Spaniards. . . . Finally, they passed that highway and found in a street a house of masonry like a fortress 23 steps high, so wide that ten persons abreast could ascend to the top. . . . They went on by another street where they found another fortress of masonry, a small one from which they saw an Indian emerge with a small wooden chest on his shoulders. (In Wagner 1942b:48-49)

Finally Landa (Tozzer 1941:108) notes the presence of private oratories and shrines associated with the houses of nobility.

Thus a wide range of location is documented for religious structures. With the exception of certain locations, such as on top of pyramidal substructures, this wide range means that location per se is not a useful means of functionally identifying these structures. Yet location coupled with other factors (e.g., size, construction materials, and associated features) can yield such an identification. Thus diminutive isolated masonry structures found along the coast of Cozumel have a strongly justified identification as *cues* or shrines. Furthermore, where other factors justify a religious identification, location can provide qualifications relating to the public or private nature of the ritual activities taking place in and around the structure.

Size

In the Maya area, the term *shrine* is used as a gloss for a small religious structure, *temple* for a large religious strucutre (Lothrop 1924; Pollock 1965; Proskouriakoff 1962). As was noted in the context of ground plans, the Spaniards likewise used these and other glosses. In addition to size references in the previous quotations, the following observations exist:

> Likewise they have their shrines and temples with raised walks which run all around the outside and are very wide: there they keep the idols which they worship . . . which they honor and serve with such customs and so many ceremonies that many sheets of paper would not suffice to give Your Royal Highness a true and detailed account of them all. And the temples where they are kept are the largest and the best and the finest built of all the buildings found in the towns. (Cortes in Pagden 1971:35)

> We saw the place [southeast point of Cozumel] was full of sand banks and reefs, so we went close to the other side where we saw the white house more plainly. It was a small tower which seemed to be as long as a house, 8 palms long, and the height of a man. (Juan Diaz in Wagner 1942a:69)

Religious structures undoubtedly did vary in size, and it seems reasonable to suspect that this affected the kinds of activities that took place inside them. Bernal Diaz del Castillo, for example, states:

> At that moment, there sallied from another house, which was an oratory of their Idols, ten Indians clad in long white cotton cloaks, reaching to their feet, and with their long hair matted together, that it could never be parted or even combed again, unless it were cut. These were the priests of the Idols. (Diaz del Castillo in Maudslay 1908:19-20)

This quotation gives the impression that the interior space of relatively large religious structures may have been restricted to the activities of priests or specialists. Similarly an account of propitiations to the goddess Ix Chel in her temple on Cozumel notes the mediation of a priest with the Idol (Duran in Roys *et al.* 1940:5). However, Cogolludo's account of this temple (Roys *et al.* 1940:6) indicates that pilgrims directly voiced their requests to the Idol.

Altogether the evidence concerning who was allowed inside religious structures is inconclusive. There is no doubt that the priesthood was large and well organized (Lopez Medel in Tozzer 1941:223) and that the interior space of religious structures was especially sacred. Yet there is no reason to believe that members of the general populace, once ritually prepared by fasting and prayer, could not enter such buildings and participate in activities within.

From historical accounts we know that the greater proportion of rituals took place in plaza areas in front of the structures. Those ceremonies involving substantial use of interior space, such as the rituals of the Katun idols (Tozzer 1941:168) and those of the Nacom or war captain (1941:165), are major community- and supra community-level festivals. Thus in addition to the possible correlation between the size of the structure, the complexity of the ritual activities, and the number of participants, there is a possible correlation between size and the importance of the activities to the community as a whole. The particularly important festival of Kukulcan, however, which focuses on the courtyard of that deity's temple rather than on the temple itself (Landa in Tozzer 1941:158), may be an exception and demonstrates the difficulty of supporting such a generalization without specific qualifications.

Associated Features and Furnishings

Some of the quotations given above include descriptions of the interior decorations and furnishings of religious structures observed in Yucatan at the time of contact. Prominent among these are idols, wooden chests containing ceremonial paraphernalia, altars for sacrifice, and wall paintings. We also have this description of furniture: "To celebrate [the new year] with more solemnity, they renewed on this day all the objects which they made use of, such as plates, vessels, stools, mats and old clothes and the stuffs with which they wrapped up their idols" (Landa in Tozzer 1941:151). This matter of wrapping the idols is brought up by other observers, and apparently so wrapped, the idols were stored in the wooden chests noted in some of the religious structures. Cortes adds, "[the temples] are much adorned with rich hanging cloths and featherwork and other fineries" (Cortes in Pagden 1971:35).

From all accounts, the most obvious function of religious structures in Yucatan was that of housing idols displayed on altars or stored, as well as housing other ritual paraphernalia and sacred objects. A second, concomitant function of these structures was as places for sacrifice to the idols they housed.

Unfortunately most of the items mentioned are perishable, and the idols and altars that are not perishable are found in a variety of contexts other than supposed religious structures throughout the Maya area. Hence idols and altars are usually sporadic criteria that must be used with caution when functionally identifying shrines and temples. How-

ever, these descriptions allow further qualification of the function of religious structures that have been identified as such on other grounds. It should be noted that on Cozumel, unlike the rest of the Maya area, altars rarely occur outside the context of identified religious structures (Leventhal 1974: 68). Those that do occur outside religious contexts differ formally from those that do not. Hence altars on Cozumel can be used to support the identification of religious structures.

General Considerations

In addition to descriptions of buildings, we have several general observations, particularly by Bishop Landa, on not only the kinds of religious structures used by the native societies but on the status of organized religion as well. These observations are important in the identification of types of religious structures as well as in interpreting the disposition of such buildings in settlement patterns.

As mentioned previously, several glosses for religious structures are used in the accounts. Cortes, for example, speaks of *temples* and *shrines*; Landa of *temples*, *oratories*, *chapels*, and *sanctuaries*. In the literature on Yucatan, nowhere has there been any discussion of native names for different kinds of religious structures. Thus it is difficult to assess the extent to which the categories given in historical sources reflect the native categories, the categories of Christian Spain, and/or those of foreign religions with which the early observers may have been familiar, such as Moorish Islam. A full elucidation of this problem would require a monograph in itself. At this point we merely wish to point out that the names applied to such buildings have problematic referents and cannot be taken at face value. Hence we must examine buildings assigned such names in terms of the criteria given above and their associations with observed activities.

The subject of organized religion cannot be easily extricated from that of functional types of sacred buildings. A general analog model of organized religion to a large degree determines the particular identification of the functional types of sacred buildings. This in turn yields a qualification of organized religion. Although the argument is potentially tautological, it is not necessarily so. Most students of the Late Postclassic would agree that religious organizations had undergone some significant changes since Classic times in the Maya area. Tozzer (1941:108-109), for example, goes so far as to assert that the temple cult was largely abandoned in Landa's time, partially basing his inference on the following quotation: "They had a very great number of idols and of temples, which were magnificent in their own fashion. And besides the community temples, the lords, priests and leading men had also oratories and idols in their houses, where they made their prayers and offerings in private" (Landa in Tozzer 1941:108). No doubt private worship was well developed in the Late Postclassic, there are similar allusions to the idols of commoners. However, Landa's specific reference to "community" temples here is only one of many statements that give the impression of a well-organized priesthood, public ceremonies, and the dedication of buildings to particular gods of community and regional importance (Tozzer 1941, for temples dedicated to gods: 109, 158, 168, 183; for the organization of the priesthood and its functions: 27, 98; for descritpions of public ceremonies and the role of the priest in them: 151-170).

In-depth discussion of the temple cult during the Classic period and subsequent changes in religious organization in the Postclassic would be tangential at this time. It should be noted, however, that although there is good evidence for private worship in the context of the home and therefore grounds for identifying religious buildings associated with household groups as "private," there are equally good grounds for arguing that the majority of religious buildings that occur outside such contexts were used and maintained by communities.

Nonetheless, the situation is by no means cut and dried. The sources give the impression that wooden idols were often, if not usually, privately commissioned and were prized heirlooms passed down the family line. Clay idols, on the other hand, were mass produced and expendable. Although wooden idols were housed in family shrines in the context of the home according to Landa, it seems equally possible that many of the idols housed in public religious structures were privately commissioned wooden sculptures.

A passage from Scholes and Roys's work on Acalan-Tixchel is pertinent to this discussion:

No description of the temples of Itzamkanac has come down to us, but a passage in the Text telling of the burning of the idols in 1550 gives us a better idea of religious organization than the equivalent section in the Spanish version. In the former we read: "Then they began to remove their devils: Cukulchan, the devil of the ruler, the devil of Tadzunum, that of Tachabte, that of Atapan, Tacacto, and the other devils. . ." From this it would appear that the god of the head chief was housed in the principal temple and that each of the patron deities of the four quarters had its own sanctuary. (Scholes and Roys 1948: 56)

Later in Scholes and Roys we learn that the other deities included Ix Chel, Ik Chuah, and Istabay. Granted this interpretation, it seems possible that although the idols housed in public sacred buildings represented deities of community and regional importance, they were privately commissioned by leaders in the community and were in some way identified with the leaders. To what degree they were identified with the rulers themselves more than the polities represented by the rulers is impossible to determine. This association between principal men and idols in the public domain may have been extended to the commissioning of small religious structures in the public domain. Some of the shrines on Cozumel therefore may have been commissioned by wealthy pilgrims to house their "representatives" on the island, which was itself a great sanctuary.

Although the historical justification for this line of reasoning is admittedly tenuous, there are other kinds of evidence that may support it. Proskouriakoff (1962:91), for example, notes the presence of oratories in the central civil-religious zone at Mayapan that are no more elaborate than those found in identified household groups. Certainly the wealthier members of society, especially if they were drawing on funds supplied by their constituents, could individually have borne the expense involved in constructing these buildings. Presumably these structures, although they remained identified with their patrons and their idols, became upon completion part of the public domain, open to everyone for worship, as was the idol of Kukulcan in Tixchel.

In summary, the status of organized religion in the Late Postclassic is a complex issue. Despite the relative wealth of historical description, the ranges of size, location, plan, and associated features presented in this section demonstrate the impossibility of using any single set of justified criteria in the identification of sacred buildings, forcing us to rely on positive configurations. The single attribute inspiring most confidence is masonry construction. It is associated with religious buildings in almost every account and is positively identified with this functional class more than with any other class in the literature. Even with regard to this attribute, identifications must be justified by demonstrating that structures exist at the particular intersections of criteria ranges associated with sacred buildings.

STRUCTURE TYPES

TYPE 1: GENERAL DISCUSSION

MAJOR CRITERIA
Single-roomed masonry structures with single doorways.

DISCUSSION
Ranging in size from about $3m^2$ to about $20m^2$, these structures correspond to descriptions given of *small towers, chapels,* and/or *shrines.* Without exception the early observers attributed a primary religious function to small masonry structures. The size range of these structures is substantially smaller than that of modern dwellings and those identified on Cozumel. Similarly these structures are masonry, whereas the accounts emphasize the perishability of construction materials used in dwellings, despite the occasional exception of elite residences. Thus, size, ground plan, and construction materials all point to a primary religious function for these structures.

Structures on the low end of the size range are barely large enough to admit a single individual, whereas the larger structures in this group could have accommodated several individuals at one time. The descriptions of items found in the interior of such structures and the limited floor space in this type lead us to infer that these structures were used primarily for the housing of idols and the storage of ritual objects. The amount of actual ritual activity in the interior must have been

severely limited. Only a few witnesses, for example, could have attended a sacrifice inside the structure. Additionally, from the inside, the single doorway focuses attention directly on the space in front of these structures. This space is often defined by the presence of a small plaza area and/or a staircase.

Leventhal (1974:73) has argued:

> An important characteristic uniting all of these structures is a narrow access area leading to a small enclosed space. This feature of religious buildings on Cozumel creates the concept of the privateness and non-public aspect of interior religious space. . . . In the Maya religious ritual, the common man was a viewer and nonparticipant. . . . The limited access area emphasizes both its sacredness and its association solely with the priesthood and not with the common man.

However, we do not believe that restricted visual access and interior space necessarily reflect a priestly monopoly on mediation with divine beings. Given this ground plan and the defined space in front of these structures, there are three possible ritual arrangements: (1) a few worshippers carrying out sacrifices inside the structure; (2) a large number of worshippers attending a sacrifice outside the structure, with delegates making the offering inside to the idols; and (3) a large number of worshippers attending preliminary rituals outside the structure, with delegates performing the actual sacrifice inside it. The three possibilities represent a range of equally likely alternatives. That the interior space was more sacred than its surrounding exterior space seems reasonable enough, but direct mediation with the supernatural by commoners is well attested in the literature. Furthermore, the small religious structures in household contexts on Cozumel vary more in construction materials than in interior arrangement. In the Late Postclassic period with its spatial dispersion of religious foci and consequently greater accessibility to sacred space, there is no reason to suspect that nonpriests viewed the interior space of religious structures as generally taboo.

TYPE 1a

MAJOR CRITERIA
Isolated location (Figure 12).

STRUCTURES
C5-1-a, C8-2-a, C9-1-a, C18-21-a, C18-27-a, C33-1-a, C4-1a, C6-1a, C12-1a, C19-1a, and C17-1a.

DISCUSSION
The only isolated masonry structures noted by the early Spanish explorers were identified as sacred buildings for the housing of idols. Bernal Diaz del Castillo gives the most explicit description as noted earlier. Another description is given by Oviedo: "They saw along the coast near the sea some small houses, some distance apart. They were white and about the height of a man, a little more or less. These, as it afterward appeared, were houses of worship, where the Indians kept the idols they adored" (Wagner 1942b:93). Therefore the physical isolation of structures in Type 1a enhances their identification as primarily religious buildings.

Additionally, C5-1-a, C8-2-a, and C9-1-a have altars set against the back wall facing the doorway. It seems probable that these altars dominated activities in the interior given the limited floor space within the structures. C18-21-a probably had an altar as well because it has been selectively looted in such a way that only a section of the back wall and floor have been removed.

Three of the structures are located on elevated support substructures: C9-1-a, C18-27-a, and C33-1-a. Individual elevated support substructures are exclusively associated with religious buildings in the historical literature.

Although these structures may have served as houses for idols, on another level they can be seen as defining the space around and between settlements in sacred terms. Given the dispersion of religious foci as a characteristic of Late Postclassic settlement pattern, on Cozumel such religious definition of space was taken to the point of bounding the entire island as sacred.

C9-1-a, for example, is located at the northeast point of the island (Plates 3c and 3d). It faces south toward the small settlement of Aguada Grande (C27) and has a section of *sacbe* emanating from its support platform in the general direction of that settlement. As a *sacbe* leads away from the center of C27 to the north, C9-1-a may have been connected to this settlement by a trail that was only partly paved. As with other structures located on *sacbes* clearly outside settlements on Cozumel, we believe this structure relates more to the sacred definition of the island as a whole than specifically to the sacred perimeters of Aguada Grande.

The same argument holds for C33-1-a, which is located on a *sacbe* running from San Gervasio to the northeast coast. This is the second of four small religious structures that punctuate that *sacbe* as far toward the coast as we were able to trace it. C35-1-a is situated on the northern side of the *sacbe* facing east toward the sea.

C5-1-a (Plate 4c) and C8-2-a (Plate 4d) are both located on the northeast coast, facing the sea. C8-2-a lies directly seaward of the settlement of La Expedicion (C25). A substantial settlement was reported (Carlos Vivas, personal communication, 1973) to exist in the interior behind C5-1-a but we could not find it. We have noted above that in several cases where settlements were located some distance inland, religious structures stood between them and the coast. Although these two structures may have been part of the sacred perimeters of Cozumel as a whole, they also were part of the individual settlements located near the coast.

In addition to the structures discussed above, several other structures that apparently have the same plan were noted in isolated locations. For the most part, these structures, which include C4, C6, C12, C19, and C17, were virtually destroyed by the time we observed them. All these are located on the coast facing seaward. Inland from C6 is the settlement of Chencedral (C23); inland from C12, the settlement of Buena Vista (C18). Although important settlements were reported to exist inland from C19 and C3 (presumably another coastal shrine but it was so completely destroyed that we have no idea what it looked like), these sites were not discovered in the course of survey. The description given of the site inland from C19 indicates the presence of a formal plaza group that may have been the nucleus of an important settlement. The same argument given for the better-preserved structures above applies to these coastal structures.

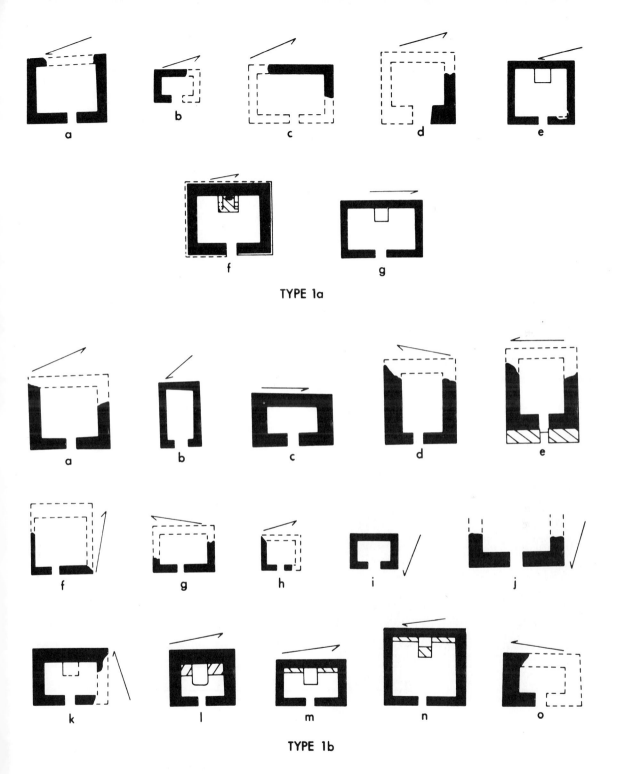

TYPE 1a

TYPE 1b

Figure 12 Masonry structures. Type 1a: (a) C18-21-a; (b) C4-1a; (c) C6-1a; (d) C18-27-a; (e) C9-1-a (after Escalona Ramos 1946); (f) C5-1-a; (g) C8-2-a (after Sanders 1955). Type 1b: (a) C18-23a; (b) C18-24-b; (c) C15-14-a; (d) C27-1-c; (e) C27-1-a; (f) C27-2-a; (g) C27-1-a; (h) C31-5-b; (i) C10-1-b (after Sanders 1955); (j) C10-1-a (after Sanders 1955); (k) C22-37-a; (l) C22-34-d; (m) C31-5a; (n) C23-3-b; (o) C18-19-a. (Scale 1:200).

Plate 3 (a) C7 (El Real) (photograph by Loring Hewen). (b) C7; note that the front stairway has been looted at some earlier date (photograph by Loring Hewen). (c) C9-1-a (Cactus). (d) C9-1-a, showing the upper facade (photograph by Loring Hewen).

Plate 4 (a) C1-1-a (Caracol) (photograph by Loring Hewen); (b) C1-1-a, showing miniature shrine and copula on the roof (photograph by Loring Hewen); (c) C5-1-a (La Palma) (photograph by Loring Hewen); (d) C8-2-a (Janan I) (photograph by Loring Hewen).

In contrast to the coastal location of the other structures in Type 1a, C18-21-a and C18-27-a are located on the periphery of the Buena Vista settlement zone—the first to the east, the second to the west of the main complex of agglutinated substructures. They both face this main complex and thereby help define the sacred periphery of Buena Vista.

TYPE 1b

MAJOR CRITERIA

Location in nondomestic groups containing other religious structures (Figure 12).

STRUCTURES

C10-1-a, C10-1-b, C15-14-a, C18-19-a, C18-24-b, C18-23-a, C22-34-d, C22-37-a, C27-1-b, C27-1-c, C27-2-a, C31-5-a, C31-5-b, and C23-3-b.

DISCUSSION

About 40% of the single-room, single-access structures we planned occur in what Anthony Andrews (personal communication, 1973) has termed *shrine groups*. These groups are characterized by the presence of several religious structures and the absence of identifiable dwellings. Such groups were noted by Bernal Diaz del Castillo (see quotations above) at Cape Catoche, Boca de Terminos, and possibly at Isla Mugeres. Furthermore their archaeological presence is well attested at Xelha, which may have been a point of embarkation for Cozumel's pilgrims (A. Andrews, personal communication, 1973).

The location of several relatively small religious structures in a nondomestic group presents us with an interesting problem in functional analysis. Bernal Diaz del Castillo's description gives the impression that several idols, possibly representing several deities with a variety of faces, were housed in each of these religious buildings. We know that certain important religious buildings were dedicated to certain deities. It is possible that smaller religious structures were similarly dedicated and the various idols represent aspects of a deity. Although it is possible that a variety of deities were represented in each of these smaller religious structures and that the structures themselves were identified with different groups within the communities, the acceptance of one or the other

alternative is functionally inconsequential because we know that particular gods were associated both with districts within communities and with particular occupational and kinship groups. This fragmented identification with the supernatural is confirmed by the proliferation of small religious structures and idolatry in the Late Postclassic. Consequently the clustering of several small religious structures in one location may represent the symbolic integration of communities in religious terms. Although each faction or group may have identified with a particular structure, several groups would have identified with that particular location and thereby would have recognized the communality of their religious devotion.

It follows from this reasoning that these structures were representative of groups within communities. This interpretation contrasts with that for the structures of Type 1a, which were identified with entire communities, if not with Cozumel as a whole. The Type 1a structures are markers of perimeters of settlements and connecting routes between places on the island. This function is more important than their probable dedication to individual deities. It should be noted that shrine groups and isolated religious buildings are often found in analogous locations. Thus shrine groups can perform the same function of marking perimeters as individual shrines do.

As with the Type 1a structures, we have some corroborating evidence for religious function in Type 1b. Five of the 15 Type 1b structures have altars set against the back wall, facing the doorway.

TYPE 1c

MAJOR CRITERIA

Location in noncentralized household goups (Figure 13).

STRUCTURES

C22-23a, C25-10a, and C31-2-a.

DISCUSSION

These three diminutive structures (size range 3-9m) apparently are associated with noncentralized households, and hence relate to Landa's description of private worship in the context of the home. However, the association with identified dwellings is only clear cut in the case of C25-10a. C31-2-a is located on a noncentral platform supporting the fragmentary remains of several perishable structures that presumably are dwellings. C22-23a is situated on a field wall near some large, low rubble platforms in the general vicinity of the group defined by C22-27-a and C22-25-a at San Gervasio. Because its association with any given household is problematic, C22-23a might be better viewed as defining the sacred perimeters of that large group. Its location on a field wall that connects it with another religious building, C22-24a, and the westward orientation of both structures toward the central focus of the group support this interpretation. C25-10a is also located on a field wall separating household groups. Thus the two functions of household shrine and marker of sacred perimeters may not be necessarily exclusive.

MISCELLANEOUS TYPE 1

C22-87-c is unusual in that it is located in a central formal plaza group at San Gervasio (Figure 13). It is the only Type 1 structure that we can positively associate with such a group, although C22-4-a may prove to be a second example. Because "idol houses" stood in such groups, its presence is expectable. However, this particular combination of plan and location is unusual. From its location, we presume that its function was in many respects the same as other more complex religious buildings found in this context. Yet the simple ground plan precludes the flexibility in spatial definition of ritual associated with the more complex religious structures. In this instance, we may have a household shrine that was elevated to community or district importance and yet was not a theater for certain of the complex rituals of community-wide significance.

C18-7-a apparently was a Type 1 structure at Buena Vista that we did not map. It is located on a small support substructure, facing west, on top of the main complex of agglutinated platforms. Because it is the only religious structure directly associated with this complex and it is not associated with observable remains of other structures, the locational significance of this building is problematic. Furthermore, it is neither large nor complex enough to be considered the religious focus of the settlement, and there are several other more substantial religious structures located on Buena Vista's periphery.

C18-28-a, like C18-7-a, is a single-roomed masonry structure situated on an elevated substructure. It is located on a field wall that marks the northeastern boundary of the main complex of agglutinated platforms at Buena Vista. It is not, however, on one of those large platforms. It faces eastward toward an extension of that complex which, in turn, lies directly east of the formal plaza group at that site. This extension was not mapped by the plane table crew or ourselves. Although C18-28-a is not associated with a particular group of structures, it may well be a boundary marker at the edge of the main complex. If so, it is the only such marker at the edge of the complex because the other religious structures that define the perimeter of the settlement are located at some distance from the main complex.

TYPE 2: GENERAL DISCUSSION

MAJOR CRITERIA

Single-roomed masonry structures with multiple accessways not formed by columns (Figure 13).

DISCUSSION

In our discussion above, we noted an explicit reference by Lopez de Gomara to a religious structure with multiple accessways not formed by columns, that is, with single accessways on several sides. This quotation refers to the important shrine of Ix Chel. Although this description portrays a rather more complex structure than those in Type 2, and there are other more complex multiple-access structures on Cozumel, the structures in Type 2 and the shrine of Ix Chel are sufficiently similar in other respects for us to utilize the description of the shrine as an analogical justification for identifying the Type 2 structures as religious. In terms of ground plan, the Type 2 structures are within the expected range of variation. Similarly the size range ($9\text{-}25\text{m}^2$) is at the lower end of the size range for structures on Cozumel. Additional corroborating evidence for a religious function includes the sporadic occurrence of mouldings, iconographically associated with religious structures (Proskouriakoff 1962:Figure 3d), and altars.

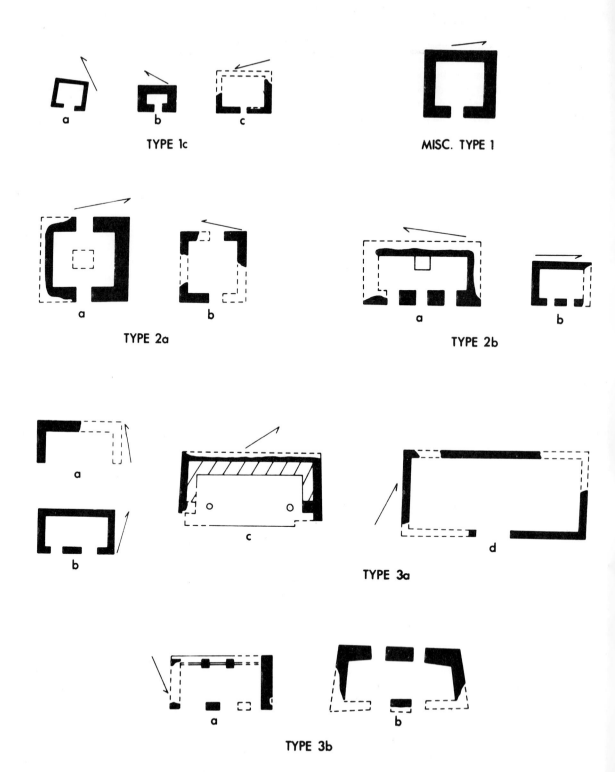

Figure 13 Masonry structures. Type 1c: (a) C25-10a; (b) C22-23a; (c) C31-2-a. Miscellaneous Type 1: C22-87-c. Type 2a: (a) C22-32-a; (b) C35-1-a. Type 2b: (a) C22-50-a; (b) C29-1a. Type 3a: (a) C15-14-c; (b) C1-2a; (c) C22-34-b; (d) C18-20-b. Type 3b: (a) C22-6-a; (b) C31-1-b. (Scale 1:200).

The particular functional significance of the Type 2 plan is that the exterior space on more than one side is rendered ritually important by multiple accessways. That this function was clearly recognized by the builders is brought out in the Lopez de Gomara quotation that mentions four staircases ascending the supporting pyramid.

TYPE 2a

MAJOR CRITERION
Isolated location (Figure 13).

STRUCTURES
C22-32-a and C35-1-a.

DISCUSSION
These structures have doorways on both the east and west faces. Both straddle the *sacbe* leading from San Gervasio to the northeast coast. C22-32-a (Plate 2a) is the first religious building on the *sacbe* outside San Gervasio. C35-1-a, situated next to a *cenote* that holds water throughout the dry season, is the last one we discovered on the *sacbe*. In both cases, the two doorways seem to be a function of the fact that the *sacbe* virtually ran through the structures. We infer that ritual activity took place on the east and west sides of the structure as well as in the interior. The multiple accessways, however, indicate more than multiple ritual exterior spaces because they also clearly punctuate the *sacbe* and emphasize its sacred nature. Someone traversing the *sacbe* would be almost compelled to move through the sacred interior space of the structures and consequently to propitiate the deities housed therein.

Furthermore, there was apparently a table altar situated in the center of C22-32-a. Although the altar clearly dominated the interior space, there was ample room to move around it. It could be approached from either direction and worshippers could easily leave by the door opposite the one they entered.

In contrast to the other two structures on this *sacbe* that are located on the edge of the *sacbe*, C22-32-a and C35-1-a definitely encourage the use of interior space.

TYPE 2b

MAJOR CRITERION
Multiple accessways on one side of the structure (Figure 13).

STRUCTURES
C22-50-a and C29-1a.

DISCUSSION
These two structures have multiple doorways formed by masonry piers. With regard to size, location, and chronological position, they are dissimilar.

C29-1a is a small structure located on the northeast coast, seaward of the settlement of Zuuk (C31). Large fragments of a Late Postclassic effigy censer were discovered directly in front of it on the surface. In terms of location, this structure defined the perimeter of Zuuk and acted as part of the sacred perimeter of Cozumel as a whole, as did several other coastal shrines. The interior space of this structure is very restricted and we believe the multiple doorways in this case were designed to allow more visual access into the building. Thus most ritual activity took place outside and in front of the structure.

C22-50-a, in contrast, has been dated through excavation to the Florescent Period. It is located in the central acropolis group, comprising Structures 47-54 at San Gervasio (C22). Although it is possible that this building was still in use during Decadent Period times, we have no direct evidence to support this. As with C29-1a, the multiple accessways may have provided increased visual access but the substantial interior space in this structure leads us to suspect that the doors played some role in defining ritual movement in and out of the structure. The differences between these structures in size and location discourage any argument of continuity from Florescent to Decadent times.

TYPE 3: GENERAL DISCUSSION

MAJOR CRITERIA
Long, rectangular masonry structures with multiple accessways and single rooms (Figure 13).

DISCUSSION
These structures are formally distinguished from other single-roomed masonry buildings by

their long, rectangular shape, and their relatively larger, more accessible interior space. It is worth noting that none of these structures shows any evidence of an altar, although this fact may not necessarily be significant, given the sample size and the problems of using negative evidence.

These buildings are consistently associated with formal central plaza groups or shrine groups. The association of shrines with long masonry buildings is reported by Oviedo (Wagner 1942a: 98). Unfortunately Oviedo does not clearly state to which buildings the columns he describes belong, although they probably belonged to the smaller ones.

Colonnades are clearly associated with formal plaza groups and temples. Empirically, however, colonnades are not associated with shrine groups on Cozumel. This may be significant.

The frequent association of Type 3 buildings with other identified religious buildings in the context of shrine groups may indicate that they have a function in some way analogous to colonnades. Yet they are distinctive in that shrine groups containing Type 3 buildings are not centralized with respect to settlements, and Type 3 buildings are on the whole smaller than colonnades ($11\text{-}60\text{m}^2$). Thus the Type 3 buildings may have had more limited functions than those attributed to colonnades. They did not, for example, serve as public residences for men and boys, religious schools, priests' quarters, barracks, or arsenals. Rather they may have been foci for ritual activity not directly involved with sacrifices or the propitiation of idols, such as ritual meals, all-night vigils, and drinking bouts. It should be noted that these activities are the more specifically religious activities attributed to colonnades. Thus the Type 3 buildings were associated with most of the religious but few of the civic activities reputedly carried out in colonnaded structures and therefore may be called *public ritual houses*.

Certain structures called *complex shrines* by A. Andrews (personal communication, 1973) are found on the coast of Quintana Roo opposite Cozumel. These are long, rectangular structures with substantial access to the exterior (e.g., Lothrop 1924:Figure 150) and small shrines built into the interior against the back wall. They may combine the functions of idol house and public ritual house. With the possible exception of C22-25-a,

a palace, this type of structure was not observed on Cozumel. The locations of these complex coastal shrines vary but the structures apparently occur frequently in either shrine groups or in isolation. Either location is reasonable if this type indeed combines the various spaces required by the activities that were separately housed in small shrines and public ritual houses on Cozumel.

TYPE 3a

MAJOR CRITERIA
Access on only one side and location in shrine groups (Figure 13).

STRUCTURES
C1-2a, C15-14-c, C18-20-b, and C22-34-b.

DISCUSSION
These structures fit the general characterization for Type 3 structures as a whole given above.

TYPE 3b

MAJOR CRITERIA
Access on two sides and location in formal plaza groups (Figure 13).

STRUCTURES
C22-6-a and C31-1-a.

DISCUSSION
These two buildings are located in formal plaza groups and are the only structures in those groups that definitely provide access to both the plaza area and the ground level outside it. Perhaps certain ritual occasions demanded direct entrance into these structures from outside the plaza group. If a small number of people were moving through a sacred circuit, direct movement into or out of such structures may have been required. All of this is, of course, pure speculation. There is, however, a possible modern analogy in the Chapel of the Senor de Esquipulas in Zinacantan, Chiapas (Vogt 1969:361). On some occasions the activities in this shrine are not directly coordinated with those activities in the nearby church of San Lorenzo, which is on the same plaza area. The shrine is oriented away from the plaza of the main church to avoid interference with rituals

in the church on such occasions. Similarly, direct access to and from the plaza group on Cozumel would have accomplished the same end of isolating two different ritual occasions occurring at the same time.

Although C22-87-d may fit into Type 3, its plan is very unclear. If it belongs to Type 3, C22-87-d straddles Types 3a and 3b, as it is in a formal plaza group but gives access only to the plaza area. Such a variation would not be at all surprising, but naturally would further complicate our attempts to identify its function.

TYPE 4: GENERAL DISCUSSION

MAJOR CRITERIA
Two-roomed masonry structures with a concentric plan (Figure 14).

DISCUSSION
Concentric plan, multiple-roomed masonry structures are a common feature of the Late Postclassic on the East Coast. The Cozumel examples are relatively simple in comparison to others in Quintana Roo (e.g. Lothrop 1924:Figure 125), although the shrine of Ix Chel may have been more complex. Lopez de Gomara (Simpson 1966), for example, mentioned that each door in this shrine had a "sill or gallery."

The symbolic value of this plan seems relatively straightforward. The encasing of the central ritual focus, be it an altar or idol, in several layers of walls enhances the esoteric quality of the innermost space. Whether or not this arrangement played a significant part in the spatial definition of ritual is difficult to determine. If it did, the arrangement may have been involved with patterns of access to the various interior spaces.

TYPE 4a

MAJOR CRITERION
Access to the outer room on four sides (Figure 14).

STRUCTURES
C22-38-a, C25-38-a, and C1-1-a.

DISCUSSION
C22-38-a, the simplest of these structures,

almost has a single room. It is included in this subtype because it seems to be the simplest on a continuum of forms with concentric plan and access on several sides. The complex altar, situated in the center of the room, encourages this assignment. There are two buttresses on the north and south sides of the eastward-facing altar that impede visual access from these directions. Apparently the buttresses reached the beam-and-mortar roof. The altar itself has substantial back and side screens and a two-level surface. This elaborate enclosure of the altar seems to replicate the inner walls of the more complex concentric plan buildings.

Although C22-38-a itself faces in four directions, the altar faces east toward a *cenote* directly in front of the structure. This arrangement indicates that exterior ritual activity, such as processionals, moved in and took place all around the structure, whereas actual propitiation of the idols and sacrifice took place only on the east side of the structure between the altar and the *cenote*. Thus there is a clear distinction between the ritual activity associated with the building as a whole and activity directly focused on the altar and the interior space.

C25-38-a, situated on a pyramidal substructure north of the settlement of La Expedicion, exhibits the next stage of complexity in this plan. As with C22-38-a, the inner sanctum faces east whereas the outer room has doorways on all four sides. This structure, which has been *Cincos Manos, Las Grecas,* and *Santo Tomas* in the literature, had been destroyed by dynamite at the time of our survey. Consequently our plan is taken from Escalona-Ramos (1946; see also Mason 1924). The location of this structure on a pyramid, presumably with a walkway around it, and apparently a single stairway on the eastern face, demonstrates the deliberate inclusion of four accessways. The ritual significance of the four doorways is implied by the rather awkward approach to the west door, for example. Spinden (field notes on file in the Peabody Museum, Harvard University) reports that he found a clay "idol" inside the inner structure.

C1-1-a (Plates 4a and 4b) is the most elaborate Type 4a structure, and varies in some respects from the other two. Originally a single-roomed structure with four doorways, it was later ex-

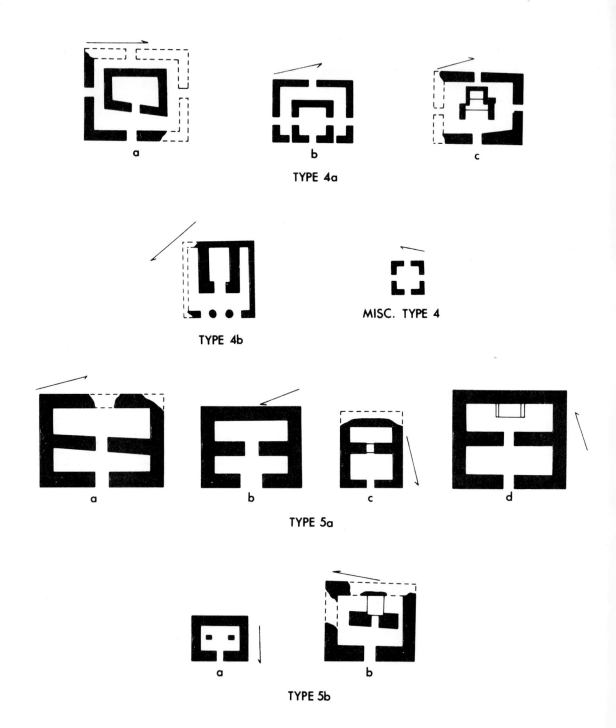

Figure 14 Masonry structures. Type 4a: (a) C25-38-a (after Escalona Ramos 1946); (b) C1-1-a (after Sanders 1955); (c) C22-38-a. Type 4b: C22-24-a. Miscellaneous Type 4: C22-34-f. Type 5a: (a) C7-1-a (after Sanders 1955); (b) C15-1-a (after Sanders 1955); (c) C16-1-a (after Sanders 1955); (d) C22-34-a. Type 5b: (a) C34-1-a; (b) C22-41-a. (Scale 1:200).

panded into a two-roomed building by the construction of an outer chamber on three sides. The outer chamber has doorways corresponding to those of the original building. The mouldings above the doorways are different on the two structures, the latter being a single three-member type, the earlier, a two single-member type. On the southern face, the two moulding styles are juxtaposed, a point that apparently did not concern the builders but which is of chronological significance because Lothrop (1924:172) thought the single-member type was a later development, following the three-member type. The presence of a loot hole in the precise center of the inner chamber indicates the possible existence of a central altar.

The four-way orientation of C1-1-a is further emphasized by the presence of a miniature shrine on the roof, which also has four doorways and a cupola on top. The cupola is hollow and has four lines of conch-shell trumpets embedded into it in such a manner that a strong wind sounds them.

The primarily symbolic nature of the four-way orientation of C1-1-a is indicated by its diminutive size ($20m^2$) despite its complexity. Even the short-statured Maya must have had to crawl through the doorways and in the interior. Therefore most ritual activities probably took place around the exterior of the structure.

The inner sanctum of C1-1-a, unlike those in the other Type 4a structures, is as accessible as the other interior spaces because it has a doorway directly linking the inner sanctum to the exterior. Although this may well be a peculiarity created by the asymmetrical modification of the original building, it is noteworthy that the sanctum is least accessible from the side facing the small plaza area on which the structure is situated.

Orientation to the four quarters so pervades Maya cosmology that it is difficult to associate these Type 4a buildings with any deity or ceremony. Roys (1943:76), however, observes that although round temples were associated with Kukulcan, some of the deity's most prominent temples were rectilinear with access on four sides. As god of the winds, Kukulcan may not have been associated with any one of the four quarters but rather with their nexus, the center. Thus his temples may have been oriented to all four direc-

tions, or to none of them, as in the case of round structures. More important, the particular association of C1-1-a with the winds exhibited in its cupola indicates an association of this building with Kukulcan.

Alternatively, from a more general perspective, it might be argued that the orientation to the four directions indicates an association of these structures with the *Uayeb* or other rituals that were organized in terms of these directions (Tozzer 1941:142).

The peripheral location of the Type 4a structures would seem to controvert ethnohistorical descriptions associating rituals organized in terms of the four directions with central places. However, peripheral location may in fact have been more sacred or have had more general community-level associations than some centralized religious foci. This would replicate the peripheral location of Cozumel as a major pilgrimage center vis-à-vis the capitals of northern Yucatan (see V. Turner 1974 on the peripheral location of modern shrine centers in Mexico).

TYPE 4b

MAJOR CRITERION
Orientation to one direction (Figure 14).

STRUCTURES
C22-24a.

DISCUSSION
C22-24a initially appeared to be unique on Cozumel in its combination of concentric plan, two rooms, and orientation to a single direction. Holmes (1895-1897:65; also see Freidel 1975: Figure 27) and later Lothrop (1924:155-156), however, describe a structure north of San Miguel with a similar plan (C11, Miramar) that was subsequently destroyed, and the inner two chambers of another structure, C22-25-a, have the same plan. Apparently in all three cases the two rooms were built at the same time. The width of the outer chamber along the sides is slightly narrower than the doorway into the inner sanctum. Because these side areas lead nowhere, it seems possible they functioned for storage. Although the role of the outer chamber may have been largely symbolic rather than functional, the space between the

inner and outer doorways may have been of some ritual significance.

Precisely what the arrangement symbolized is impossible to determine. Certainly it lends an air of esoteric seclusion to the inner chamber and may have had a meaning similar to the arrangement of A. Andrews's complex shrines and those structures of similar plan mentioned on Cozumel in Type 3. Although C22-24a does not have the functional floor space in the outer chamber found in the other two structures just mentioned, the chamber may still have symbolized similar ritual associations. Furthermore, a tendency toward miniaturization as a symbolic medium has already been pointed out in the case of C1-1-a (Type 4a) and is well attested generally in Late Postclassic architecture on the East Coast.

The combination of the colonnaded, wide outer doorway with the restricted access created by the inner doorway makes this plan similar to tandem-plan masonry structures with the same access arrangements. It is possible that C22-24a shared some of the functions of structures in Type 6.

MISCELLANEOUS TYPE 4

C22-34-f is situated on top of a circular truncated pyramid in a shrine group at San Gervasio (Figure 14). At the time of observation, only fragments of the walls of this small single-room structure remained. This created the impression that the structure was round and it was so planned on the group map. Although small, round masonry structures are known on the coast of Quintana Roo (A. Andrews, personal communication, 1973) and are therefore not out of the realm of possibility for Cozumel, Escalona-Ramos (1946:619) plans this structure as square with doorways on all four sides. Because he saw this structure in a much better state of preservation, in retrospect we accept his identification of the plan as square.

C22-34-f is the simplest structure on the Type 4a continuum and it seems rather contrived to create a separate subtype for the structure on the basis of its single-room plan. However, from the perspective of the East Coast in general, this plan does merit a separate subtype. Several examples of the plan exist in the literature (Lothrop 1924: Figures 171 and 173). Additionally the association of a building facing in four directions with

pyramidal substructure combines two of the proposed material criteria for religious buildings dedicated to Kukulcan. Perhaps in this case, more so than in many others, we can argue for an identification of a religious building as sacred to a particular deity.

TYPE 5: GENERAL DISCUSSION

MAJOR CRITERIA

Tandem plan two-roomed masonry structures with single outer and inner doorways (Figure 14).

DISCUSSION

On Cozumel, the two primary ways of partitioning interior space in masonry structures are the concentric and the tandem plan. Leventhal (1974:74) is of the opinion that both of these arrangements achieve the same effect—to create an outer, more visually accessible space and an inner, less visually accessible space. In the discussion of concentric plan buildings (Type 4), we have already pointed out that a more complex interpretation of such plans is possible. Here we focus on the notion of visual accessibility as employed by Leventhal.

Leventhal generally argues that the function of narrow doorways is to constrict visual more than physical access. Constricted visual access symbolized the sacred and remote nature of the space within. This notion provides a useful approach to the Type 5 buildings. In the three out of five Type 5 buildings that contain altars, the altar is located on the central axis of the building directly behind a doorway in the medial wall. Rather than shielding activity in the immediate vicinity of the altar from view, the medial wall and doorway focus attention from the outer chamber upon it. The medial wall, however, does block from view the items and activities to either side of the altar. Furthermore this arrangement discourages physical ritual participation by people in the front room because they must stand well behind the medial doorway in order to view activities around the altar.

It is possible that the medial doorway was covered with a screen. However, in contrast to evidence on several exterior doorways of masonry buildings, no trace of cord-holders was found near the medial doors. Perhaps some altars were visually accessible and others were not, as Villa Rojas (1945:98) described for the modern Tix Cacal Indians:

> The patron cross of the village is kept in the village church, a building constructed of the same materials as houses but larger and better made. The altar on which the cross rests occupies a small room at the far end of the church called the Gloria, which is separated from the rest of the space by a screen of poles. In the village churches, unlike the sanctuary at the shrine village, the sacred precinct is open and the cross visible to all.

Although mediation is direct in the small village churches of these Indians, at the sanctuary of the talking cross mediation is always indirect through a church official. Despite the unknown factors separating modern from ancient use of religious buildings in Quintana Roo, the analogy is consistent with the archaeological and historical evidence.

In summary, occurrence of the tandem plan in miniature structures with virtually unusable interior space indicates the plan had some symbolic value. Because it also occurs in larger structures with usable interior space, the tandem plan may have defined ritual activities along specific lines. Moreover the restricted visual access from the exterior found in these structures indicates that activities within were not for observation from without. Thus there is a demarcation between activities outside the buildings and those inside. On this basis the Type 5 structures can be related to the Type 1 structures. Leventhal likewise viewed these two types as related.

TYPE 5a

MAJOR CRITERIA
Tandem plan two-roomed masonry structures with single outer and inner doorways (Figure 14).

STRUCTURES
C7-1-a, C15-1-a, C16-1-a, and C22-34-a.

DISCUSSION
These structures fit the general plan discussed above. Ranging in size from 16 to 46m^2, they are on the whole larger than structures of the first three types. They are not found in any formal plaza groups, but rather occur in isolated locations along the coast, on *sacbes*, and in shrine groups that have been associated with religious buildings.

This range of location, coupled with the sporadic occurrence of exterior mouldings and facades (C7-1-a [see Plates 3a and 3b], C15-1-a, and possibly C22-34-a), altars (C7-1-a and C22-34-a), and other construction details (vents and roof ornaments) indicate that Type 5a structures are within the formal range of religious buildings on Cozumel.

These four structures are given a subtype designation primarily to distinguish them from two other Type 5 buildings that are distinctive enough to warrant separate classification.

TYPE 5b

MAJOR CRITERION
Multiple interior accessways (Figure 14).

STRUCTURES
C34-1-a and C22-41-a.

DISCUSSION
C34-1-a (9m^2) is virtually a miniature structure. Two masonry piers inside effectively divide the severely restricted interior space into two tandem rooms with three visually accessible openings to the back room. Although it might well be argued that these piers are simply a pragmatic device for holding up the roof, which is made of roughly dressed flat slabs overlain with mortar, the fact that there were alternative roofing techniques that might have been employed makes it likely that the piers had some symbolic value as well. By focusing attention on the center of the back wall, the placement of the piers creates the general effect characteristic of Type 5 buildings. In this case, the effect of the severely restricted interior was probably intended to be real as well as symbolic. The ritual activities at C34-1-a, located on the *sacbe* running from San Gervasio to the northeast coast, were therefore probably carried out in front of the building.

C22-41-a (Figure 15) was originally a single-room structure with an altar either against the back wall or set out a small distance from it. The structure was later modified by construction of a medial wall. This medial wall was built not only to incorporate the front part of the altar, but to leave a miniature doorway or niche in the front of it as well. By simply terminating the medial wall before it reached the exterior ones, accessways to the back part of the structure were left at the sides. Thus, someone standing in the front room could see whatever was placed on the altar, but nothing to its sides. Such a plan epitomizes the visual control function of the medial wall in the Type 5 buildings by eliminating the ingress-egress function of the central interior doorway. This function is relegated to side doorways. It is clear from the construction history of the building that this modification was deliberate and represents a functional modification of the interior space.

The affinity between the plan of C22-41-a and that of the shrine of Ix Chel as described by Lopez de Gomara (Simpson 1966) has been

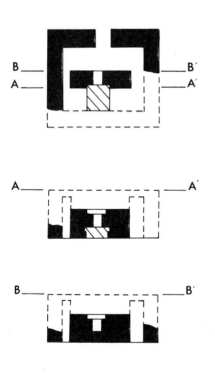

Figure 15 C22-41-a plan and sections.

discussed by Freidel (1975). Apparently the temple of Ix Chel was a complex tandem-plan structure, the focus of which was a lifesize hollow idol. This idol was fastened to the medial walls in the front room. A small, secret door in the medial wall permitted access into the idol from which a priest could speak to the worshippers. The back room, described as a *sacristy*, was open only to priests.

In C22-41-a, however, the altar, not the idol, is the ritual focus and the medial doorway functions to allow visual rather than physical access. Thus the same effect, on a more modest dramatic scale, could be achieved in C22-41-a by a priest standing next to an idol on the altar or in the back room. If this is the case, the temple of Ix Chel would be innovative in shifting the religious focus to the front room, restoring the medial doorway as a means of physical ingress and egress, turning the religious focus into a lifesize idol, and placing the priest inside rather than next to it. This argument hinges on the association of idols with altars in religious buildings and on the belief that the idol of Ix Chel was not unique in her ability to speak.

Features that have been called *altars* in the archaeological and historical literature occur in a variety of contexts other than inside religious buildings. Those that do occur inside such buildings seem to have functioned as places of sacrifice, thrones for idols, and places for offerings. According to Bernal Diaz del Castillo's description, quoted above, of an interior altar used for sacrifices, this feature was quite accessible. Thus the altar in C22-41-a would have been ill suited as a place of sacrifice because the sacrificer would have had to lean through a niche doorway, or approach the altar from the side in the narrow back room. On the other hand, the altar could have been used as a place for offerings. However, in the descriptions of ceremonies involving offerings, the offerings were placed in front of the idols. Alternatively idols were placed on altars inside shrines and temples. The combination of awkward physical access and easy visual access to the altar surface makes it likely that the altar was meant to be viewed rather than approached. Because the primary religious foci associated with altars in Late Postclassic Yucatan were idols, it seems likely this was the function of C22-41-a.

Given the importance of talking crosses in modern and historic Quintana Roo (Villa Rojas 1945:21), it is tempting to infer a persistence of precontact religious practices in the area. Victoria Bricker (personal communication, 1974), however, has discouraged simple correlations of modern and ancient talking "deities," arguing that the intervening factors (including possible encouragement of such native practices by Christian priests) are complex. Additionally any attempt to establish the prevalence of talking idols in precontact times is hampered by the scarcity of references to them. Nevertheless, the *chilanes* (prophets) were capable of direct verbal communication with the supernatural, specifically the deity floating in the rafters of the *chilan*'s house (Roys 1933:182), idols were "fed" the blood of sacrifice, indicating that they may have been viewed as living entities, and as late as the seventeenth century there was a talking idol among the Itza. Avendano, for example, gives the following speech when his life is threatened by a Cacique Covoh:

> just as there is a time marked out and determined for you to become Christians, so also are the times determined for me to die for love of Him; and if it were left in your hands, as you think, and say such things, you would have carried it out, or the devil Pakoc (this is an idol who speaks to them very frequently) whom you adore and who dictates such things to you; but here you shall know how slight is his strength in my presence, since he only dares to speak of it to you and not to come and execute it upon me. (Means 1917:145)

It is highly unlikely that the religious practices of the pagan Itza were influenced by their Christian brethren to the north, even if such Christian natives were encouraged to have talking crosses, as Bricker believes. If the Itza talking idol cannot be attributed to postcontact diffusion, then it indicates a strong, if geographically sporadic, tradition of such entities in the area.

It is possible that the function of the medial wall in C22-41-a was simply to create a more isolated and secluded space around the altar, thereby heightening the altar's sanctity. Other plans on Cozumel, such as C22-24a, achieve such an effect, but they also block visual access to the central focus or altar. It is the combination of visu-al access to the altar and blocked visual access to the sides of the altar that was important in Type 5 buildings and particularly in C22-41-a.

Just as the shrine of Ix Chel represents an elaboration on C22-41-a, so C22-41-a is a modification of the basic Type 5 plan. The shift in this case involves the separation of the physical and visual access functions of the central doorway in front of the altar, the relegation of physical access to the sides, and the creation of a central doorway in the medial wall, which is only accessible visually.

This shift from the single medial doorway found in Type 5a buildings to the three medial doorways with distinct uses need not have been sudden. Unfortunately we lack both the chronological controls and historical analogies to support such a seriation and the formal architectural variability in small masonry structures on the East Coast is broad enough to support any number of seriational patterns.

In any case, C22-41-a was certainly an important religious structure. It rests on a pyramidal substructure about 4m high with a single staircase on the western face. This substructure is connected to the large rectangular enclosure at San Gervasio by a small *sacbe*. The fact that large pyramidal substructures are rare on Cozumel seems to indicate that the structures resting upon them were of notable importance.

TYPE 6

MAJOR CRITERIA
Two-roomed tandem-plan masonry structures with colonnaded, multiple-front doorways (Figure 16).

STRUCTURES
C18-24-a, C22-4-a, C22-4-b, C25-1-a, C25-1-b, C25-1-c, C31-1-b, and C22-6-c.

DISCUSSION
Although there are larger individual structures, as a type these structures are the largest and most substantial masonry structures found on Cozumel ($28\text{-}54\text{m}^2$). In contrast to the Type 5 structures, they are found, with one exception, in formal plaza groups. Bernal Diaz del Castillo (Maudslay 1908:112) clearly distinguishes idol houses from chambers and large halls. If the three Type 6 struc-

tures in the major formal plaza group at San Gervasio (C22-4a through C22-10; see Figure 18) are idol houses, Diaz del Castillo's description fits this group perfectly. A variety of other sources, such as Landa's general description of a Yucatecan town (Tozzer 1941:62), describe central plaza groups as expectable locations for community religious buildings. The majority of masonry structures (7 out of 10) that occur in centralized formal plaza groups belong to Type 6. Although we cannot preclude a religious function for other types of buildings found in such groups, it seems likely that the Type 6 structures represent the larger masonry religious structures described as temples.

Sporadic criteria, such as mouldings and location on raised substructures, relate this type to others identified as religious buildings. However, none of the Type 6 structures shows evidence of altars. The absence of altars is puzzling, as the Type 6 structures are the best candidates for centralized temples. The discrepancy may be explained by the association of these structures with small rectangular platforms in the center of the plaza groups that functioned as group altars.

Although Type 6 shares an orientation to one direction, tandem plan, and limited access to the chamber with Type 5, it is distinguished from that type by its visually and physically more accessible front room, as pointed out by Leventhal (1974: 80-81). Although it might be argued that the tandem plan is shared with Mayapan-style dwellings (our Perishable Type 15), the Mayapan-style dwellings are open across the entire front room and on Cozumel are associated with outbuildings rather than colonnades and "chambers." Furthermore, the tandem plan is associated with masonry religious structures long before the rise of Mayapan.

The distinctive feature of the plan is its open access in the front room. Unlike religious buildings oriented to a single direction with a single constricted doorway, there is no physical demarcation of the exterior space in front of the structures and the interior space of the front room inside them. Apparently the objects, people, and activities inside the Type 6 structures were intended to be viewed and integrated with those on the plaza areas in front of them.

In the few explicit descriptions of ritual activities associated with temples, there are some indications of this kind of integration. According to Landa (Tozzer 1941:164-166), the festival of the *nacom*, or sacred war captain, was celebrated in the month of *Pax*. This festival was a major community ceremony that drew the local leadership in the outlying towns and villages to the main center. The festival was described as follows:

> And they bore [the *nacom*] in great pomp, perfuming him as if he were an idol, to the temple, where they seated him, and burned incense to him as to an idol. And thus he and they remained until the five days were passed, during which they ate and drank the gifts which were offered in the temple, and they danced a dance with a long martial step, and so they called it in their language, *Holkan Okot*, which means the dance of the warriors. (Landa in Tozzer 1941:165)

Clearly the sacred character of the *nacom* was heightened by his treatment as an idol, censed, and placed in the temple. Although there is no direct reference to whether or not the *nacom* reviewed the dances and other proceedings in the plaza before him, it is implied in the description. In practical terms, it would certainly be less awkward to carry the *nacom*, and possibly his litter, through the wider doorways of Type 6 structures than through the narrow ones of other types of religious structures. In fact, it would be impossible to carry someone in and out of the structures with single accessways on one side. This is also true of the medial doorways in most of the Type 6 buildings. Thus the *nacom* would be placed in the front room during such ceremonies.

A more tentative indication of the integration of ritual activities within and in front of the temple is seen in a festival held in honor of all the gods:

> During this month of Yaxkin, they began to prepare, as was their custom, for a general festival which was celebrated in Mol . . . in honor of all the gods. . . . . After they had collected in the temple and performed the ceremonies and burning of incense, which they had done in the past (festivals), their purpose was to anoint with the blue bitumen, which

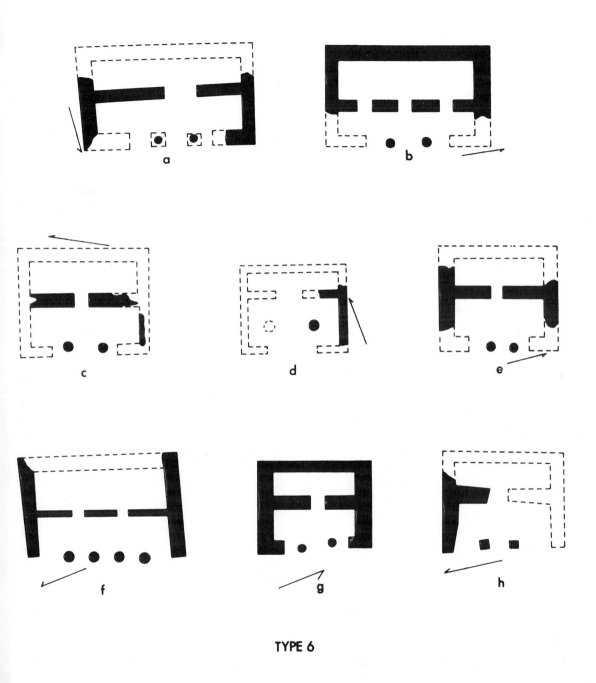

TYPE 6

Figure 16 Masonry structures. Type 6: (a) C25-1-b; (b) C22-4-b; (c) C22-6-c; (d) C18-24-a; (e) C22-4-a; (f) C25-1-a; (g) C25-1-c; (h) C31-1-a. (Scale 1:200).

they made, all the appliances of their pursuits, from the priest to the spindles of the women and the wooden columns of their houses. For this feast they collected all the boys and girls of the town . . . they struck each of them on the joints of the backs of the hands . . . they gave them these blows so that they might become skillful workmen in the professions of their fathers and mothers. The end of this ceremony was a good drunken feast. (Landa in Tozzer 1941:158-159)

Unless they removed the doorposts from the house for this ceremony, it seems probable that the activities began at the temple and emanated to dwellings. Thus there would be continuity in the ritual activity within the temple, in the plaza, and beyond. Although other kinds of religious structures could certainly have been used, the Type 6 structures are best designed for such continuity.

Undoubtedly more esoteric, less-public rituals were held in centralized community temples. Besides possibly serving as storage places for ritual paraphernalia, as described in the Ix Chel temple, back rooms of community temples may well have served as places for more exclusive ritual activities that involved only community leaders (see Leventhal 1974:75). Thus, such a combination of relatively open and inaccessible interior space is appropriate to the centralized temples that presumably served as contexts for a wide variety of ritual activities.

C18-24-a is the only structure in Type 6 that was not located in a formal plaza group. Because it was badly damaged at the time of observation, our plan is an extrapolation from scanty remains. It lies in a shrine group to the north of the main settlement zone of Buena Vista. The peculiarity of its location outside a formal plaza group is heightened, moreover, by the absence of Type 6 structures from the main plaza group at the settlement. Apparently the principal religious foci at Buena Vista were located at the periphery of the settlement rather than in its center. Given the disposition of the overall settlement, C18-24-a seems to have shared the community functions of other Type 6 structures, and its location can be attributed to the unusual organization of Buena Vista, which is discussed in Chapter 6.

MISCELLANEOUS MASONRY STRUCTURES

C8-1-a is a transverse plan masonry structure with two rooms. The structure was so ruined that it was impossible to locate the doorways (Figure 17). Those given on the plan are hypothetical and are based upon the location of an altar set against the medial wall in the west room. As altars consistently face doorways in other masonry structures, it is likely that the doorways were in the end walls. The location of this masonry building on the northeast coast leads us to suspect that it was religious in function. The peculiar arrangement may have had some special ritual significance related to the eastern and western orientation of the rooms.

C2-1-a is another transverse plan masonry structure with three rooms and five doorways (see Fernandez 1945). This plan is so unusual (Figure 17), both for Cozumel and the East Coast in general, that it is difficult to relate it to other masonry structures. Because it is situated on the southeast coast, it would seem to be a religious structure. However, it is unlike any of the structures we have identified with this function. Thus, given its location on the coast in front of the important settlement of Buena Vista, it may have served some defensive function. The coastal shrines on Cozumel seem generally to have been used as defensive lookout posts in times of attack, as when the Spanish arrived (Wagner 1942a). Possibly in this case the defensive function overrode the religious and the structure housed a small garrison.

C27-3-b, estimated at $200m^2$, is without question the most unusual structure on Cozumel (Figure 7a). It is included in the masonry structure category because its walls seem to have been primarily of stone. However, these walls are uncut rubble, set presumably in mud mortar, and probably did not extend all the way to the roof. It has an estimated six small rooms (depending how one divides up the interior space) connected by a meandering corridor.

Located in the center of Aguada Grande and dated by ceramics to very late in the Decadent period, the structure may well date to Conquest times. It does not, however, reflect any identifiable Spanish influences. It is situated next to C27-4a, which was identified as an oven of some kind in Chapter 2. Perhaps C27-3-b was a work-

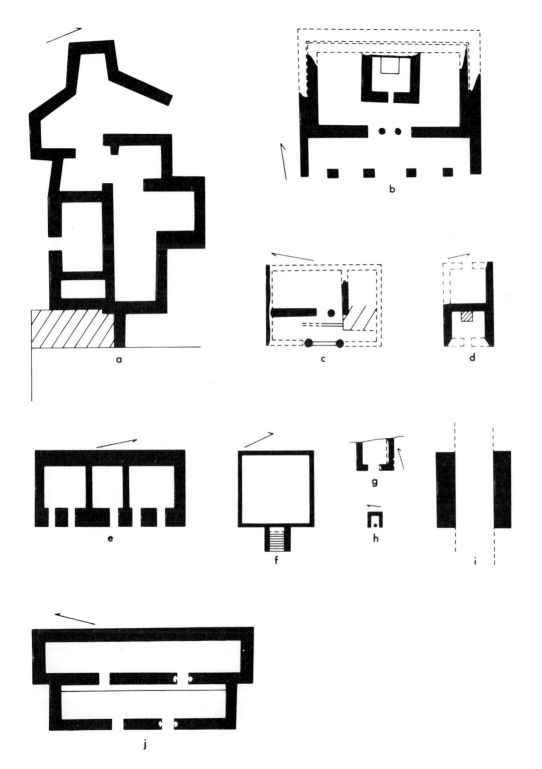

Figure 17 Masonry structures. Miscellaneous: (a) C27-3-b; (b) C22-25-a; (c) C22-30-a; (d) C8-1-a; (e) C2-1-a (after Fernandez 1947); (f) C22-10; (g) C32-1a; (h) C23-3-a; (i) C22-31; (j) C22-48-a. (Scale 1:200).

shop for mass-manufactured idol censers that were fired in the oven. Unfortunately no excavated remains support such a function for either feature. Alternatively it may have served as an inn for pilgrims or as a storage house for commodities relayed through Aguada Grande from the north coast to the center of the island, but this is pure speculation.

C22-48-a is considered here not only because it has an unusual plan (Figure 17j), but because it appears to date to the Early period on architectural grounds (see Gregory 1975:Figure 22). The structure has two long, tandem rooms (total area is 95m^2), and two medial and two front doorways. The walls are made of very finely cut rectangular blocks that are dressed on all surfaces and laid in regular courses. Each wall consists of a double course of such blocks with virtually no hearting between them. The rooms were vaulted and the vault is laid in very regular steps about 8.0cm wide. There is a single, massive rectangular moulding running around the outside of the structure just above the level of the lintels. Above the moulding, a facade of flat, square blocks is carved in a stepped-pyramid motif reminiscent of the facade on the Early period "Palace" at Acanceh in Yucatan.

Whatever the function of this structure may have been before, during the Late Postclassic it was used as a place of worship and sacrifice. Bones of small mammals and birds as well as censerware dating to the Late Postclassic were found on the floor level below the roof fall. C22-48-a, however, does not appear to have been replastered or otherwise remodeled during the Late Postclassic.

C22-25-a (Plate 2b), in its final form, compares well with the palaces at Tulum (Lothrop 1924:Figure 25: Structures 20, 21, 25, and 34) and the more substantial dwellings at Mayapan. Yet it is clear that C22-25-a underwent important modification during its history. Leventhal (1974: 84) believes that it was originally a Type 1 shrine, subsequently modified into a complex shrine of the kind found on the coast opposite Cozumel, and finally elaborated into a palace with combination tandem-concentric plan. We, on the other hand, think that the structure began as a single-roomed domicile that was subsequently modified to include a shrine along the back wall and a colonnaded front room. Although the entire back wall of the structure has collapsed, certain circumstantial evidence supports this interpretation. The entrance to the shrine has a definite depression in the floor because the level of the shrine room is lower than that of the room it adjoins. This arrangement would make sense if the builders of the shrine had to accommodate an already extant beam-and-mortar roof over the original single-roomed dwelling. In order to fit the roof of the shrine into the building, they had to lower the level of the shrine relative to the floor level of the original structure. The colonnaded portico is clearly a subsequent addition because its walls are not bonded into those of the original single-roomed structure. In sum, we suggest that this rather substantial masonry walled, single-roomed dwelling was modified to fit the tandem-plan and interior shrine arrangement typical of "palaces" as found at Mayapan and Tulum.

Smith (1962:231) noted the similarity between Mayapan elite dwellings and East Coast palaces, explaining the absence of bench areas at Tulum by their location under roof fall. In a plan of a palace structure at Ichpaatun given by Escalona-Ramos (1946:582), there are clearly L-shaped bench areas in the front room. The rise of the roof fall up the medial wall in the front room of C22-25-a indicates bench areas might similarly be present. Unfortunately the room was not cleared.

C22-25-a is part of a group connected to the main plaza group at San Gervasio by a *sacbe* (Figure 17b). This relationship is shared by two substantial residential groups. If C22-25-a is primarily religious in function, then its group is of the shrine type. Although shrine groups are found connected to other groups by *sacbes* on Cozumel, in other instances they are located on the periphery of settlement zones. Thus a residential function for the group would be more consistent with the rest of the pattern at San Gervasio.

Finally a large domestic midden was found and excavated immediately west of C22-25-a. The high occurrence of utilitarian wares, animal and fish bone, broken ground- and chipped-stone tools, and the notable lack of censerware indicates the debris was domestic. If the group that included C22-25-a was oriented primarily toward religious ritual, this seems an unlikely location for a domestic midden.

C22-30-a, located in a group with one of the Mayapan style dwellings, is identified as a private oratory (Figure 17c). It is included here because the plan is unusual in that it combines aspects of concentric and tandem plans. The inner sanctum is a compartment in the northeast corner of the building. The structure has two accessways formed by columns and a possible bench area in the southeast corner. Although the structure does not contain an àltar niche as found at Mayapan, the colonnaded doorways and bench area relate this building to oratories found there. As Mayapan style oratories go, this one is quite elaborate with its masonry walls and beam-and-mortar roof.

C32-1a is a small Type 1 structure built into a shallow cave (Figure 17g). The location of altars and small shrines in caves is not unusual on the East Coast (A. Andrews, personal communication, 1973; Lothrop 1924:Figure 132; also see Miller 1977). Although there are no descriptions of rituals in caves, during the Colonial period large numbers of idols were found in them. In general, both depth and height are sacred to the Maya. Therefore, just as "exalted" locations are and were appropriate for religious buildings, so are caves. There are indications that caves were used for other ritual purposes on Cozumel, such as the primary deposition of the dead.

MISCELLANEOUS MASONRY STRUCTURE CLASSES

There are three general classes of structures that do not form internally consistent types on the basis of architectural criteria: miniature shrines, group altars, and masonry arches. Nevertheless, they seem to reflect three general functional categories and are therefore considered as miscellaneous classes.

MINIATURE SHRINES
C23-3-a, at $0.9m^2$, is the smallest masonry structure on Cozumel. It has a column in the doorway with its own diminutive capital. The walls are roughly dressed blocks, a single course thick, and the roof was slab. A good sample of effigy censerware was found in front of the doorway and around the structure, and a cache was discovered below it. Along with C23-3-b, a larger shrine, C23-3-a constitutes the central group at

Chen Cedral and probably housed a single idol. Like C25-30a (below), C23-3-a probably functioned as a group altar.

C22-6-d, a diminutive niche chamber at the southern edge of the staircase in front of C22-6-c, and C25-30a, a group altar at La Expedicion, may be two other possible miniature masonry religious structures on Cozumel. C25-30a contained a crude limestone carved figure and a rich cache below it.

GROUP ALTARS

STRUCTURES
C1-1-c, C18-1-f, C22-10a, C22-26a, C22-30-b, C22-34-c, C22-90-c, C22-95-c, C25-1-f, C25-30a, and C31-1-e.

DISCUSSION
For the most part, the features called *group altars* on Cozumel are small rectangular masonry platforms situated in the plazas of important groups. As at Mayapan (Smith 1962:221), such altars, when found in residential groups, are often oriented to the axis of the most important dwellings. They are also found oriented to the temples (Type 6 structures) in formal plaza groups.

In addition to two miniature masonry structures described above that functioned as group altars, two of the group altars (C22-10-a and C18-1-f) are more elaborate than the others. C22-10a was originally a small Type 1 structure. Later it was filled in and refaced. A three-member superior moulding and a staircase on the eastern face were added and the staircase oriented the structure to the *sacbe* that enters this plaza group from the east.

C18-1-f, in the formal plaza at Buena Vista, was apparently a small, square colonnaded structure. It is too small to fit into the established types for colonnades and its location indicates a religious function. C18-1-f is the one break in an otehwise consistent form-function correlation for open-sided colonnaded buildings. Although the structure is unique as a religious focus on Cozumel, it is consistent with the relegation of masonry religious structures to the periphery of the Buena Vista settlement zone.

That group altars functioned as religious foci may be inferred from several oblique references in Landa's *Relacion*. Part of the ceremony surrounding the making of wooden idols involved placing the finished figure in an arbor in the yard where all present could worship it (Tozzer 1941: 160). During the Uayeb rituals, idols of the four year-bearer gods are placed temporarily in the households of principal men: "and to celebrate [the festival] they made a statue of a god, which they called Bolon Dzacab, which they placed in the house of the *principal* adorned in a public place where everyone could go to it" (Tozzer 1941:140). Although this public place may well have been an oratory, group shrine, or the front room of tandem-plan buildings, the most accessible location would be the group altar.

Additional support for their function as religious foci is found in the features sporadically associated with them. A tomb was located beneath C22-95-c, a burial beneath C22-26a, and definite caches under C23-3-a and C25-30a. The cache under C23-3-a, the miniature shrine, may have been related to the structure, but dates to the Early Postclassic or Modified Florescent period. Thus it may be related to an earlier structure on the same spot. Alternatively, the shrine group at C23 may date to the Modified Florescent but continued in use into the Decadent.

The group altar in front of C1-1a is unusual in that it is a single carved block resembling a phallus or mushroom. Phallic imagery is less rare in the Decadent period of Yucatan than in other periods and may be indirectly connected with the cult of the *plumeria* (Roys 1933) and erotic practices generally attributed to Mexican influences.

MASONRY ARCHES

Masonry arches have been known to occur on Cozumel for a long time. The recognized examples are at the settlement of El Cedral (C15) that were observed, planned, and illustrated by Holmes (1895-1897:68) and most subsequent investigators of Cozumel's ruins. Holmes describes one arch (C15-5-e) situated at the northwest corner of a large formal plaza group as being in good condition and notes that the feature was probably attached to a building to the east at one time. He identifies the arch as a portal access onto the plaza and describes a second arch in badly ruined condition at the northeast corner of the group. The vault of C15-5-e is smooth rather

than stepped and has a clear outset at the spring. These characteristics of masonry architecture at El Cedral are commonly associated with Florescent and Modified Florescent architecture in Yucatan. Test pitting in the vicinity of C15-5-e and C15-14-a, the Type 1 masonry religious structure, yielded a small sample of Modified Florescent ceramics in sealed contexts. It is possible that the masonry structures at El Cedral were built prior to the Decadent but were in use up to the Contact period.

However, both smooth vaults and portal arches are also found in Decadent contexts. Although it runs under structures in the group, a vaulted passageway at Mayapan (Smith 1962: Figure 21h) functions as a portal arch and exhibits both smooth and stepped vaulting. Portal arches in the outer and inner walls at Tulum (Lothrop 1924: 68-74) are roofed with vaults or beam-and-mortar construction. Thus, although portal arches have their roots in Florescent architecture, they appear to persist into Decadent times.

Apparently portal arches functioned as elaborate accessways. In the case of the encompassing walls at Tulum, the portal arches control access to the settlement and inner enclosure. In the Mayapan example and at El Cedral they restrict access onto the plaza. At El Cedral, however, there were other accessways onto C15-5. Thus these arches seem to have been of ritual as well as pragmatic significance.

Another arch was discovered in the course of survey at San Gervasio. This arch, C22-31, straddles the intercommunity *sacbe* (C22-S-1) at that site and is the first feature on the *sacbe* outside the main formal plaza group where it originates. C22-31 had a masonry vault that has collapsed and is substantially larger than those at El Cedral. Given the fact that all the structures in the main formal plaza group and all the shrines on the *sacbe* are ceramically dated to the Decadent, it seems that C22-31 too was built duirng this time period.

Unlike the accessways through the walls at Tulum, or perhaps the plaza group portal archways, the arch on San Gervasio's main *sacbe* cannot have restricted physical access in any way. Hence its function must have been purely symbolic. Because its location on a *sacbe* and its formal similarities to other arches indicate that it did function as an accessway, it may have been a symbolic entrance to the settlement zone of San Gervasio. If this identification is correct, then its presence on a *sacbe* strengthens the general identification of *sacbes* as an important means of ritually defining socially discrete territories and relationships between them. That is, it helps identify *sacbes* as remains of ceremonial circuits within and between settlements on Cozumel.

As noted above, the *Provinciae* mentions the presence of a "large stone arch" at the southern end of Cozumel. This feature was apparently associated with a shrine and some thatched huts, but not with a formal plaza group. This isolated disposition of the arch is similar to that of C22-31. Although further exploration by the Spanish of this little settlement did not reveal the presence of a *sacbe*, its arch still may have ritually defined space for ceremonial processions. From this it follows that the location of this arch at the southern extremity of the island on a headland overlooking the sea indicates the presence of a ceremonial circuit encompassing the coastal shrines, which are some distance from major settlements in the interior. Because such arches are apparently rare on Cozumel, the one mentioned in the *Provinciae* probably marked an important terminus of a cermonial circuit running to the interior and/or along the coast.

SUMMARY AND CONCLUSIONS

The kinds of variation found in the masonry structures on Cozumel are to some degree made expectable by the descriptions of religious structures left by the Spanish in the Contact period. Therefore all these structures, with the noted exceptions, have been identified as primarily religious in function.

Fortunately, the types we have isolated on Cozumel show sufficient internal consistency for us to infer a consistency in the factors generating formal variability. We have argued that the variability selected for discussion relates to the disposition of ritual activities in and around these structures. In this sense, the formal types are also functional ones.

It is difficult to discern the specific associations such formal variability had in the minds of the builders. In some fortunate instances, certain deities such as Kukulcan appear to be associated with the material forms and certain interior designs with specific functions, as in the case of the talking idols. However, in most cases, we lack such correlates. Moreover, although it is likely that certain formal types were more appropriate to some ritual activities than to others, it seems just as likely that ritual was modified to fit the structure on occasion.

Furthermore, from the historical evidence, it is quite possible that in the minds of the natives religious buildings ran from plain to fancy. If this is the case, the design selected for a particular building would depend as much upon the expense to the sponsors as upon the desirability of a particular plan.

Perhaps stronger analogical identification can be developed on the basis of relative location than on form. Certainly the combination of the two is the most promising means to a functional identification. It is possible that the degree to which a formal type shows locational consistency is a measure of the consistency of associations with that type in the minds of the builders and users. Table 5 correlates types with location on Cozumel. Types 2, 3, and 6 show greater locational specificity than do Types 4 and 5, whereas Type 1 is clearly the all-purpose religious building. Private oratories, group altars, and arches are other forms specialized by location.

We have defined five locations for masonry religious buildings on Cozumel: isolated, on *sacbes*, in shrine groups, in central formal plaza groups, and in household groups. Historically the last two locations are well established as relating respectively to public community usage and private usage. The first three locations relate to an analogical scheme that we have briefly alluded to in the previous pages but must now spell out—ceremonial circuits that ritually define geographic territories and their interrelationships.

Coe (1965) and Vogt (1968) have worked out some of the details and the broader aspects of this model. They argue that the typically dispersed settlement pattern of the Maya must have been accompanied by some strong integrative forces and some means of defining the territorial units that functioned as sociopolitical entities. Both of these needs were satisfied in the ceremonial movement of people in, around, and between territorial units that range from the holdings of a family

Table 5
Correlation of location with formal masonry structure types.

Type	Isolated	Shrine group	Formal plaza group	Household group	Sacbe
1	X	X	X	X	X
2	X				X
3		X	X		
4	X	X		X(?)	
5	X	X			X
6	X		X		

group to entire communities or provinces.

Vogt (1968, 1969) bases his argument primarily on ceremonial circuits observed in the modern Maya community of Zinacantan, Chiapas. The rituals are organized and directed by specialists (called *hz'lotetik*, or shamans) and involve the sequential visiting of cross shrines, caves, mountains, and waterholes. These religious foci mark not only the sacred topography of territorial groups, but also their social boundaries. Periodic rituals held for the blessing of lineage groups, waterhole groups, hamlets, and the entire community, involve circuits of ascending geographic scale. Throughout the year, pilgrimages along these circuits, also conducted by shamans, form an integral part of curing ceremonies.

In addition to these activities, major fiestas in the hamlets and community center require the virtually continuous movement of religious officials, specialists, and participants to and from the center. Some of this movement involves elaborate processions, for example, the reception of visiting saints.

Vogt (1969:391) summarizes his functional interpretation of these circuits:

> The functions of the circuits appear to involve a set of boundary maintaining mechanisms in the Zinacanteco social system. When groups of cargo-holders make a circuit around Zinacantan Center they are symbolically saying (on behalf of all Zinacantecos) "this is our sacred center through which the holy river flows and around which live our ancestral gods watching over and guarding all of us." When the members of a waterhole group make a circuit that involves the waterhole and the sacred places around the waterhole, they are symbolically saying "this is our waterhole." When the members of a spa make the K'in Krus circuit around the lands they have inherited from their patrilineal ancestors, they are saying symbolically "these are our lands." When a circuit is made around a maize field it likewise marks off the boundary symbolically, or when a counterclockwise circuit is made around to four corners of a new house, this also says symbolically "here is our new house in which we are going to live." Hence each circuit symbolically designates property rights and marks off crucial social spaces in the Zinacanteco world.

Of particular interest are the material concomitants of the system: the geographically dispersed location of permanent, imperishable religious foci. Similar systems with the same concomitants are found in other highland Maya groups.

Coe (1965) interprets the *Uayeb* rituals described by Landa not only as a model of community organization among the Maya of Yucatan, but also as a model of rotating power within and between communities along the lines of the *cargo* system found in modern highland Maya groups. More important, these rites involve processions from the center of communities to the peripheries and back. The gods of the *Uayeb* ritual were associated with the cardinal directions and images of the gods were placed ceremoniously at the entrances into settlements. Each community ideally had four entrances at the four cardinal directions, and, over a 4-year period, the rites went to each entrance in turn, apparently in a counterclockwise circuit.

Landa describes such foci on the periphery of settlement zones as piles of stone upon which the images of gods were placed (Tozzer 1941:139-140). We found no piles that we could identify as boundary markers, but such amorphous features could have been easily missed in the bush. On Cozumel, however, there are identifiable religious foci on the periphery of settlement zones—masonry religious structures. The association of these buildings with settlements is indicated by their proximity to them, their occasional orientation toward them, and by the presence of *sacbes* connecting some of them to settlements. Furthermore, where they are connected to communities by *sacbes*, these structures are located roughly north, south, east, or west of the main settlement zones. Landa confirms the association of roads with these peripheral religious foci: "the lords and the priest and the men of the town assembled together had having cleared and adorned with arches and green the road leading to the place of heaps of stone where the statue was, they went all together to it with great devotion" (Tozzer 1941:140). The correlation of *sacbes* with masonry religious structures is high on Cozumel, and where these *sacbes* are punctuated by such structures or terminate at them, a firm case can be made for the ritual significance of *sacbes*. Although they are essentially the remains of ceremonial circuits, this does not preclude an additional secular function as highways.

If *sacbes* indicate ceremonial circuits on Cozumel in the Late Postclassic, then the possibility that other isolated shrines and shrine groups were points on ceremonial circuits is enhanced. This argument is elaborated in our discussion of *sacbes* and community settlement patterns in Chapters 4 and 5. For the moment let us say that we doubt very much that any of our "isolated" religious structures or religious groups were truly isolated. We think each of them contributed to the ritual definition of territorial and social boundaries at both the level of the community and the island as a whole.

The presence of several idol houses, however, has the added implication of a multiplicity of social referents. Such an arrangement indicates that these groups were sacred to more than one deity or component of society, depending on how one interprets the specific associations of the individual structures. These groups were, therefore, probably ritual central places, despite their peripheral location to central formal plaza groups and the main concentration of structures in settlements.

In the last analysis there are architectural forms with ritual significance and locations with ritual significance on Cozumel. That these vary independently to a substantial degree indicates the lack of any rigid emic categories for religious buildings. Instead we infer a basic repertoire of appropriate forms and locations from which builders could select a particular concrete expression. We have tried to tie down the functional referents in these repertoires. Any attempt to generalize form-locational correlations into ideal functional types obscures the facts, which indicates the Maya did not usually think in such terms. We say usually because the degree of association between form and location is not arbitrary. Although there is no perfect correlation, there is no perfect independence.

The following generalizations can be made about the functional types of religious structure on Cozumel in the Decadent period.

Centralized community temples are associated with Type 6 and are located in central plaza groups. Historical sources are fairly consistent in locating important community religious buildings in the central plazas of settlements, and the correlation between Type 6 and the central plaza groups is relatively good on Cozumel. The form is appropriate not only to integrated use of interior and exterior ritual space, but to more exclusive use of interior space as well. In several accounts there are implications of such integrated use by large groups of people in the context of community-level festivals.

Notable exceptions are the central plaza of Buena Vista, which lacks masonry religious buildings, and the central plaza group comprising structures C22-87-a through C22-87-d, which has a Type 1 masonry structure. A Type 6 structure, however, occurs on the periphery of the Buena Vista settlement zone.

Possible variations on Type 6 are found in perishable structures C22-95-a and C22-34-e. The first is on an elaborate pyramidal substructure in a central location, appropriate to a community temple. Unfortunately the plan is very fragmentary. Although C22-34-e lacks columns in the front doorway, the plan otherwise conforms to Type 6. However, it is located in a shrine group rather than in a central plaza group. The situation is complicated by associated ceramics that indicate that this shrine group was probably built and used during the Modified Florescent period. C22-34-e may have been an addition to the group in the Decadent period. This group probably continued in use during the Decadent.

Noncentralized community temples, associated with Types 4, 5, and 6, are found in isolated locations, on *sacbes*, or in shrine groups. If we call *temples* those structures within which sizable groups could participate in rituals, then these forms make up a functional type. By weighing size, the distinctions made on the basis of plan are crosscut; that size is a factor to some degree independent of plan is confirmed by the ranges in size within types formed on the basis of plan. As in the case of central community temples, it would seem that structures capable of holding a large party inside were deliberately so designed. The available descriptions indicate that ritual activities involving large groups of people were of community-level importance.

In an earlier discussion, these isolated locations were identified with ceremonial circuits. The fact that the natives of Cozumel placed some of their most important religious foci on these circuits either outside or on the edges of settlements indicates the importance of ritual definition of social and geographic space to them.

Centralized community shrines are associated with Type 1 and are located in centralized groups. Type 1 structures are found in central locations at three settlements: San Gervasio, Chen Cedral, and Aguada Grande. Smaller structures with more restricted interiors are appropriate to a small number of individuals attending rituals inside them and thus shrines are grossly distinguished from temples on the basis of size.

Restricted interior space, however, in no way precludes the possibility of large ritual gatherings in the vicinity of small structures. If we presume that large ritual gatherings took place primarily at centralized religious foci, as Landa's observations partially support, then it seems likely that these structures were used for such community celebrations despite their small size. The presence of such small, relatively simple masonry structures

as centralized community religious foci demonstrates the lack of any mechanical determination of form by function. This situation points to the possibility that factors other than ritual use may, on occasion, have served as determinants of form and size. These might have included size and disposition of the group sponsoring the construction of a religious building.

Noncentralized community shrines are associated with Types 1, 2, 4, and 5 and are located in isolated places, on *sacbes*, or in shrine groups. This is clearly a most flexible formal and locational grouping. The inclusion of the many structures that share these attributes in a single functional category follows primarily from our identification of ceremonial circuits on Cozumel.

The notion that these structures were constructed for public or community use is supported by the extreme rarity of masonry religious structures in the context of private households. Although private religious foci occur on Cozumel, they are constructed primarily of perishable materials.

Furthermore, the majority of buildings in this category are found on the periphery of settlements. Notable exceptions are some of the coastal shrines and the *sacbe* shrines between San Gervasio and the northeast coast. There are at least 17 coastal shrines along the northern, eastern, and southern edges of the island. Juan Diaz and others in the sixteenth century counted another 14 shrines along the western coast. From the smoke and drum signals sent up from the vicinity of these buildings as the Spanish explorers sailed along the coast, one might infer a secondary function as watchtowers. These signals and the ubiquity of the shrines indicate none of the shrines was very far from settlements. Hence even the most isolated of these structures were incorporated into an overall definition of space in ritual and social terms as part of ceremonial circuits on Cozumel. Moreover, the dispersion of religious buildings in these locations functioned not only as a means of lending an air of privacy and seclusion to them, but also as a means of reinforcing territorial definition and relationships within and between communities.

Public ritual houses are associated with Type 3 and are located in shrine groups. The case for identifying Type 3 structures as places for religious activities indirectly associated with the propitiation of idols, such as vigils and ritual drinking bouts, has already been made under the discussion of that formal type.

A possible, although quite tenuous, analogy for this type of structure is reported to exist at the village of Tix Cacal in Quintana Roo (D. Schuman, personal communication, 1975; Villa Rojas 1945:43). Apparently there is a structure located next to the church of the sacred cross, which is used by men participating in ritual activities for drinking bouts following ceremonies in the church.

Private shrines and oratories are associated with Type 1 and miscellaneous masonry structures and are located in household groups. Location is strongly weighed in forming this category and both perishable and masonry structures have been identified as private shrines and oratories. Generally these structures share a simple, one-room plan with constricted access. An exception is C22-30-a, which is an elaborate two-roomed oratory. On the whole, religious buildings in the context of private households are relatively modest on Cozumel. In fact, in many cases more investment appears to have been placed in the small, raised support substructures than in the superstructures of private shrines, for example, C22-13-c and C25-6-d. C22-13-c is a small raised substructure with evidence of plaster flooring in a household group at San Gervasio. The facade of the substructure is unusually elaborate, being constructed of flat, squared, finely dressed blocks that look very much like Puuc-style veneer stones. Additionally the substructure has a single-member moulding below the facade as well as a sloped lower facade that gives a *talud-tablero* effect. C25-6-d is also a small raised substructure but is attached to a substantial dwelling.

The relatively low level of investment in private shrines and oratories on Cozumel may indicate a different religious organization from that found at Mayapan. At the capital, the dispersion of religious foci seems well correlated with increased worship in the context of the home, which is well corroborated by Landa. On Cozumel, this dispersion seems to relate to ceremonial circuits rather than to households. Although it is possible that Cozumelenos were in the habit of building their private household shrines at some distance from the house compound, this seems highly unlikely, given what we know about modern and historical practices. Perhaps some of the dispersed shrines were identified with certain segments of the community that, in turn, were represented by an important family on ritual occasions, as is implied in the historical accounts. Unfortunately we have little control over this grey area between public and private domains.

CHAPTER 4

SUBSTRUCTURES, *SACBES*, AND FIELDWALLS

Substructures, Platforms, and Terraces

The vast majority of architectural features on Cozumel are raised and leveled areas with rubble, trash and dirt fill. These features have stone retaining walls of varying construction quality. In the literature of the area, such features are termed *platforms, substructures,* and *terraces.* Varying connotations have been applied by different students of the region. We generally follow the terminology of Smith (1962:224) in labeling the whole category substructures. Smith further distinguishes platforms and terraces within this category. Smaller and relatively well-defined raised areas underlying superstructures are platforms or support substructures, whereas terraces are the larger and often amorphous raised areas that support superstructures and their platforms. These platforms are often arranged in groups. Terracing, as a principle, usually takes advantage of natural rises by expanding and leveling them. As used by Smith, however, terraces would also include large raised and leveled features that do not necessarily take advantage of the terrain. They are often modified and expanded by the construction of new retaining walls and the dumping of new fill behind them.

Most recognizable superstructures on Cozumel have support platforms. Although Smith's *terrace* is useful as a general category distinct from *support platform*, we find it necessary to break it down into the two subcategories of *group substructures* and *agglutinated substructures.* Group substructures show traces of superstructures ranged around a plaza area on top. In contrast, agglutinated substructures are large, amorphous features with multiple, rectilinear areas on top of them distinguished by varying height (see Figure 18). In some cases, however, group substructures seem to form the nucleus of agglutinated substructures. The fact that this is not true in the majority of cases may well be due to the necessity of identifying group substructures on the basis of superstructural remains. Nevertheless, the presence of agglutinated substructures that clearly did not support plaza arrangements characteristic of group substructures indicates that this distinction is not entirely an artifact of preservation.

There is strong analogical and archaeological evidence for a positive correlation of substructures with superstructures in the Maya area. In the case of small, well-defined platforms without preserved superstructural remains, the extrapolation of a supportive function per se is reasonable. The problem of identifying such features as house platforms has already been considered in Chapter 2. Using size, location, and elaborateness, we have already identified some small structures as supporting private shrines. Unfortunately such identifications are very tenuous and on the whole attempting functional specificity for platforms without extensive control through excavation is a rather futile exercise.

Granting a supportive function, and applying the principle of abundance, substructures are a prime source of empirical evidence for the regional breadth and temporal depth of the characteristically dispersed Maya settlement pattern. Qualifying this pattern has become largely a matter of measuring the density of substructures in settlement

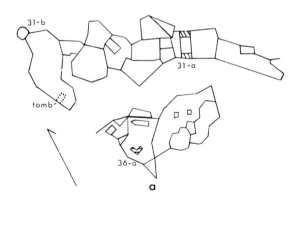

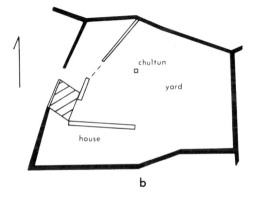

Figure 18. (a) Agglutinated substructures at La Expedicion, (b) a household group at Buena Vista (C18).

zones and analyzing their relationships to civil-religious architecture. At this level of analysis, the sheer number of substructures and their spatial organization become important. They will be considered in more detail in Chapter 5.

Agglutinated substructures, in contrast, are distinctive enough to be regarded as a consistently functionally specialized class, as are formal plaza groups and shrine groups. They are not only a type of substructure, but are also characteristic of only some settlements on Cozumel. Varying from being relatively minor features at San Gervasio, to moderately important at La Expedicion, they characterize the entire settlement of Chen Cedral. Because they are functionally specialized characteristics of settlement, we discuss agglutinated platforms in Chapter 5.

Sacbes

Sacbes, prepared stone paths or roads, have cropped up repeatedly in our discussion of masonry religious structures and ceremonial circuits (Figure 19). Intrasite *sacbes* are well documented in Classic contexts in both the southern and northern Lowlands and in Florescent contexts in the northern Lowlands. Intersite *sacbes*, from Classic and Florescent times, are also reported from the northern Lowlands (Kurjack 1974b; Villa Rojas 1934). Thus, although it is a little surprising that *sacbes* are rare in important late settlements such as Mayapan and are not reported for Tulum, it is not unexpected that they should eventually come to light in Decadent contexts on Cozumel. *Sacbes* are still being built in the Maya Lowlands. At the village of Chinoox, Belize, for example, rubble roadbeds are prepared, capped with white marl, and leveled with large logs (D. Birdwell, personal communication, 1975).

Like other architectural features on Cozumel, the *sacbes* are modest in construction compared to those reported elsewhere. The most substantial *sacbe*, C22-S-1, reaches a maximum width of only 4m and a maximum height of approximately 50cm over low ground. Even this *sacbe*, after passing C22-31-a, quickly narrows down to about 1.5m and remains a narrow stone path for the rest of its length. In general, Cozumel's *sacbes* average between 1.5 and 2m wide and range between ground level and 50cm in height. There is a general tendency for widening at the point of termination.

Construction technique, observed on the surface and through minor clearing operations, varies from a layer of flat, roughly dressed slabs set in the ground with vertically set edging slabs to layers of very large slabs of cap-rock built up to 50cm high with no retaining walls. In some cases, as on C22-S-1, a layer of gravel and small rock caps the bedding of slabs. In another case, C22-S-4 terminates in a ramp leading up to the plaza of a household group. The ramp has rubble and small stone fill and retaining walls of dry, horizontally laid, roughly dressed slabs. These variations in technique sometimes occur in the same *sacbe* and seem to correlate with shifts in the height of the land traversed. Dry laid large slab sections (see Plate 5a), for example, occur in low-lying seasonally inundated areas, whereas slab-paved and

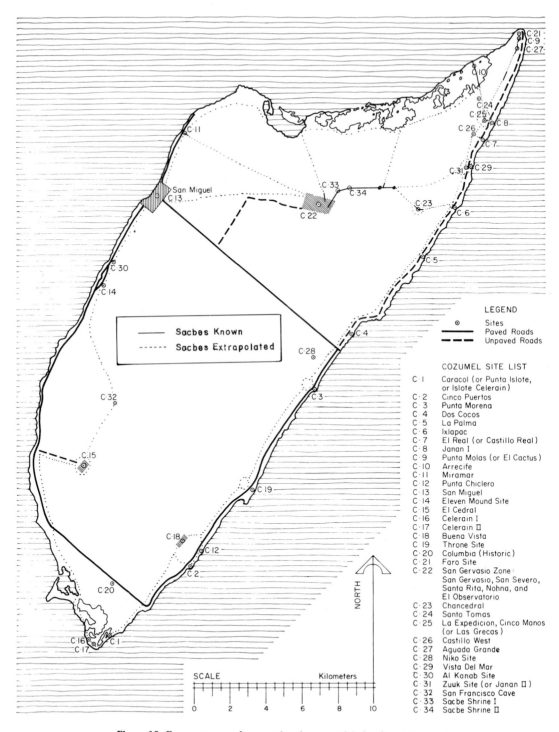

LEGEND

⊙	Sites
——	Paved Roads
– – –	Unpaved Roads

COZUMEL SITE LIST

C·1	Caracol (or Punta Islote, or Islote Celerain)
C·2	Cinco Puertos
C·3	Punta Morena
C·4	Dos Cocos
C·5	La Palma
C·6	Ixlapac
C·7	El Real (or Castillo Real)
C·8	Janan I
C·9	Punta Molas (or El Cactus)
C·10	Arrecife
C·11	Miramar
C·12	Punta Chiclero
C·13	San Miguel
C·14	Eleven Mound Site
C·15	El Cedral
C·16	Celerain I
C·17	Celerain II
C·18	Buena Vista
C·19	Throne Site
C·20	Columbia (Historic)
C·21	Faro Site
C·22	San Gervasio Zone: San Gervasio, San Severo, Santa Rita, Nohna, and El Observatorio
C·23	Chancedral
C·24	Santo Tomas
C·25	La Expedicion, Cinco Manos (or Las Grecas)
C·26	Castillo West
C·27	Aguada Grande
C·28	Niko Site
C·29	Vista Del Mar
C·30	Al Kanab Site
C·31	Zuuk Site (or Janan II)
C·32	San Francisco Cave
C·33	Sacbe Shrine I
C·34	Sacbe Shrine II

Sacbes Known
Sacbes Extrapolated

SCALE   Kilometers

0   2   4   6   8   10

NORTH

Figure 19. Fragmentary and extrapolated ceremonial circuits on Cozumel.

a   b

Plate 5 (a) Portion of the northern *sacbe* at C27 (Aguada Grande) (photograph by William T. Sanders, courtesy Peabody Museum, Harvard University). (b) Field wall on Cozumel (photograph by Loring Hewen).

gravel-capped sections occur on higher ground. Although it seems likely that these roads were capped with white marl, we found no clear evidence of this procedure.

The major intersite *sacbe* at San Gervasio, C22-S-1, and intrasite *sacbes*, C22-S-2, 3, and 4 can be dated to the Decadent by their associations with Decadent period features. The structures and plazas connected by the *sacbes* are dated to the Decadent by ceramics, with the exception of the residential group terminating C22-S-4. Historical corroboration for the existence of *sacbes* at the time of Spanish contact can be found in a statement by Las Casas (Wagner 1942a) and in the description of Cozumel given by Juan Diaz. He mentions stone roads raised at the sides and concave in the middle (Wagner 1942a:71).

Some of the fragmented *sacbes* on Cozumel, however, may date to earlier periods. The *sacbe* at El Cedral, which apparently runs from C15-1 to C15-5, probably dates to the Modified Florescent because C15-1-a most likely dates to this period. Although the date is problematic, it is not a formidable obstacle to functional analysis be-

cause C15-1-a exists now and El Cedral was definitely occupied during the Decadent. In contrast, C22-S-5 at San Gervasio, which runs from an important shrine group to the settlement zone, appears to have been intentionally destroyed. The stone path stops just short of a field wall that crosses it. Clearing around this termination showed that the break in the path was caused by the deliberate removal of the stone slabs. The ensuing stones were probably removed to build the field wall crossing the *sacbe*. Unfortunately there is no sound method of dating this particular field wall. However, it forms part of the wall network that in this vicinity is in many instances associated with Decadent period construction. Thus this particular *sacbe* appears to have fallen into disuse sometime during the Decadent.

This situation makes it difficult to assume that all the *sacbe* fragments running between sites or terminating at shrines or shrine groups were part of a synchronic network of stone paths during the Decadent. Nevertheless, if we can establish a general function for *sacbes* on Cozumel, then only the particular configuration of *sacbes* for any given period, rather than the existence of such networks or their implications in one time period, is called into question.

Generally, *sacbes* can be identified as roads and paths of particular ritual importance. This is suggested by historical descriptions (e.g., Landa in Tozzer 1941:174) of ceremonial processions to and from various localities within settlements during the colonial period. Las Casas, quoted earlier, gives the strong impression that nonpaved streets or paths were functionally distinct from the paved roadways. Although the ambiguous description weakens the association of *sacbes* with masonry religious structures also mentioned by Las Casas, it does indicate that intrasite paths were not paved as a rule. The failure of Montejo to mention *sacbes* in the course of his *entrada* into northern Yucatan and Landa's implication (Tozzer 1941:174) that the *sacbes* were constructed in ancient times negatively corroborates this rule.

The fact that *sacbes* are generally rare both in the Decadent and in historical descriptions may obliquely support their special ritual importance. Furthermore, if their function is primarily ceremonial, Cozumel, as a major religious sanctuary, might well be expected to have a higher occurrence of these features. It is significant that the most famous *sacbe*, which runs from Yaxuna to Coba (Villa Rojas 1934), is specifically identified as a major pilgrimage route to Cozumel Island:

> There are remains of paved highways which traverse all of this kingdom and they say they ended in the east on the seashore where it crosses an arm of the sea for the distance of four leagues which divides the mainland from that island. These highways were like the *caminos reales*, which guided them . . . so that they might arrive at Cozumel for the fulfilment of their vows, to offer their sacrifices, to ask help for their needs, and for the mistaken adoration of their false gods. (Cogolludo in Tozzer 1941:109)

Molina Solis says of this particular route, "The journey was a true pilgrimage. During its course the pilgrims visited the temples along the route, the ancient monuments and the abandoned ruins, where they paused to burn copal the sacred incense reserved for the expressions of the cult" (in Villa Rojas 1934:207-208). Although this observation is replicated in modern worship at

abandoned ruins, it relates equally well to the shrines punctuating the intersite *sacbe* at San Gervasio.

A quotation from Lizana describes the *sacbes* at another pilgrimage center, Izamal:

> There they offered great alms and made pilgrimages from all parts, for which reason there have been made four roads or causeways to the four cardinal points, which reached to all the ends of the land, and passed to Tabasco, Guatemala and Chiapas . . . So great was the concourse of People who assisted at these oracles of Itzamut-ul and Tiab-ul that they had made these roads. (in Villa Rojas 1934-189)

Although Lizana's opinion of the length of these *sacbes* is undoubtedly incorrect, the one intersite *sacbe* associated with Izamal runs from that center to Ake and is vaguely oriented to the cardinal directions. The presence of this *sacbe* lends some credence to Lizana's statement concerning the function of such features. Furthermore, his allusion to cardinal orientation links these causeways to processional routes within settlements mentioned by Landa (Tozzer 1941:146).

These quotations indicate *sacbes* had a primarily ceremonial function during Decadent times. Intersite *sacbes* were used as pilgrimage routes, whereas intrasite *sacbes* were constructed for processions. Nonetheless, *sacbes* could have served more prosaic purposes, such as transport routes for goods and people. Unfortunately direct reference to this use is lacking and such a function can only be generally inferred from the association of pilgrimages with commercial enterprise. Certainly *sacbes* could accommodate movement across low-lying areas in the rainy season, and would allow faster movement of large numbers of people than would narrow dirt paths. If *sacbes* were really important to commerce, for example, one might expect to find more mention of them in historical documents, but descriptions of such commercial centers as Chauacha make no reference to them. It is always possible, moreover, that good analogies for the commercial use of *sacbes* are lacking because commerce had shifted its primary emphasis from land transport to sea transport by Decadent times. This hypothesis could only be tested through comparative analysis of artifact inventories at sites dating to earlier periods that are connected by *sacbes*.

Returning to the association of *sacbes* with religious structures, in addition to the quotation given from Molina Solis, we can add that Villa Rojas found several isolated platforms next to the Yaxuna-Coba *sacbe*. He thinks these may have been used as places for rest and prayer. Unfortunately these platforms were devoid of superstructural remains. Villa Rojas (1945:43) provides another possible approach to this association in his discussion of settlement patterns in the village of X-cacal: "At one side of each of the principal entrances to the settlement there is a small oratory containing its own cross where visitors customarily pause a moment to pray and cross themselves before entering the holy village." D. Schuman (personal communication, 1975), who spent six weeks in this village during the summer of 1975, has provided some additional information on these oratories. According to informants, there are ideally four of these structures at the periphery of the community. The actual number may vary, however, depending on what paths are frequented into the village. During Schuman's stay, one of the oratories was moved from its place on an old path to the intersection of the path with a newly constructed road in order to obtain maximum coverage of traffic going into the village. Schuman had an opportunity to examine this particular oratory and describes it as a wooden-walled, thatched-roof building, about 4-5m on a side. The structure is open across the front. Two small crosses dressed in *huipiles* stand in a wooden box on the altar. The altar is set against the back wall. With the exception of open visual access, this structure compares well in size and disposition of the altar with the structures identified as shrines on Cozumel.

Despite all the intervening historical factors, which necessarily qualify the analogical potential of these oratories, their arrangement does bear a resemblance to the patterns inferred for Cozumel during the Decadent. In both cases there are religious buildings on the periphery of settlements defining community boundaries. The location of the oratories in X-cacal, however, seems to be dependent upon the disposition of important communication-transportation routes into the village. Although they are used occasionally for processions carrying the sacred cross of X-cacal on visits to the crosses of nearby communities (D. Schuman, personal communication, 1975), these routes are primarily secular in character. This does not undermine our argument that the motivation behind *sacbe* construction in Decadent times was religious. Rather it supports the notion that intersite *sacbes* also followed important, established communication-transportation routes. The only indication that the *sacbes* were in themselves sacred comes in the description given by Las Casas. Apparently the natives put up considerable resistance when the Spanish wanted to cross a *sacbe*, although their movement on unpaved streets was unimpeded.

In another respect, the sacred definition of X-cacal resembles the pattern described by Landa (Tozzer 1941:140). Villa Rojas (1945:43) observes that four stone piles with crosses on them are set at the intercardinal points at the edge of the church plaza. These crosses explicitly define the sacred precincts of the church in the natives' minds.

Although Landa states that his rock piles are "at the entrance of the town, on all four sides of the town, that is to say, at the East, West, North, and South" (Tozzer 1941:39), it seems possible that he is describing one variation on a theme of ritual definition of community space rather than the general pattern for Yucatan. The X-cacal pattern, with rock piles and oratories defining the sacred plaza and the community respectively, and the Cozumel pattern, with formal plaza groups and peripheral shrines, may be additional variations on the same theme.

Although the majority of *sacbes* on Cozumel run between structures or groups, there are two cases (C22-87 and the group platform of C18-20) where *sacbes* run between one edge of the plaza and structures at the opposite edge. These instances preclude identification here of a pragmatic transportation function as the *sacbes* can only have served a ceremonial, processional function. Specifically, at Buena Vista the *sacbe* (C18-S-2) connects with another that runs between the group plaza and a raised shrine, and at San Gervasio the *sacbe* ends at a staircase leading off the plaza.

Due to both the exigencies of field priorities and the fragmentary nature of the features, our control over intersite *sacbes* on Cozumel is weak. However, we can offer some general inferences as to the nature of these *sacbes* that may be of some use to future investigations (Figure 19). There are fragments of intersite *sacbes* at three sites: San Gervasio (C22), Aguada Grande (C25), and Chen Cedral (C23) (see Figures 20 and 35; also see Sabloff and Rathje 1975b:Map 2). Some of the massive field walls at Buena Vista, discussed below, may also have served as *sacbes*.

The best preserved intersite *sacbe* at San Gervasio, C22-S-1, runs toward the northeast coast. Despite the fact that traces of the *sacbe* were lost several kilometers before reaching the coast, one of the several coastal settlements seems to have been its final destination. At C33-1-a, the second shrine on the *sacbe* from San Gervasio and several kilometers from the settlement, a secondary *sacbe* diverges and runs to the north. Because this *sacbe* was only followed for about 50m, it was not determined whether it continues to the north coast or ends somewhere in the northern interior.

The second intersite *sacbe* at San Gervasio, C22-S-6, runs northward from the shrine group on C22-34. The *sacbe* begins at a small rectangular masonry feature that yielded various items of exotic materials indicating the presence of a cache. The *sacbe* was followed for about 150m before being lost in the dense undergrowth. It heads in the general direction of Laguna Ciega on the northern coast.

The presence of shrines on the northern coast with *sacbes* extending southward (e.g., Arrecife [see Freidel and Leventhal 1975:Figure 10]) indicates it is reasonable to suppose that these two *sacbes*, C22-S-6 and the branch of C22-S-1, head for the coast.

At Aguada Grande, there are two *sacbe* fragments located to the north and south of the main settlement zone (see Plate 5a). Both are oriented north-south and run through aguadas that are seasonally inundated. These *sacbe* segments terminate at the opposite edge of the aguadas, giving the impression that they served to facilitate movement into and out of the community during the rainy season.

Although the two *sacbe* fragments at Aguada Grande are on opposite sides of the site, they line up north and south. Thus they were probably part of a path running north-south through the community, passing in front of the three shrines that form the community's central focus. This partially paved road may end at C9-1-a to the north. The structure faces south and has a *sacbe* running

south from it. South of the settlement, fragments of *sacbe* oriented north-south were found between Aguada Grande and La Expedicion, the next community down the coast, suggesting that the *sacbe* fragments at Aguada Grande may connect the two sites.

At Chen Cedral, a section of *sacbe* leaves the settlement and heads east toward the coast. This *sacbe* was only followed far enough to determine that it probably did not terminate in a shrine on the periphery of the settlement. On the western edge of the settlement, we found a gateway and wall-lined path leading into Chen Cedral. Although an informant familiar with the area said that C22-S-1 terminated at this site, we were unable to find any evidence of the *sacbe* on this western edge.

From both the spotty information and allusions by native informants to *sacbes* in the southern lagoons and the vicinity of Castillo Real (C7) on the northeast coast and our survey, we have the general impression that intersite *sacbes* linked settlements to each other and settlements to shrines on the coast. The positive association of such paved paths with shrines or temples supports the inference that ceremonial circuits formed extensive networks on the island. Undoubtedly, *sacbes*, the concrete expression of an important ritual link between settlements, served to strengthen economic, political, and social ties between these communities.

Generally intrasite *sacbes* on Cozumel run from the central areas of settlements toward more peripheral shrines and shrine groups. C22-S-2, 3, and 4 are notable exceptions in that they connect residential groups with a civil-religious plaza group. The disposition of particular intrasite *sacbes* are better dealt with in the context of settlement pattern descriptions. Let us say for now that their function seems to be related to ritual processions as the difficulties of traversing short distances within settlements are not noticeably relieved by paving paths.

The Field Wall Network

On Cozumel there is a network of low stone walls that traverses all but a fraction of the island's surface and divides it into roughly rectilinear plots. Cozumel's landscape is, therefore, artificially defined in a manner that is quite extraordinary for

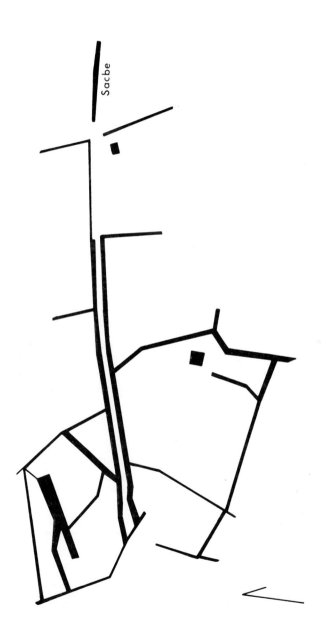

Sacbe

Figure 20. Wall section and *sacbe* northeast of C23.

the Maya Lowlands. Despite the fact that this wall system has been noted in the literature of the region for some time (Arnold and Frost 1909:174; Lothrop 1924:156; Escalona-Ramos 1946; Sanders 1956, 1960; Mason 1927), it has had a negligible impact on notions of ancient Maya land tenure or subsistence technology. Ironically this situation might be understood as one in which historical and ethnographic information has served to blind us to possibilities rather than to enlighten us. The historical and ethnographic literature strongly suggests a community of land ownership commensurate with a swidden subsistence economy.

Recent investigations in other parts of the Maya Lowlands (Harrison 1975; Harrison and Turner 1977; Seimens and Puleston 1972; B.L. Turner 1974) corroborate the evidence of extensive artificial definition of terrain in the Maya area offered by Willey and his colleagues in 1965. This rapidly growing literature generally implies that such modifications of the landscape are the remains of intensive agricultural systems. If continuing research supports this inference, the ramifications may substantially alter our understanding of Maya socioeconomic development. In this context, the wall network on Cozumel is ripe for presentation and analysis.

Unfortunately, our information on the wall network is rather meager. We have mapped the walls inside La Expedicion and inside and around Aguada Grande. On other parts of the island we have small samples of the network and general observations as to its configuration and extent (Chen Cedral; Figures 20 and 48). What we can offer are the implications of the data at hand in hopes of encouraging further research on this problem along the northeast coast of Yucatan.

The walls themselves vary in both size and construction technique. Today, the simplest and smallest ones appear as low (20-30cm) ridges of dry rubble where they have collapsed. On rare occasions, sections of these simple walls are preserved to a height of about 1m (Plate 5b). This is probably close to their original maximum height. On the average they are 1m wide. Larger walls, also of dry-laid rubble, now appear as ridges about 30-50cm high and 1.5-2.0m wide. Finally the most substantial walls have maximum preserved dimensions of 2m high by 2m wide and a core of rubble and gravel retained by roughly shaped slabs. Addi-

tionally, there are even more substantial features that appear to form an integral part of the network. These are long, low platforms up to 100m long and over 2m wide. Although they look much like other rubble substructures in construction and in some places are large enough to have supported structures, these features are aligned with the wall network and are interconnected by smaller walls. Thus they are easily distinguished from the amorphous rubble substructures that are dispersed throughout the network and that apparently supported structures of some kind.

The simplest type of wall was found all over the island. The more elaborate forms, on the other hand, were only found in the vicinity of Chen Cedral and Buena Vista. Where these elaborate wall types occur, they are combined with the simpler wall type in a fashion that superficially appears to be random. Thus all the various wall types can be found surrounding a single lot. Intuitively we believe there is some method in this madness, but lacking maps of large sections of the network in the vicinity of these sites, we could perceive no empirical pattern.

Initially we thought the large walls with retainers were *sacbes* because an exploration of the wall network to the east of Buena Vista demonstrated that one could walk along these larger walls to within 500m of the coast. Ramps running off the wall to ground level were also observed during this traverse. At one point the wall terminated in a modest rubble pyramid about 4m high, only to continue on the other side of it. A small settlement was found next to this pyramidal substructure. Hence it seems quite plausible that where these larger walls interconnect, they were used as walkways. This would make sense during periods of seasonal inundation. However, in other places these large walls are only short sections connected to smaller walls that could not have been easily walked. Although B.L. Turner (1974:120) considers the walls running parallel to the slopes in his terraces as walkways, we think these walls had the additional functions discussed below.

Analysis of aerial photographs of Cozumel (see, for example, Sabloff and Rathje 1975a:78), observation by light plane, and on-the-ground exploration indicate that the network extends right through the shallow lagoons bordering the northern coast, and that walls are found throughout the swampy areas to the south of the lagoons. There are only three areas that are not traversed by the network: (1) the deep lagoons at the northern and southern ends of the island, (2) a zone extending 100-200m along the coasts, and (3) a region of extremely rough and rocky terrain between El Cedral and Buena Vista. Although the exact extent of this last region is unknown, it appears to be about 2km wide and covers a minimum of several square kilometers. Additionally the network is not presently found in the modern communities of El Cedral and San Miguel. Here its lack may well be attributed to use of the stone in modern construction.

The entire wall network is roughly oriented to the main north-south axis of the island, that is 20-25° east of north for walls running north and south. Inside the settlement of La Expedicion the network shows considerable distortion, but only slight distortion is evident within Aguada Grande's settlement zone.

Although Sanders (1955) noted the presence of the field wall network at the site of Aguada Grande and concurred with Escalona-Ramos (1946) in thinking the lots were probably agricultural fields, he believed that the network was probably postcontact. This inference was based on his dating of Aguada Grande to the late facet of the Decadent and on the possibility that it persisted as a settlement into the colonial period. The preliminary ceramic analysis of the Cozumel Project corroborates the generally late date for the settlement, but indicates that it has some time depth in the Decadent period. For Cozumel as a whole, the network shows accommodation to features dating to Decadent or earlier times. In spite of evidence of occupation postdating the conquest at these settlements, there is no evidence of major construction dating to the colonial period.

It seems highly unlikely that the Spanish would have introduced the wall network. Cozumel suffered not only the drastic population reduction characteristic of the whole peninsula during the early colonial period, but also the collapse of its economic system, which was based on long-distance trade and religiotourism, soon after the establishment of Spanish hegemony. Cozumel was, for all practical purposes, abandoned within 100 years of the conquest. Thus it does not seem reasonable to postulate a short period of tremendous effort or

a longer period of regulated effort on the scale required by the wall system during the early colonial period.

Although the historical information on stone walls is rather scanty, the Motul Dictionary lists a term for stone field or houselot walls, *ticin cot* (Wauchope 1938). The Maya at the village of El Cedral still use this term for both new and old field walls in their settlement. Additionally, Las Casas (in Wagner 1942a) reports the presence of houselot and field walls in his history of the conquest. Although the observations are supposed to pertain to Cozumel, the report is garbled and he could also be referring to either Ecab or Champutun. Nonetheless the location of the town described is of less consequence than the fact that such walls were being built at the time of the conquest.

Archaeologically, houselot walls dating to the Decadent are reported from Mayapan (Bullard 1952, 1953, 1954; Smith 1962:Figure 1) where they apparently do not extend beyond the city limits but rather are generally confined to residential districts. Recently field and houselot walls have also been discovered in a variety of locations on the East Coast of Quintana Roo: at Xelha (A. Andrews, personal communication, 1973), Coba (G. Stuart, personal communication, 1974), and Tancah (discovered by Arthur Miller; personal communication from P. Harrison 1975), as well as in the Rio Bec region (R.E.W. Adams, personal communication, 1979; also see Garza T. de Gonzales and Kurjack 1980). Those at Xelha, which Freidel has observed, are similar to those on Cozumel and define relatively small rectangular plots roughly oriented to the cardinal directions. It would seem that, by contact times, the entire coastal area and much of the interior of Quintana Roo was spatially defined by ridged fields, terraces, and field walls.

Unfortunately there is no way of determining how long the field wall network may have been in use during and prior to the Decadent period. Instances of field walls that cut across earlier features and isolated fragments of walls are quite rare. Modification by dividing up an existing lot seems to have occurred at both Aguada Grande and La Expedicion. Although these walls could be arranged sequentially, there is no way of determining an absolute chronology for them. Similarly, judging by the presence of wall fragments within the lot, modification by expansion seems to have occurred in a large lot at the northern end of the Aguada Grande survey area, but again temporal placement is only relative. There is, however, no evidence of drastic modification of the network that might indicate disjunction in its growth following the initial establishment of rectilinear lot form and rough orientation to the cardinal directions. In light of the lack of contrary evidence, the network must be considered a synchronic phenomenon contemporary with the latest structures in the settlements investigated. In short, it is a Decadent period phenomenon.

It seems reasonable to suppose that the wall network is somehow related to the subsistence practices in the Decadent period. Unlike ridged fields and terraces, however, the field walls probably did not function as a means of soil retention, soil renewal, or irrigation. Although the walls themselves may have had some practical function, such as shading plants next to them (M. Pohl, personal communication, 1973), the retention of water, or the growth of vine plants, these are minor advantages that do not warrant such a tremendous output of labor. The demarcation of space provided by these walls must have had some practical utility, as postulated by Escalona-Ramos (1946) and Sanders (1960). Nevertheless, because the wall network includes settlements on Cozumel and is found within the city of Mayapan but not in the countryside around it, it may also relate to a cultural perception of land quite different from that portrayed in the early historical documents.

In the last analysis, such a cultural perception may well have been the motivation for the wall network. Although the shallow, lateritic soils of the island are suitable for swidden agriculture and horticulture, only isolated sinkholes with deep soil accumulations and higher moisture content are suitable for intensive cultivation. A more regulated, shortened fallow cycle, which might be made possible through careful plot demarcation, would probably lead to rapidly decreasing yield unless accompanied by fertilization for which we have no archaeological evidence.

Regulation of land use in a manner foreign to modern Maya subsistence practices is clearly manifested in the wall network. Control over where and how much farmers planted may have been a matter of individual ownership, or com-

munity- or even island-wide regulation. The consistency of the grid pattern where mapped and observed and the lack of noticeable breaks in the grid between neighboring communities give the impression that the construction of the network, and hence regulation of land, were under some kind of centralized authority. Certainly this would correlate better with what is known historically of Maya attitudes toward land than would individual ownership. Centralized or even community regulation of land use may have had the dual practical benefit of discouraging a prodigal overexploitation of a limited land base and encouraging the movement of people into service occupations thereby gaining income from off-island resources.

One possible key to the problem of utility is the consistently small size of plots relative to modern milpas. Where mapped, lots range from less than a tenth of a hectare within communities to about 1ha outside them. Observation elsewhere on the island and on the mainland confirms the relatively small size of the fields defined by walls (Figure 21). Steggerda (1941:113) gives the average size of milpas in the Chichen Itza region as 99.23 *mecates*, whereas those reported by Redfield (in Steggerda 1941:113) at Chan Kom averaged 72 and 63 mecates in consecutive years. The fields outside settlement zones on Cozumel average 10 mecates or 10-20% the size of those reported in Yucatan. Modern farmers on Cozumel and the mainland, who are well aware of the ancient field walls, consistently remarked on the small size of the lots enclosed by them. Small field size may have some intrinsic value sufficient to offset the obviously greater effort entailed in maintaining many small scattered plots rather than one or two large ones. Redfield and Villa Rojas (1971:52) note in passing that the smaller milpas at Chan Kom gave somewhat larger yields. It is impossible to determine whether or not this is a spurious correlation based on a sample with short time depth or the result of other factors, such as the planting of smaller milpas on richer soils. Smaller plot size may positively affect secondary regrowth of vegetation on fallow land because decreasing plot size means increasing proximity of any given section of cleared land to the surrounding forest. Depending on the degree to which proximity affects secondary regrowth (and we do not have any positive evidence that it does), smaller plot size

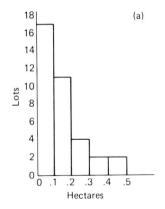

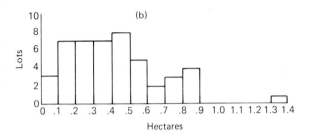

Figure 21. Frequency histograms of field lots by size in hectares at (a) Aguada Grande and (b) La Expedicion.

could measurably lessen the length of time required to produce adequate secondary growth on fallow land.

Chronologically, there is no need to presuppose that such demarcation of land was introduced with the Putun Maya during the Postclassic period, or that it derives from foreign concepts of land use. Peter Harrison's (personal communication, 1975) Uaymil survey discovered vestiges of an extensive system of massive walls (2m high by 4m wide) in southern Quintana Roo. These walls surrounded low mounds and the latest material on these mounds were late Early Classic ceramics. Although surface ceramics are only a very tentative indication of chronological placement, it may not be purely coincidental that the massive walls on Cozumel were found associated with settlements that show clear indications of occupation during the Florescent or Late Classic periods. Additionally, B.L. Turner (1974) gives some slight indications that plot size is substantially smaller than that of modern milpas in his discussion of

Late Classic terraces near Becan. In one measured example, terraces at Becan vary in width from about 20 to 40m, according to the slope angle. The cross walls, which he calls *walkways,* are shown in one photograph in his article (1974: Figure 5). In combination with terrace walls, these give the impression of small lot size comparable to those found on Cozumel. In the case of terraces and ridged fields, small lot size may be related to intensive agricultural practices. On Cozumel, where agriculture can only be intensified by shortening the fallow cycles, small lot size may be vestigial from earlier practices.

At the moment, too little is known of land demarcation along the eastern side of the Yucatan Peninsula to do more than speculate on temporal and geographic developments. Nevertheless, the Cozumel information supplies two more pieces of the puzzle: (1) land demarcation continues into the Decadent in Quintana Roo and (2) demarcation itself, disassociated from such practical benefits as land reclamation and water control, was valued and maintained. Thus it is highly likely that the walkways Turner found among his terraces and Harrison's possible late Early Classic wall systems in Quintana Roo were significant beyond their practical utility.

The apparent lack of field walls in northwestern Yucatan simply may be a reflection of our lack of information on the Late Postclassic outside of Mayapan. It may, however, reflect a true lack of these features in that region as historical records of land tenure given by informants from that region consistently report communal land ownership, swidden agriculture, and a definite lack of field markers except in the case of cacao groves or other "improved" lands (Roys 1939). If the second alternative is correct, the houselot walls at Mayapan take on new meaning. On Cozumel, as noted above, the walls pervade settlements. Those lots in settlements are smaller on the whole than those outside but still in the vicinity of settlements (compare lot size at Aguada Grande with lot size at La Expedicion in Figure 21). This correlation of lot size with settlement implies that those lots within communities were perceived as houselots whereas those outside were agricultural fields. The walls at Mayapan enclose houselots, like those in Cozumel's settlements. If the Mayapan walls are anomalies in northwestern Yucatan, the notion of bounded houselots may have been introduced into the city from the East Coast. The general affinities between Late Postclassic materials on the East Coast and those at Mayapan and more specific affinities in house plan and settlement enclosure tend to support this hypothesis. Empirical confirmation of the lack of field walls in northwestern Yucatan would allow a stronger statement to be made concerning the long-distance relationships between communities on the East Coast and Mayapan than has been allowed to date because of the weighted nature of the available evidence (Pollock 1962:12).

These various lines of evidence, fragmentary and limited as they are, converge to indicate that the wall network on Cozumel was not simply the technical by-product of more intensive subsistence practices. It also reflects a conception of land that, once in operation, actively determined land use and therefore the distribution of permanent facilities on the landscape. Thus the implications of a completely defined landscape go far beyond those of a more-regulated use of land for agricultural purposes. The location of house, outbuildings, shrines, and other buildings must also have been more regulated.

Only one allusion in the historical literature is pertinent to qualifying the cultural perception of land defined as property, be it of individuals or of communities. Landa (in Tozzer 1941:189) gives a detailed account of salt pans and salt gathering along the northern coast of Yucatan: in passing he mentions that "they had for this purpose their places marked out in the lagoon itself, which

were the most productive of salt and with the least mud and water." As noted above, the wall network on Cozumel extends out into the northern lagoons. Some parts of these lagoons are producing rock salt even today. In Yucatan, these marked-off areas occur in association with a nonagricultural resource, whereas on Cozumel they appear to be simply an extension of the network into the lagoons. It is possible that the natives of Cozumel felt much the same way about land as the natives of Yucatan felt about salt pans. However, if the wall network was the result of accumulated individual enterprise, we would expect to find both a more irregular patchwork of individual holdings and more evidence of modification as lots were bought, sold, divided, and consolidated by individual owners. Such irregularity and modification is evident within the settlement zone of La Expedicion where private ownership may well have been operative, but not outside this settlement.

Unfortunately the information is insufficient to allow any solid confirmation of either private or public ownership of land outside settlement zones. Nevertheless, given the regularity of the grid, some form of public ownership seems more likely. In fact, as argued above, the lack of breaks between communities argues for centralized island-wide administration or control. To anticipate somewhat the interpretations of settlement organization in the following chapters, it is possible that although sections of the island around communities were turned over to the elite families for use and management, the land was owned by the entire "community" of Cozumel.

CHAPTER 5

STRUCTURE ASSEMBLAGES

The Synchronic Analysis of Features

All settlement pattern analyses must deal with the problem of which features are contemporary and which are not. The degree of chronological control depends on how features are dated and, in the case of the Cozumel survey, what proportion of features are dated. The dating used in this settlement pattern analysis relies on temporally diagnostic ceramics from controlled excavation, looted construction fill, and surface collections. With the exception of controlled primary depositional contexts, ceramics provide only a tentative dating of associated features, a *terminus ante quem*. Unfortunately most of the sherds gathered in the course of the Cozumel survey come from secondary contexts or the surface. Therefore good chronological control over many features is lacking and we must extrapolate from formal characteristics associated with dated features to those of uncertain age. This extrapolation can be augmented in certain cases by *sacbes*, walls, and other features that associate undated structures with dated ones. On the whole, this is a highly questionable procedure, but, in addition to being the best one available given the limitations of our field research, the dated structures indicate that settlement patterns did not undergo radical reorganization between Modified Florescent and Decadent times. Formal plaza groups, shrine groups, *sacbes*, and agglutinated substructures all seem to be present in Modified Florescent times, and most of those earlier structures that are still standing seem to have been used during the Decadent. Thus, although the particular picture may not be entirely correct, the general picture presented of Cozumel's settlement patterns is probably valid.

Although ceramics dating to the Formative, Early period, and Florescent are found in fair quantities at some sites on the island, the data are too scanty to give an adequate understanding of settlement patterns in these periods. Therefore the individual features dating to these periods, particularly the Early period and Florescent, are taken into consideration in the overall assessment of the settlement patterns in which they occur.

Settlement patterns observable in the Decadent period apparently reflect spatial principles of organization established at least by Modified Florescent times. Although this is not a confirmed observation, there is some evidence to support it that is presented in the context of individual settlements.

The Group Types in General

Three types of structure groups have been dealt with in the analysis of perishable and masonry structures on Cozumel: formal plaza groups (Table 6), shrine groups (Table 7), and household groups (Tables 8 and 9). The sample for each group type is quite small. The scarcity of formal plaza groups is probably a reasonable reflection of settlement dynamics. Generally there was one of these groups in each settlement. The scarcity of shrine groups is probably as much a reflection of their often isolated location and the consequent failure of the survey to locate some of them as it is of their rarity on Cozumel. The especially small number of household groups is a more complicated matter.

Table 6
Formal plaza groups on Cozumel

Group	Structure	Figure number	Formal type	Functional type
C22-4	4-a	18	6 Masonry	Community Temple
through	4-b		6 Masonry	Community Temple
10	5-a		12 Perishable	Public Building
	6-a		3 Masonry	Public Ritual House
	6-b		7 Perishable	Meeting House
	6-c		6 Masonry	Community Temple
	7-a		13 Perishable	Public Building
	8		Platform	?
	9		Problematic	?
	10		Misc. Masonry	Group Altar
C22-87	87-a	19	13 Perishable	Public Building
	87-b		9 Perishable	Dwelling
	87-c		1 Masonry	Community Shrine
	87-d		3 Masonry (?)	?
C31-1	1-a	20	6 Masonry	Community Temple
	1-b		3 Masonry	Public Ritual House
	1-c		11 Perishable	Dwelling
	1-d		Misc. Masonry	Group Altar
	1-e		11 Perishable	Dwelling
C25-1	1-a	20	6 Masonry	Community Temple
	1-b		6 Masonry	Community Temple
	1-c		6 Masonry	Community Temple
	1-d		6 Perishable	Kitchen (?)
	1-e		8 Perishable	Dwelling
	1-f		Misc. Masonry	Group Altar
C18-1	1-a	19	4 Perishable	Priest's House (?)
	1-b		12 Perishable	Public Building
	1-c		10 Perishable	Dwelling
	1-d		13 Perishable	Public Building
	1-e		11 Perishable	Meeting House (?)
	1-f		Misc. Masonry	Group Altar
C15-5[a]			Misc. Masonry	Arch
			Misc. Masonry	Arch
			4 Perishable	—
			Perishable	—
			Perishable	—
			Perishable	Group Altar

[a]Missing data from Holmes 1895-1897.

Empirically, small perishable structures grouped around raised plaza areas are indeed quite rare on Cozumel. In this respect the patterns on Cozumel seem to deviate not only from the general situation in the Southern Maya Lowlands (Bullard 1960; Carr and Hazard 1961) but also from

Table 7
Shrine groups on Cozumel

Group	Structure	Figure number	Formal type	Functional type
C1-1	1-a	22	4 Masonry	Shrine
and 2	2-a		3 Masonry	Public Ritual House
	3			
C10-1	1-a	22	1 Masonry	Shrine
	1-b		1 Masonry	Shrine
C15-14	14-a	24	1 Masonry	Shrine
	14-b		1 Masonry (?)	Shrine
	14-c		3 Masonry	Public Ritual House
C18-18	18-a	23	3 Masonry	Public Ritual House
and 20	19-a		1 Masonry	Shrine
	20-a		3 Perishable	Perishable Shrine
C18-24	24-a	21	6 Masonry	Community Temple
and 25	24-b		1 Masonry	Shrine
	25-a		1 Masonry	Shrine
C22-34	34-a	21	5 Masonry	Temple
and 35	34-b		3 Masonry	Public Ritual House
	34-c		Misc. Masonry	Group Altar
	34-d		1 Masonry	Shrine
	34-e		Misc. Perishable	Temple
	34-f		Misc. Masonry	Shrine
	35-a		3 Perishable	Shrine
C22-37	37-a	23	1 Masonry	Shrine
and 38	38-a		4 Masonry	Shrine
C27-1	1-a	34	1 Masonry	Shrine
and 2	1-b		1 Masonry	Shrine
	1-c		1 Masonry	Shrine
	2-a		1 Masonry	Shrine
C31-5	5-a	23	1 Masonry	Shrine
	5-b		1 Masonry	Shrine
	Altar		Misc. Masonry	Group Altar
C23-3	3-a	22	Misc. Masonry	Shrine
	3-b		1 Masonry	Shrine

well-investigated Late Postclassic settlements such as Mayapan (Smith 1962). Cozumel is more like Tulum, which also lacks household groups (Lothrop 1924).

To some degree the lack of clear household groups reflects the manner by which such groups were identified in the field. Most of the observations pertained to superstructures with visible foundation walls. Often, where such remains were found, the usual small support platform was lacking and the structure rested directly on a large group substructure. Therefore in those cases where

Table 8
Household groups on Cozumel

Group	Structure	Figure number	Formal type	Functional type
C22-1 and 3	1-a	26	15 Perishable	Dwelling
	2		Misc. Masonry	Group Altar
	3-a		3 Masonry	Oratory/Shrine
C22-12	12-a	25	3 Perishable	Oratory/Shrine
	12-b		Platform	Dwelling (?)
C22-13	13-a	26	14 Perishable	Dwelling
	13-b		4 Perishable	Priest's House
	13-c		Misc. Masonry	Shrine
C22-25 and 28	25-a	26	Misc. Masonry	Palace (?)
	26		Misc. Masonry	Group Altar
	27-a		Misc. Perishable	Oratory/Shrine
C22-29 and 30	30-a	25	Misc. Masonry	Oratory
	30-b		Misc. Masonry	Group Altar
	30-c		15 Perishable	Dwelling
	29-a		Misc. Perishable	Dwelling
C22-90	90-a	25	13 Perishable	Dwelling
	90-b		7 Perishable	Ritual Meeting House
	90-c		Misc. Masonry	Group Altar
C25-7 and 9	7-a	36	Semicircle	Outbuilding
	8-a		9 Perishable	Dwelling
	9-a		Misc. Perishable	Dwelling
C25-10 and 12	10-a	40	1 Masonry	Private Shrine
	11-a		9 Perishable	Dwelling
	12-a		Platform	Outbuilding
C25-5 and 6	5-a	30	1 Perishable	Outbuilding
	6-a		Misc. Perishable	Dwelling (?)
	6-b		Misc. Perishable	?
	6-c		Misc. Perishable	?
	6-d		Misc. Masonry	Shrine
C25-30 and 31	29	30a, 40	Platform	Outbuilding
	30		Misc. Masonry	Group Altar
	31		11 Perishable	Dwelling

superstructures were destroyed by root action and slumping it was impossible to ascertain the presence or absence of a plaza group arrangement. Some of the groups presented in Tables 8 and 9 are reconstructed on the basis of the proximity of structures or their inclusion within houselots defined by walls, rather than on the basis of a plaza arrangement. Thus despite uncertainty as to the magnitude of household-plaza group rarity, such rarity is empirically real on Cozumel.

Table 9
Possible household groups on Cozumel that have one identified structure

Group	Structure	Figure number	Formal type	Functional type
C25-23	23-a	28	Misc. Perishable	Dwelling
C25-24	24-a	29	2 Perishable	Dwelling
C25-27	27-a	28	2 Perishable	Dwelling
C31-4	4-a	27	9 Perishable	Dwelling
C22-40	40-a	—	9 Perishable	Dwelling
C22-36	36-a	—	6 Perishable	Dwelling

(See Sabloff and Rathje [1975b:Map 2] for illustrations of C22-40 and C22-36.)

Because location plays a crucial role in the identification of structure function, the identified functions of group types and of the individual structures comprising them are necessarily interdependent. Nonetheless, they are not altogether interdependent as independent ethnohistorical and ethnographic analogies support the identification of formal plaza groups as centralized administrative headquarters for communities, shrine groups as important religious foci, and household groups as precisely that. Similarly, independent analogies have been brought to bear on some of the individual structure types. On the whole, however, the identification of group function has played a more determinative role in assigning function to individual structures than vice versa.

As might be expected, this logical interdependence has resulted in some "normalizing" of the structure functions given briefly in the tables. Although an attempt was made in the individual analyses of structures to evaluate the pros and cons of each identification, in some cases, particularly outbuildings in household groups, the identification was based primarily on the association of larger and smaller structures. Nonetheless, the group types still reveal a considerable amount of internal variability. This variability, especially in the case of formal plaza groups, is a significant aspect of settlement patterns on Cozumel.

The Formal Plaza Groups

There is strong ethnohistorical support for the presence of centralized administrative facilities in northern Lowland Maya communities at the time of the conquest. As several quotes pertinent to the identification of such facilities have already been given in the chapters on perishable and masonry structures, here we will only summarize the descriptions of buildings, their functions, and spatial arrangements.

The descriptions deal with centralized community structures that functioned as legal courts, markets, warriors' houses, arsenals, boys' houses, mens' houses, and council halls, as well as places of worship. Thus ceremonial center is clearly a misnomer for the central places in these communities. Perhaps public administrative center might be a more appropriate label. The historical literature is fairly consistent in ascribing a plaza arrangement to these central places and in some instances there are detailed physical observations of the formal characteristics of buildings in them. Unfortunately, the correlation of form with function is difficult to establish. Masonry structures on raised support platforms, however, can be identified as idol houses and long-colonnaded, open-sided structures can be viewed as flexible multifunctional public buildings. Given the difficulties of establishing such correlations, it is almost impossible to identify much of the variability in activities associated with such centers.

In this report, we control two of three main lines of independent information on structures and groups: form, and the rather scanty ethnohistorical form-function correlations. Thus the third, excavation of associated materials, supplies a potential test of hypotheses generated on the basis of the first two. The substantial variation in the composition of formal plaza groups on Cozumel has been identified as reflecting variation in functional composition. Unfortunately given the limited degree of control over form-function correlations, this identification must be considered a hypothesis rather than a demonstrated probability. However, the formal variability found in Cozumel's plaza centers is sufficiently great to make the alternative hypothesis, that formal variability merely reflects flexibility of building shape associated with a uniform set of activities in these centers, a less fruitful one. Hence we predicate our analysis on the presumption that formal variability reflects functional variability in these formal plaza groups.

The most famous description of Yucatec Maya town organization is given by Landa:

> Their dwelling place was as follows: —in the middle of the town were their temples with beautiful plazas, and all around the temples stood the houses of the lords and priests, and (those of) the most important people. Thus came the houses of the richest and of those held in highest estimation nearest to these, and at the outskirts of the town were the houses of the lower class. (in Tozzer 1941:62)

Landa's description specifically relates to the arrangement of dwelling places around the center, to the expression of social structure in space, rather than to the various kinds of activities carried out at the center. Other references tend to confirm Landa's observation that the dwellings of the elite were near, but not on, the main central plaza.

The main plaza group at San Gervasio, C22-4-10 (Table 6), consisting of temples, chambers, and colonnaded halls, fits Landa's (in Tozzer 1941:62) and Bernal Diaz del Castillo's (in Maudslay 1908: 112) descriptions perfectly. Four elite dwelling groups surround this nonresidential plaza group (Figure 22). Three of them are connected to it by *sacbes*. The other formal plaza groups on Cozumel, however, clearly deviate from the norm in that they include dwellings (see Figures 23 and 24). The analogy may refute the identification of structures in these other groups as dwellings. On the other hand, it may be incomplete. The latter alternative seems more likely because the available observations focus exclusively on the formal plazas of important towns and provide normative statements on the organization of important communities rather than on the entire spectrum of communities at the time of contact. In this respect

the analogy fits the important center of San Gervasio very well. It does not fit the other communities well because they reflect variation in the expression of social structure in communities not commented on in the historical literature. This is particularly true of the smaller and less important communities.

There are several reasons to believe that the perishable buildings in formal plaza groups served as dwellings. As previously discussed, these buildings belong to formal types embracing buildings that are clearly the main dwellings in household groups. Moreover, although these buildings occur in both domestic and formal plaza contexts, other buildings found in formal plaza groups (excepting the ubiquitous Type 1 shrines) occur in such groups or in shrine groups. This pattern suggests that although most buildings found in formal plaza groups or shrine groups were functionally specialized to serve in the public domain, the perishable buildings were designed to serve in both the public and private domains. Although it is possible that the perishable structures in formal plaza groups and in households served distinct functions, or that the obstensible dwellings in household groups are actually public buildings of some kind, the simplest explanation is that we are dealing with dwellings in the public domain. The one formal plaza group at San Gervasio where these perishable buildings are not found is precisely the one where elite residential groups are found in close association with, but outside, the central plaza. Thus the identification of these benched structures as dwellings helps to explain the variability in formal group composition found on Cozumel.

The general picture of social and political organization of Yucatan at the time of contact (Tozzer 1941:62-63) indicates the presence of a hereditary nobility that held the most important political offices. The rulers of minor centers (*batabs*) were usually related to the rulers of regional centers (*halach uinics*) and were political vassals of such regional leaders. It is possible that each of the formal plaza groups in lesser communities on Cozumel was both an administrative center and the residential group of the local noble ruler (the *batab*). This combined function of the center reflects a stronger integration of social rank and political responsibility at the level of the lesser communities than the spatially distinct elite residences and public centers

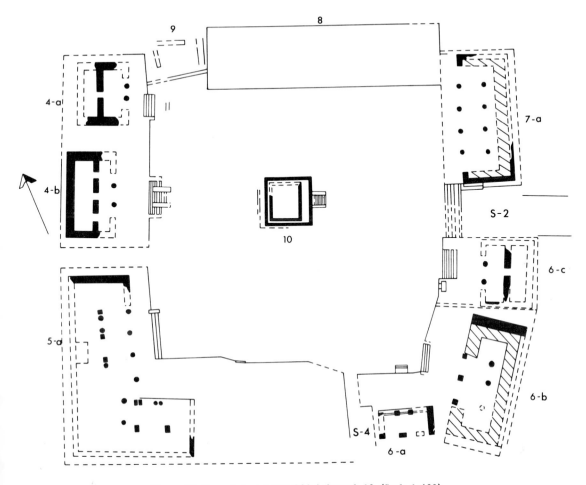

Figure 22. Formal plaza group C22-4 through 10. (Scale 1:400).

of regional or, in the case of Cozumel, island-wide capitals. In the case of San Gervasio, there appears to be a more complex relationship between political organization and social organization appropriate to the capital of the island.

The variation in structures found in formal plaza groups that were not serving as homes reflects a certain specialization of integrative institutions at the community and island-wide level. This follows from a general premise in cultural geography that variation in the function of communities showing a tendency toward hierarchical grouping reflects interdependence between these communities. From this perspective, San Gervasio's C22-4-10 appears to contain the entire range of structures found in formal plaza groups, whereas

each of the other formal plaza groups stresses some types of building over others. This feature of C22-4-10, the disposition of elite dwellings, and additional factors that are discussed in the context of that settlement makes San Gervasio a likely candidate for the capital community of Cozumel in the Decadent period. We have sketched out here the analytic approach to formal plaza groups and their crucial role in interpreting settlement organization; we provide more discussions of the settlements themselves in Chapter 6.

Shrine Groups

Shrine groups have already been discussed at some length in Chapter 3. It has been argued that

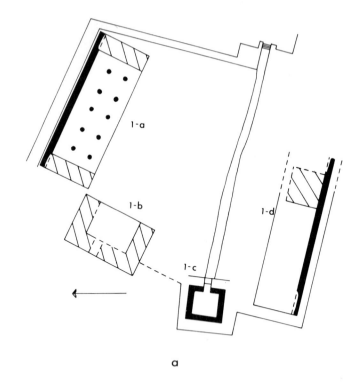

a

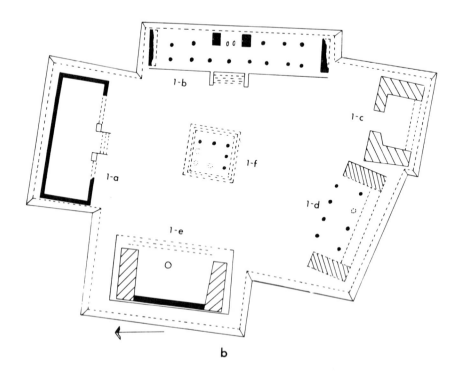

b

Figure 23. Formal plaza groups (a) C22-87 and (b) C18-1. (Scale 1:400).

these groups functioned as religious central places, that is, as major foci or terminals on ceremonial circuits running around communities or the entire island. Because both formal plaza groups and shrine groups contain religious buildings, there is some functional overlap between them. Nonetheless the contrasts in structure composition and range of location also indicate differences in the function of these group types (Figures 25-28).

Although the formal variability in structures comprising shrine groups is substantially less than that found in formal plaza groups, the variability in location is second only to Type 1 masonry religious buildings, ranging from centralized to completely isolated. The majority of structures in shrine groups belong to the Type 1 masonry all-purpose shrines, but variability is manifest in the number and complexity of shrines and the presence or absence of public ritual houses and noncentralized temples. Such variability may reflect a range of activities associated with shrine groups. The presence of public ritual houses, for example, may reflect the accommodation of the shrine group to long vigils and ritual meals. However, this variability in composition is not correlated with variation in location. The independence of location and composition in shrine groups parallels the independence in formal attributes and location observed in several masonry types. As argued at the end of Chapter 3, factors other than functional specialization would appear to be operating here, so that variability in shrine group composition may well reflect the financial wherewithal of the builders more than any strong categorization of such groups by function.

The number of structures in shrine groups and the sheer size of the groups may possibly reflect the role shrine groups played in the organization of particular communities. The largest and most elaborate shrine group is at San Gervasio, situated between the western districts and the eastern district. Its location is peripheral to both sectors but central with regard to San Gervasio as a whole. Hence its role as a social boundary marker may have been superseded by or combined with an

integrative role for the eastern and western districts of San Gervasio. Similarly, the northern and southern shrine groups at Buena Vista, in keeping with that community's general relegation of religious structures to the periphery and emphasis on dispersal of religious foci, are elaborate. The large shrine group at Aguada Grande is commensurate with its role as central focus for that community. Thus size and elaborateness of shrine groups per se may reflect the general importance of such groups to given communities and may be varying functionally by community context rather than by community composition.

Household Groups

Only a small number of household groups (see Figures 29-34) can actually be identified on Cozumel because raised plaza arrangements appear to be rare on the island. Although several of the groups listed in Tables 8 and 9 are not so arranged, there are fragmentary indications of more household groups lacking a clear plaza arrangement than those listed. These are referred to in Chapter 2. As discussed in Chapter 2, given the nature of the data, it is difficult to determine precisely what proportion of the observed structures are in plaza arrangements, in groups lacking plazas, or isolated. Only one clear pattern emerges from the data on dwellings and associated structures on Cozumel. With the exception of formal plaza groups and elite residences there is one dwelling per group. The only exception to this generalization is C25-9a which is grouped with C25-8a because they share a field or houselot. However, the distance between these two structures argues against their being considered as a group.

Recent research in the Maya Lowlands (Abrams and Webster n.d.; D. Birdwell, personal communication, 1975) is beginning to reveal that household composition and concomitant material facilities undergo change through time in a systematic fashion. To date such change is largely explained by economic factors that are clearly post-conquest, such as the introduction of commercial

Figure 24 [next page]. Formal plaza groups (a) C25-1 and (b) C31-1. (Scale 1:400).

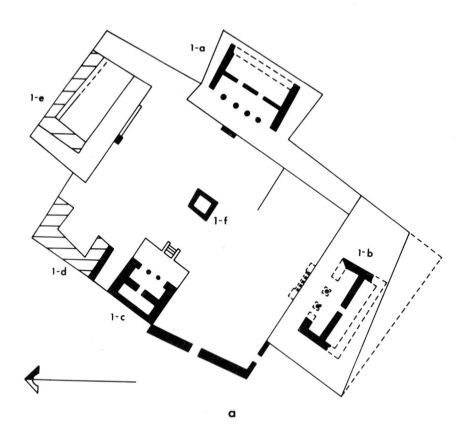

a

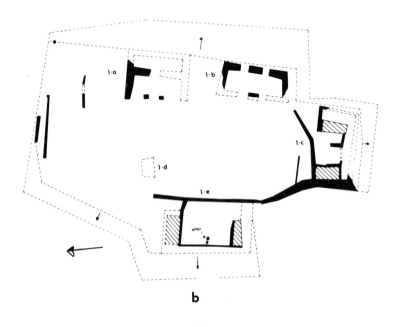

b

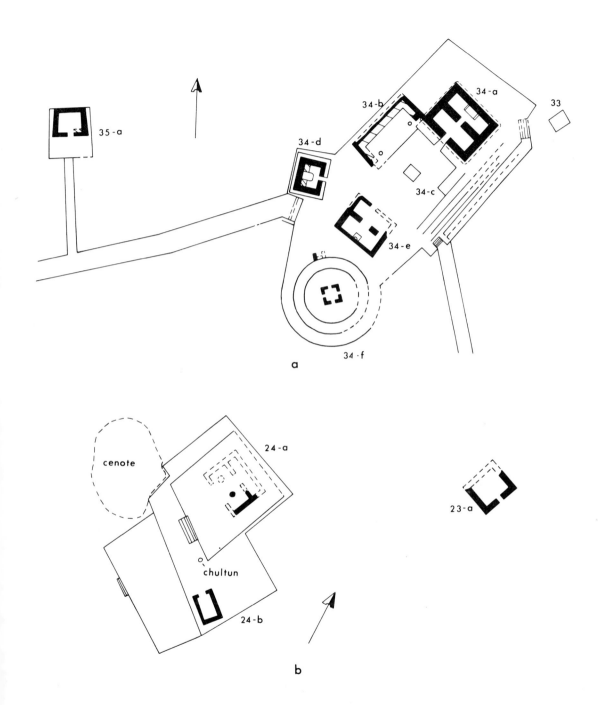

Figure 25. Shrine groups (a) C22-33 through 35 and (b) C18-23 and 24. (Scale 1:400).

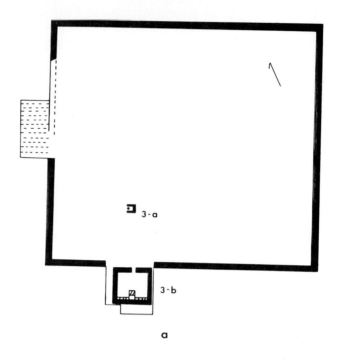

3-a

3-b

a

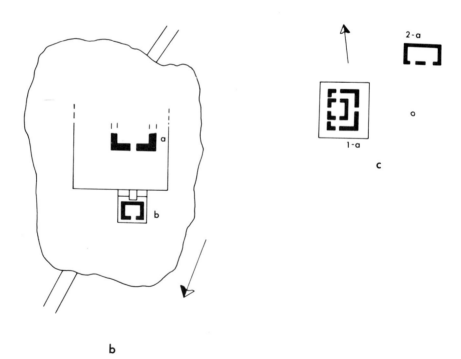

2-a

1-a

c

b

Figure 26. Shrine groups (a) C23-3; (b) C10-1; (c) C1-1 and 2. (Scale 1:400).

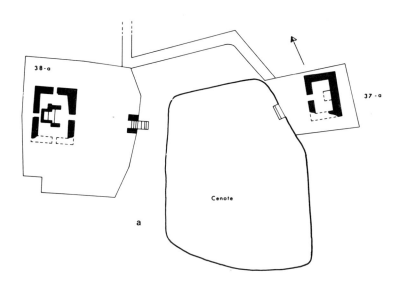

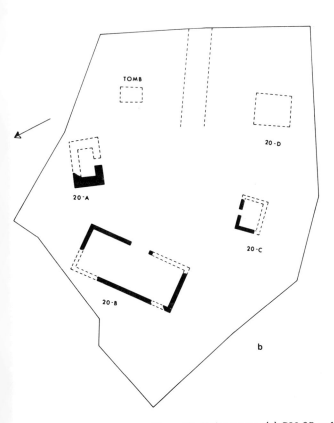

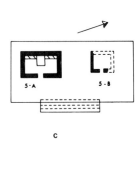

Figure 27. Shrine groups (a) C22-37 and 38; (b) C18-20; and (c) C31-5.

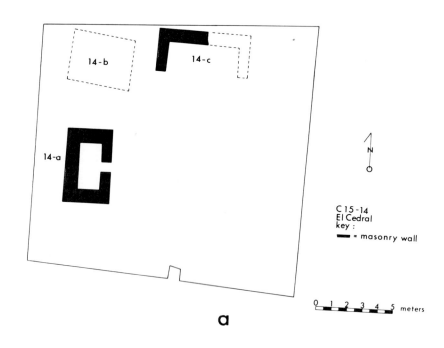

a

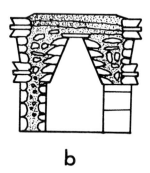

b

Figure 28. (a) Shrine group C15-14; (b) cross-section of vault of C15-14a.

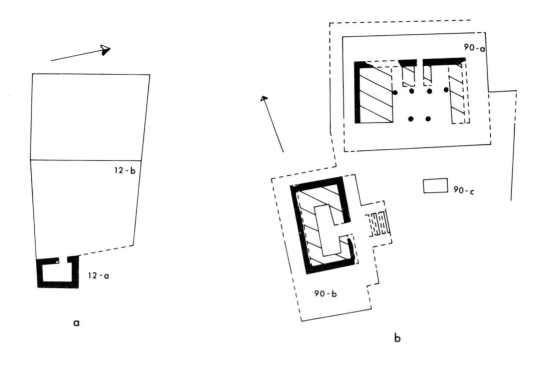

a

b

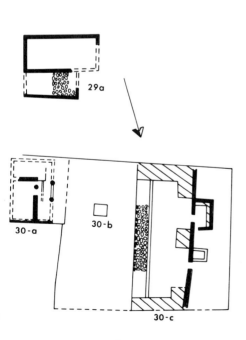

c

Figure 29. Household groups (a) C22-12; (b) C22-90; (c) C22-29 and 30. (Scale 1:400).

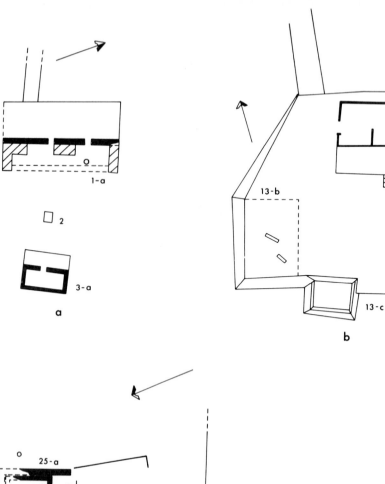

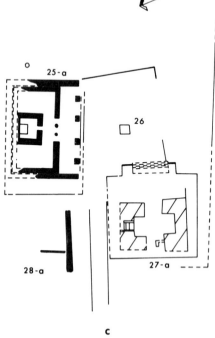

Figure 30. Household groups (a) C22-1 through 3;
(b) C22-13; (c) C22-25 through 28. (Scale 1:400).

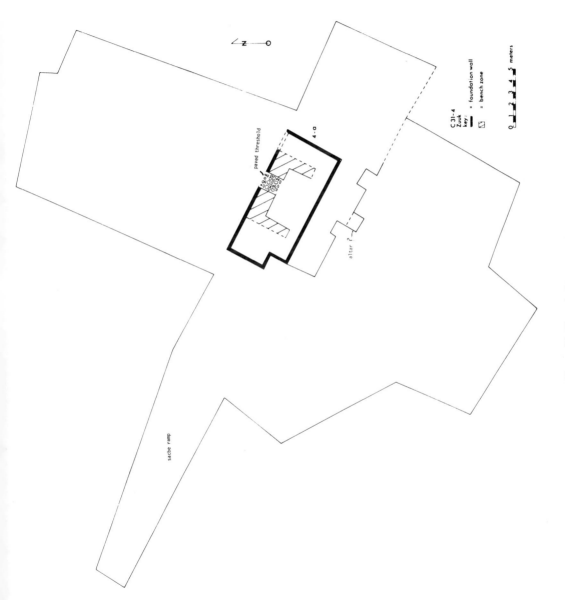

C 31-4
Zuuk
key: ▬▬ = foundation wall
      ▨ = bench zone

0 1 2 3 4 5 meters

paved threshold

4 - a

altar ?

sacbe ramp

Figure 31. Household group C31-4.

107

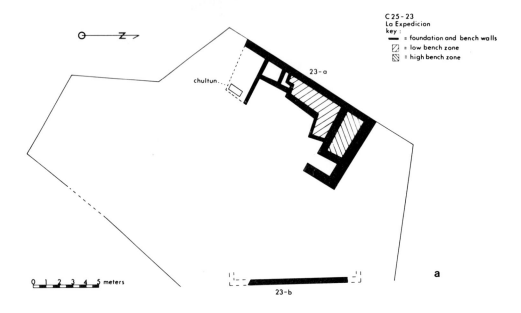

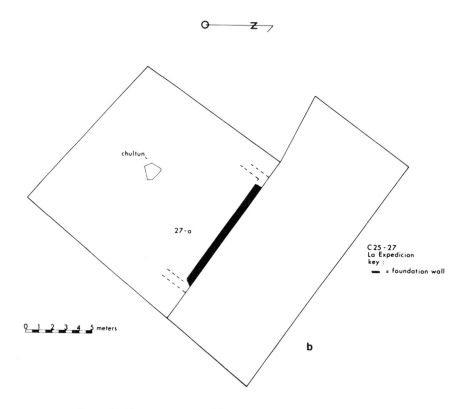

Figure 32. Household groups (a) C25-23; and (b) C25-27.

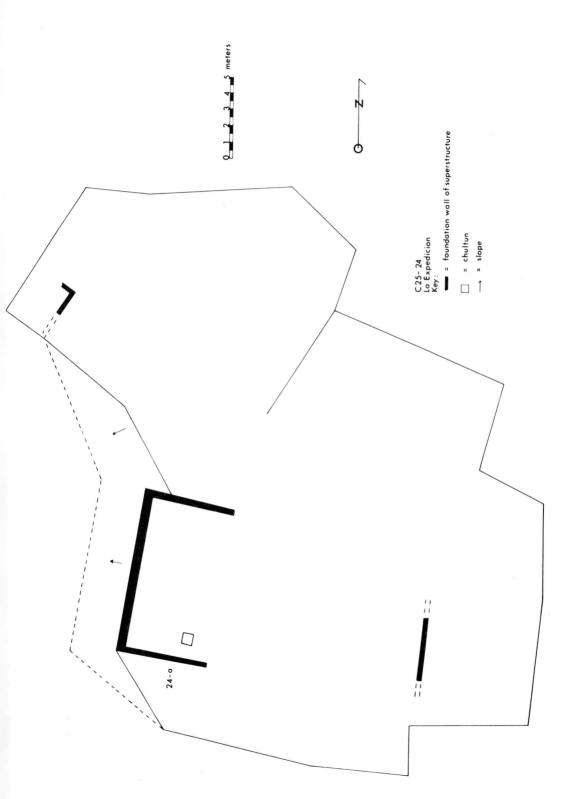

C25-24
La Expedicion
Key: ▬ = foundation wall of superstructure
□ = chultun
→ = slope

Figure 33. Household group C25-24.

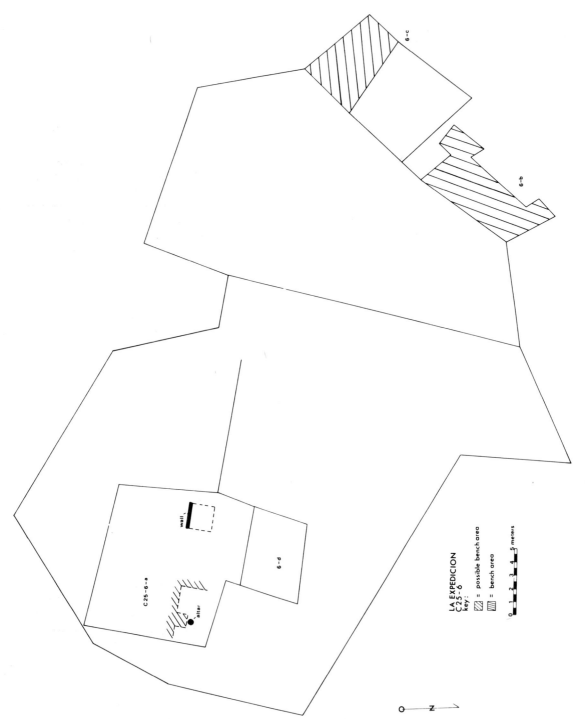

LA EXPEDICION
C25-6
key:

⊞ = possible bench area

⊟ = bench area

0 1 2 3 4 5 meters

C25-6-a

wall

altar

6-d

6-c

6-b

N

Figure 34. Household group C25-6.

cane cropping. Nevertheless, it seems reasonable to suppose that comparable dynamics of some kind were operating in antiquity. Weak analogical and archaeological control over social group organization and fission dynamics in the area make it difficult to support any general correlations between the apparent predilection for single-dwelling households on Cozumel and social organization. Nonetheless, some tentative leads on the subject can be offered.

A census taken on Cozumel in 1570 notes "these 143 couples living in only 39 houses, with two to eight couples in each house along with widowed persons, adolescents and children" (Roys 1957:155). In an earlier investigation, Roys and his colleagues (1940) observe that the practice of having several nuclear families or extended families living under one roof was not limited to the island of Cozumel because Tomas Lopez issued an edict discouraging such living arrangements in Yucatan proper.

It is possible that such large family groups inhabited single dwellings during the Decadent as well. The obvious problem here is the drastic demographic collapse of Cozumel between the time of contact and the time of the 1570 census (Roys 1957:155). This important intervening factor has been considered at some length by scholars attempting to assess continuity and change between precontact and early colonial residence and descent patterns (Haviland 1970). Curiously enough, the matter of actual material facilities has not played a major role in these discussions. As argued by Haviland (1970:69-70), it seems reasonable to suppose that some changes in residence and descent patterns resulted from demographic collapse. If large cooperating economic groups were the rule prior to the conquest, the large "ambilocal" groups on Cozumel following the conquest may be regarded as an attempt to maintain such groups in the face of rapidly declining population. However, this has no necessary correlation with the presence of large groups living in a single dwelling or in several dwellings clustered together. Although it could be argued that living in one house is more efficient economically than living in many, as a general rule peoples' attitudes towards social space are quite tenacious. Thus, compromises involving social space would be among the last made in the face of drastically changing circumstances. Certainly the families living on Cozumel at the time of the census had both the materials and the necessary labor to raise additional dwellings had they desired them. Thus reasoning both from what is known of Yucatecan practices at the time of contact and the lack of sufficient economic impetus, the single-dwelling, multifamily arrangement cannot be attributed to the postconquest demographic collapse.

If large family groups living under one roof cannot be attributed to postconquest change, then this practice provides a useful analogy for interpreting Decadent period household arrangements on Cozumel. In considering these arrangements, three questions arise: (1) How would fission operate in such circumstances? (2) What are the possible economic concomitants of this household organization? (3) How are the multiple dwellings of the elite residence-formal plaza centers to be explained?

A general review of the ethnographic literature on the Maya gives the impression that fission normally occurs through marriage when offspring move into their own dwellings. The variations in residence patterns (patrilocal, matrilocal, or ambilocal) or a sequential combination of residences can result in economic ties between domestic units that range from independent to interdependent. The fission process can express itself materially as more or less compact clusters of dwellings. Logically, it would seem that the greater the economic interdependence between nuclear families making up extended families, the greater the tendency toward compact arrangements of dwellings. Although there is no neat positive correlation between the compactness of dwellings and the degree of economic cooperation, and although exceptions can be found in many Maya communities, the correlation holds as a general tendency.

Abrams and Webster (n.d.) have found that a shift from milpa farming to commercial cane farming in a northern Belizean community resulted in increasing cooperation between domestic units making up extended families. Here the pooling of family resources yields sufficient capital to maintain profitable and expanding cash cropping. D. Birdwell (personal communication, 1975) has similarly noted that the extended families in the Maya fishing village of Chinux, Belize, who maintain economic cooperation are those in which members are involved in a variety of economic pursuits, such as fishing, fruit growing, and industrial labor, in addition to milpa farming. Thus motivation for close economic cooperation between members of extended families seems to be the opportunity to become involved in commercial systems above and beyond subsistence activities.

Although economic interdependence in no way requires the nuclear families to live together in a single dwelling, it seems reasonable to suppose that families living in such an arrangement do cooperate economically. Having eliminated demographic collapse as an explanation for the multifamily dwellings noted in the Cozumel Census of 1570, there appears to be no better explanation for this living arrangement than a strong social sanction motivated by a tradition of economic cooperation between large groups at the subsistence level. By 1570 the opportunities for natives of Cozumel to participate in suprasubsistence commercial systems were practially nil. Subsistence, however, included considerably more than milpa farming and there is good reason to suspect that fishing still played an important role in Cozumel's localized economy at this time.

Nonetheless, it seems unlikely that cooperation at the subsistence level could originally have engendered the living arrangement observed at the time of the census because there are too many instances in which subsistence activities are competently carried out by nuclear families. If this living arrangement extends back into the Decadent, and Cozumel was the scene of thriving mercantile activities as recorded in this historical literature, then it seems likely that other economic opportunities motivating extended family cooperation were operating before the conquest. Economic cooperation at the subsistence level may have been one ramification of increased economic cooperation in other activities during the Decadent period. Both opportunities for the commercial cropping of corn, cotton, fruits, and vegetables, and for occupational specialization should have been made available by the influx of religious pilgrims and merchants attracted by the island's oracle and strategic location on a long-distance trading route (Sabloff and Rathje 1975b). This line of reasoning only accounts for economic cooperation at the extended-family level during the Decadent and not for the particular living arrangement noted. However, certain

professions, such as working on a trading canoe, fishing, or transporting commodities overland on the island, might have required the absence of adult males from family groups for extended periods of time. In these circumstances, large families could have supplied protection and other services to nuclear families whose adult male was absent from the household. In the last analysis, there is no economic factor that would have required extended families to live in single dwellings, but there are circumstances under which social sanctions for such living conditions would be appropriate.

Although fission of family groups is usually a fairly straightforward process under most circumstances in the Maya area, with fairly obvious material concomitants, the fissioning of extended families living under one roof must have been a more complex affair. In such circumstances, it seems more likely that death of the paterfamilias triggered dissolution of the household than that marriage of children did (c.f., Tozzer 1941:130 on the abandonment of houses at the time of a death in the family). Under these circumstances a substantial portion of the family, younger sons, their children, affines, and so forth may have moved out and formed the nuclei of new extended families. The apparent paucity of household groups of structures on Cozumel is to some degree balanced by the presence of agglutinated substructures. One possible factor in the growth of these substructures by accretion might be the addition of new extended family dwellings at the time of fission. New extended families would build their own household platform adjoining that of their original home. Such an arrangement would be commensurate with continued economic cooperation between the segments of the original family following fission. Alternatively, given the wall network pervading the settlements, family landholdings within communities may have been severely defined and extension of the family platform may have been the best option available, short of moving to the periphery of the community. Although not all the agglutinated substructures can be explained in this way, some of them might be.

All the elite residence formal plaza groups on Cozumel contain two or more identified dwellings. There are several possible explanations for this deviation from the propensity for single-dwelling groups evident in the data. The first possibility is that only two segments of what is in fact a continuum of household arrangements on Cozumel were observed. Although this negative argument has considerable merit, accepting it necessitates assuming the present data are too limited to allow any useful patterns to be discerned.

A second inference is that the two or more dwellings found in civil-administrative centers reflect the presence of two or more families inhabiting the same plaza. These families might be related through kinship ties and in actuality represent one extended family responsible for administration of the center, or might be two distinct families responsible for different functions or offices in the center. Both of these interpretations are supported by the similarity of material inventories recovered from the horizontal excavation of two or more dwellings. Historical statements on sociopolitical organization have little to offer in discriminating between these two possible arrangements. Although towns apparently were administered by a hierarchically organized group of officials with distinct functions, there is no indication of a dual leadership at the top level that would support the inference of distinct families living in Cozumel's centers. Another aspect of the pattern on Cozumel is that where there are two dwellings on a formal plaza, one is distinctly larger than the other. This would appear to support the notion of a second related family living with the *batab* at the center and simply reflect the multiple-dwelling households found at various times in the Maya Lowlands. Thus whereas some families, the elite, were following one household arrangement, the majority were following another.

However, if multiple-dwelling households are associated with the elite on Cozumel, it might well be expected that the clearly elite residential groups surrounding the main formal plaza group at San Gervasio (C22-4-10) would have the same pattern. Although two of the five residential groups might be construed as multiple-dwelling households, this constitutes rather weak support for the expectation. Three of the elite dwellings (C22-1-a, C22-12-a, and C22-30-c) appear to be Mayapan-style structures. It is possible that their builders were emulating practices associated with that great city, but this would not explain the single-dwelling composition of two of them, because multiple-

dwelling households are most common at Mayapan (Smith 1962). The notion that multiple-dwelling households were not exclusively associated with the elite receives further support from other elite groups at San Gervasio (C22-90 and C22-40), which also appear to be single-dwelling households.

At the moment another interpretation seems to fit the available information equally well, if not better, than the possibilities given above. It is clear from Smith's (1962) research at Mayapan that social and religious space overlapped in the context of household groups. Something similar must have been taking place in the context of formal plaza centers containing dwellings on Cozumel. Nonetheless, there is a difference between religious activities taking place in what is normally private, secular space and social, domestic activities taking place in what is public, religious space. Landa (Tozzer 1941:128-129) notes that women were excluded from temples except on particular occasions, and that there were rituals in which they did not participate. Presumably the dwellings located in the formal plaza groups would be the scene of substantial amounts of ritual activity of community importance. It is possible that the smaller of the two dwellings in a formal plaza group was not the home of a distinct family, but rather the kitchen and sleeping quarters of the female members of the elite family occupying the center. This arrangement would facilitate the use of the main dwelling as a place of ritual and council for the community. At three of the formal plaza centers containing dwellings (C25-1, C31-1, and C18-1) there are two dwellings clustered at one corner of the group. This proximity is as appropriate to a division of a single household by sex as to two dwellings occupied by related families.

Although the formal plaza group of C22-87 would seem to deviate from the pattern given above, this deviation is rather minor. The dwelling on this group, C22-87-b, has a rear doorway "for the necessary service" that opens onto a lower plaza that supports an L-shaped benched structure. The structure on the lower plaza could be the second dwelling associated with the profane activities of the kitchen and women's work. Unfortunately, neither the lower plaza nor the structure were mapped due to an oversight on the part of the surveyors.

One advantage of this last interpretation is that it could be tested through excavation, elevating it to the status of a hypothesis. It would be expected that the artifact and feature inventories associated with these two kinds of dwellings would be quite distinct. There are some superficial hints of this distinctiveness. The main dwellings at La Expedicion (C25-1-e) and Zuuk (C31-1-e) both have altars associated with them. The altar is located in front of the structure at La Expedicion and inside it at Zuuk. The second dwellings do not have altars. This variability is more easily explained by the interpretation of separation of the sexes than by the other alternatives given above. Additionally, the only *chultun* associated with these elite dwellings occurs in one of the relatively smaller dwellings (C18-1-c) on the formal plaza at Buena Vista.

In this chapter some broad comparisons of structure assemblages on Cozumel and some of the inferences that can be drawn from them have been presented. Keeping these generalizations in mind, we now turn to the particular with descriptions of the settlements surveyed on the island. It will be necessary in discussing these settlements as communities to draw on the inferences made in this chapter and others given in earlier chapters.

CHAPTER 6

SITE DATA

Aguada Grande

Aguada Grande (C27) is the smallest settlement investigated by the survey on Cozumel, having a central core of approximately 3ha and a total settlement zone of less than 10ha. Aguada Grande is the northernmost settlement on the island and is located between two *aguadas* that are seasonally inundated and no doubt were an important factor in the establishment of a settlement here (Plate 6a, b). The large *aguada*, south of the settlement, contains water at the height of the dry season. The settlement is situated close to the northern lagoons and shallow protected waters bordering them. These areas are rich in marine resources, particularly large gastropods that were eaten in quantity during the Decadent period. It is, however, stiuated on the spine of high ground running up to the northern point of the island away from the low-lying swamp land that immediately borders the interior sides of the northern lagoons. Although topsoil in the vicinity is relatively thin compared to the San Gervasio, Buena Vista, or El Cedral settlement zones, it is quite capable of supporting crops if modern usage is any measure of ancient fertility. Trees with yellow flowers, locally termed *tzitzay*, are abundant in the area and farther south between Aguada Grande and La Expedicion. According to local informants, these are the primary source of nectar for honey bees. These trees are literally covered with bees when in flower. Several descriptions of Cozumel at the time of the conquest refer to "rosewood thickets" that provided nectar for the flourishing honey industry on the island. The locally available important resources included salt, fish, shellfish, and shell from the lagoons, and honey.

Our initial excavations and survey on Cozumel were begun at Aguada Grande. We chose to start there for several reasons. First of all, we hoped to obtain midden materials at what Sanders (1955, 1960) believed was a substantial ancient residential community. If we were to have any success in understanding the development of Cozumel, we had to have tight control of our chronology. The discovery and study of primary midden deposits is one of the easiest and best roads to this goal. Second, we hoped to obtain data about changing residential settlement patterns through time on Cozumel. Unfortunately, we were not too successful in these regards at Aguada Grande. Third, we believed that we would obtain more comprehensive data and more control over them by beginning our preliminary investigations at a relatively small site. Such was the case, for example, for the wall system we found on the island. Fourth, and more pragmatically, much of Aguada Grande was situated within cleared *zacate* grass fields so that the task of clearing the site was much less than would be the case elsewhere on Cozumel. Given our very small crew, these latter considerations were quite important.

Aguada Grande may have been visited by Spinden in 1926. Mason (1927:275-276) notes that Spinden crossed a *sacbe* south of Punta Molas, which almost certainly refers to the Aguada Grande causeway. Mason (1940:83) points out elsewhere that "remains of low stone walls which may have been the division walls of farms were found at several points in the coastal strip, notably

Plate 6 (a) Center of C27; (b) Aguada at C27 during the rainy season (Photograph by Mrs. K. Andrews); (c) C27-1-c; (d) C27-8.

on Cozumel Island and on the mainland at the ruins of Xkaret (Little Bay)."

The site was first formally reported by Alberto Escalona Ramos (1946) who mapped the four shrines at the center of the site. He also noted the presence of numerous low walls in the area and gave his opinion that they served as limits of cultivated fields. Sanders (1955, 1960) later revisited the site and made several small excavations inside and in front of the shrines. He also made a more extensive map than Escalona-Ramos, which included several surrounding structures, some of the adjacent stone walls, and a *sacbe*. Sanders expressed great interest in Aguada Grande because he believed that it was one of the few possible

population centers that he had located during his East Coast survey.

Date and Composition

Excavation in the settlement zone revealed that although there was some occupation of the site in Florescent times, the features observed today date from the Decadent and were in use until late in that period. Unlike other settlements where clear evidence of colonial or contact period occupation was found in the form of glass trade beads, the evidence for such occupation at Aguada Grande is equivocal. It is based primarily on the presence of very crude catenserware that is thought to persist into the colonial period (Sanders 1955, 1960). The layout and composition of the settlement argues for a primary occupation of the community during the Decadent period.

The settlement (Figure 35) is composed of the following features: (1) a central shrine group and associated structures (C27-1 through 3); (2) five large rubble substructures and a group of partially masonry structures considered to be domestic facilities (C27-6, 8, 11, 12, and 13); (3) associated outbuildings (C27-7, 9, 10, and 26); and (4) a scattering of low rubble platforms, circles, and semicircles that comprise the outer zone of the community.

The Analysis

Aguada Grande is one of two settlements on Cozumel known to lack a formal plaza group. The other is Chen Cedral (C23). The central location and size of the shrine group, C27-1, lead to the inference that this group functioned as the community focus (see Figure 35; Plate 6c). However, the lack of buildings associated with centralized civil-religious activities (public buildings, public ritual houses, and community temples), in addition to the lack of an elite residence, reflects a different mode of community organization at Aguada Grande than that found at other settlements on Cozumel.

It was argued earlier that shrine groups functioned primarily as important religious foci on ceremonial circuits. We hypothesize that the shrine group and associated route were present at Aguada Grande before the consolidation of the residential community around it. Although this does not mean that all the structures in the settlement necessarily postdate the shrines, the majority of them should. Unfortunately, excavations in C27-1 and 2 did not provide firm dating of these structures and their history (see Figure 37; Plate 7a, b), although pre-Decadent period trash was found inside C27-2.

There are several lines of evidence that support this hypothesis. A passage from the *Provinciae* (Wagner 1942a:58) describes a small community at the southwestern point of Cozumel. Structures described include a stone house that was probably a masonry shrine (Wagner 1942a:69), a large stone arch, and several *buhia* (thatched houses). If stone arches on Cozumel are associated with procession-

al entrances into formal plaza groups or with *sacbes* that functioned as processional routes, this small community was probably located there because the southern end of the island was an important terminus on an island-wide ceremonial circuit. In this case, the initial and predominant function of the shrine and arch at this community related to the ceremonial circuit rather than to the administrative needs of the community growing up around it. Perhaps, had the community continued to grow, the necessity for a more formal administrative center would have arisen.

A similar situation was probably taking place at Aguada Grande on the northern coast in the same period. This is evidenced not only by the lack of a formal administrative center, but also by the small size of the settlement and the orientation of structures to the wall network pervading it. The distortion of the grid and the process of subdividing lots witnessed at La Expedicion is just beginning at Aguada Grande (e.g., the lots associated with C27-8 and 10). The correlation of walls and structures indicated either that both were constructed at the same time or that the walls preceded the structures. Finally, although certain of the outlying structures, such as C27-18, may have served some ceremonial function, peripheral shrines usually associated with other settlements are not found at Aguada Grande. Using our interpretation of such outlying religious structures, we surmise that formal socioreligious boundaries had not yet been established at this settlement.

The structures immediately associated with the shrine group (Figure 35) include a possible group altar (C27-5), a multiroomed partial masonry structure (C27-3a and 3b), and a structure very tentatively identified as an oven (C27-4) (see Figure 38). Because the latter two structures are unique on Cozumel, they do not fit the inventory of features highly associated with formal plaza groups or shrine groups. Given the association of this shrine group with both an intersite ceremonial circuit and a small community, these two structures could relate to one or both of these. As there is an established formal inventory for structures relating to civil-religious centers, it is more likely that C27-4 and C27-3a and 3b relate more to activities associated with the ceremonial circuit than those associated with the community. Thus

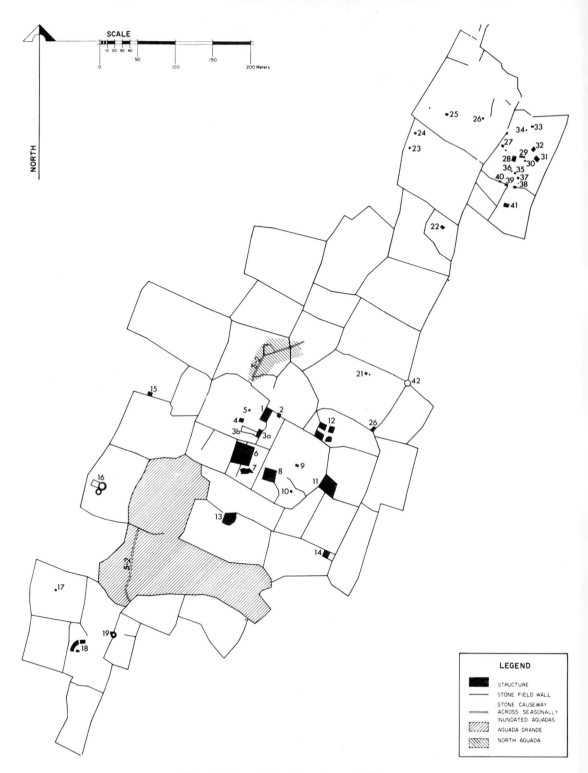

Figure 35. Aguada Grande settlement (C27).

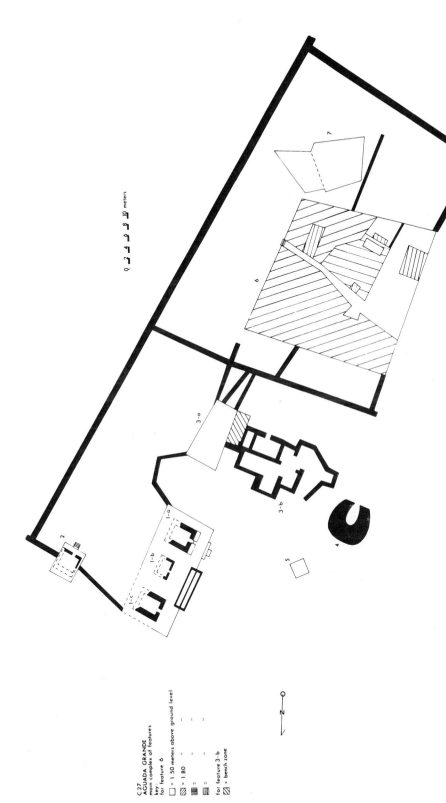

Figure 36. The center of Aguada Grande.

C 27
AGUADA GRANDE
main complex of features

key
for feature 6

☐ = 1.50 meters above ground level
▨ = 1.80   "   "   "   "
▦ =   "   "   "   "
▥ =   "   "   "   "

for feature 3-b
▨ = bench zone

0 1 2 3 4 5 10 meters

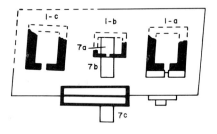

Trench 7

a

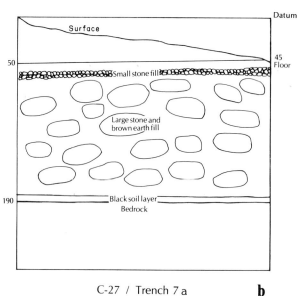

C-27 / Trench 7 a

2.80 x 84   North Face

b

0 _____ 100

c m

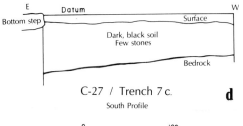

C-27 / Trench 7 c.

South Profile

d

0 _____ 100

c m

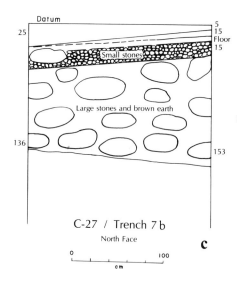

C-27 / Trench 7 b

North Face

c

0 _____ 100

c m

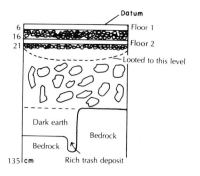

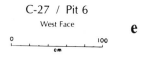

C-27 / Pit 6

West Face

e

0 _____ 100

c m

it has been suggested that C27-3b served as (1) a workshop for the local manufacture of idols fired in the nearby oven (C27-4); (2) a storage place for local products relayed along the ceremonial circuit because such routes were multifunctional; or (3) an inn for pilgrims passing through the settlement on their way around the circuit. Any one of the three alternatives is possible.

Only one fragmentary perishable dwelling, C27-8, was observed at Aguada Grande (see Plate 6d). In all other cases, the features on top of the large rectangular rubble substructures were amorphous and did not indicate their function. However, because single-dwelling households are prevalent elsewhere on the island and one of these platforms, C27-13, apparently had an associated burial in a location appropriate for a threshold (see Figure 39; Plate 7d), we identify these features as the single-dwelling households of extended families. C27-12, a group of four structures, may in fact be a multidwelling household. The structures in this group are quite unusual in that they are partially masonry with single constricted accessways. Although the formal attributes would argue for a religious function, the arrangement is more like that of a household. In this respect it is curious that the doorways of two of these structures face away from the other two toward the shrine group. Perhaps two dwellings and two associated structures are represented. Unfortunately only excavation can clear up this problem. In any case, C27-12 is considered to be the dwelling of an extended family, giving a total of six extended families in residence at Aguada Grande.

C27-6 is the largest of the rubble substructures and also the nearest to the shrine group. Perhaps this is some reflection of the historical and social primacy of this family at the settlement. Two pits in this structure were noninformative about its function.

Among the outbuildings at Aguada Grande, C27-9 has been identified as a hermitage or place of seclusion during fasting. This structure is centrally located relative to several of the households in the community, a placement appropriate to its public accessibility. The other identified hermitages, C27-24, 25, and 26 (see Figure 40; Plate 7c), lie north of the settlement zone in general alignment with the ceremonial route heading north toward the shrine at C9-1-a.

The cluster of small rubble substructures and stone piles to the north of the main settlement (C27-27 through 41) cannot be precisely dated because there were no sherds in the construction fill or on the ground around them. The tiny stone circles (e.g., C27-34) in this area look very much like modern walls protecting fruit trees against damage by pigs. There is, in fact, a grove of lime trees next to the cluster of buildings that is undoubtedly postcontact. Thus this group probably represents a relatively recent, postconquest ranch. The walls around this group are much better preserved than those nearby, standing about 1.2m high. They are indistinguishable from ancient walls in construction technique. As ancient walls have been rebuilt by the owners of the ranch at Buena Vista quite recently without any deviation from the ancient plan, perhaps these well-preserved walls were similarly rebuilt in recent times.

The features east and south of the settlement, C27-16, 18, and 19, are also functionally problematic. Excavation of C27-16 yielded small samples of Decadent period wares and a large number of small circular limestone disks (Figure 41 and Plate 8). Some of the chipped-stone disks had been worn smooth along their edges, representing a kind of wear pattern possibly associated with rubbing against softer organic materials. On analogy

Figure 37. (a) Location of Trench 7; (b) Trench 7a; (c) Trench 7b; (d) Trench 7c; and (e) Pit 6; Trench 7 was excavated on the west side of C27-1 in front of and inside the remains of the middle shrine (b). 7a was a 280 x 84 cm excavation with a depth of 190cm, 7b was 1 x 2m with a depth of 153cm, and 7c was 1 x 2.10m with a depth of 61cm. 7a and 7b revealed rubble fill below plaster floors, whereas 7c consisted of soil and small rocks below the surface. A very limited quantity of sherds, bits of shell, and an obsidian blade were uncovered in these excavations. Tests in the other two shrines on C27-1 and in C27-2 revealed sherds, censer fragments, beads, greenstone axe and figurine pieces, and shell artifacts in the fill and fall, although all these structures showed clear evidence of previous looting (see, for example, Pit 6 inside C27-2). Pit 6 also revealed a trash deposit that included pottery from the Florescent and Modified Florescent periods.

a

b

c

d

Plate 7 (a) C27-1-b; Trench 7b, showing remains of a plaster floor; (b) C27-1-b; Trench 7c; (c) C27-25; Trench 9; (d) C27-13, clearing along the side of the platform.

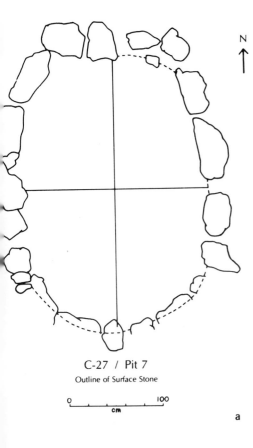

C-27 / Pit 7

Outline of Surface Stone

N
↑

0 _____ 100
cm

a

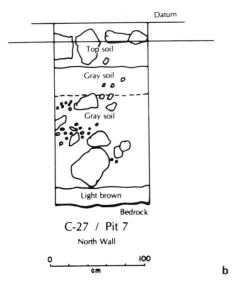

Datum

Top soil

Gray soil

Gray soil

Light brown

Bedrock

C-27 / Pit 7

North Wall

0 _____ 100
cm

b

Figure 38. (a) outline of surface stone on C27-4; (b) profile of north wall of Pit 7. Pit 7 (2 x 2.80m) was placed in C27-4, a unique structure just to the south of the major shrine platform C27-1. There was an oval arrangement of stones on the surface. Some potsherds and an obsidian blade were found near the surface. Below the surface, a fine, dark black earth fill was discovered. This fill continued until 1.70m below datum. There were a few sherds and some large rocks in the fill. It may have been burned earth inside a pit. The soil outside the probable pit was gray. At 1.70m, there was a change to a light brown fill, which lay just above bedrock.

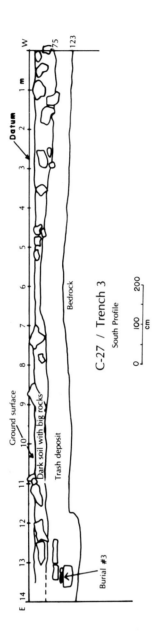

Figure 39. Trench 3 was a 14 × 1m excavation, which was placed along the east-west center axis of C27-13. This large rubble platform had well-defined edges (see Plate 9d) but no discernible features on its surface. The excavation revealed two principal levels. The first consisted of a dark soil layer with large rocks, whereas the second was a rich trash layer that sat above bedrock. On the top of the latter was a light tan clayey soil, possibly an old weathering surface. The trash deposit included sherds, animal bone, fish bone, shell, and stucco fragments (near the center of the trench). These fragments might have been from an earlier floor that was destroyed in the terminal renovation of the platform. Among the sherd fragments were Early period basal flange pieces.

A burial (Burial 3) was discovered in the trash level, lying extended on its back directly on a large flat rock 15-20cm thick. The body was parallel to the easternmost wall of the platform 30-40cm to the west of the retaining wall. The burial furniture included a polychrome vase next to the right shoulder, what may have been a wooden bowl with copper sheeting (although its preservation was too poor to tell) over the head and upper torso, and pieces of shell.

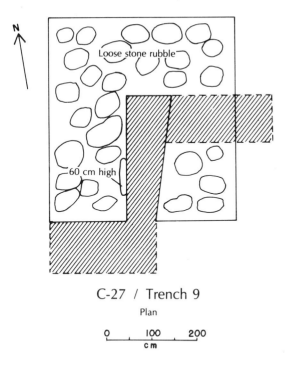

N

Loose stone rubble

60 cm high

C-27 / Trench 9

Plan

0   100   200
           cm

Figure 40. Trench 9 was placed in front of and inside the C-shaped platform C27-25. The trench had almost no depth. The loose stone rubble was placed nearly on bedrock that lay 35-45cm below the surface. A few sherds, a small figurine, and a limited quantity of obsidian were found just below the surface. An excavation in a similar structure, C27-26, approximately 53m to the west, had even less depth (about 15cm) with a few associated sherds.

with modern bee-raising practices, these disks may have been used as plugs for log hives. Modern hives employ wooden plugs daubed with *sascab* (plaster). Although the limestone disks are found in a variety of other contexts, they may, as Wallace (1978) has strongly argued, indicate that C27-16 functioned as an apiary. The complex of semicircular substructures, C27-18, contains a possible altar, indicating some type of ritual structure. The small rubble substructures found scattered in the vicinity of the settlement might be temporary field dwellings, or, more likely, given their proximity to the settlement, storage facilities.

In summary then, Aguada Grande developed late in the Decadent period around a preexisting shrine group on an established ceremonial circuit up the northeast coast. We would evaluate the small settlement described in the ethnohistorical literature at the southwestern tip of the island in the same way, though we did not find it in survey. Although the family occupying C27-6 may have been particularly important in local affairs, Aguada Grande apparently lacked a noble ruling family and the administrative accoutrements associated with the presence of such. The community probably developed here in response to a general expansion of population on the island during the Decadent period as evidenced in the proliferation of Decadent features. The site was also strategically located on an existing ceremonial circuit and on arable land near the resources of the northern lagoons. Religiously, Aguada Grande was tied into the pilgrimage rituals for which Cozumel was famous and was a node in pilgrimage circuits that went around the island. Socially, its inhabitants likely came north from La Expedicion, Aguada Grande's immediate neighbor to the south, and remained closely linked to the people of this community. It follows that Aguada Grande's political affiliations were also probably closest to La Expedicion, although, like La Expedicion and other sites on the northeast coast, it was probably also closely tied to the capital of San Gervasio. Economically, Aguada Grande may have serviced people traveling the ceremonial circuit and produced a variety of commodities, including salt, shellfish, fish, and honey, for exchange with pilgrim-traders in local markets. Although Rathje and Sabloff (1975b:13) have noted the importance of avoiding "leaks" of goods intended for long-distance trade into local economies, the principal commodities produced in the region of Yucatan (cotton cloth, salt, and honey) do not require specialized skills nor are they difficult to acquire. Additionally, descriptions of commercially important markets, such as the one at Cachi (Roys 1943), imply the exchange of local products and exotics could take place within a single institutional context. The variety of contexts in which exotics occur on Cozumel, albeit in small quantities, indicates that the local economy was to some extent oriented toward and integrated into long-distance trade moving through the island.

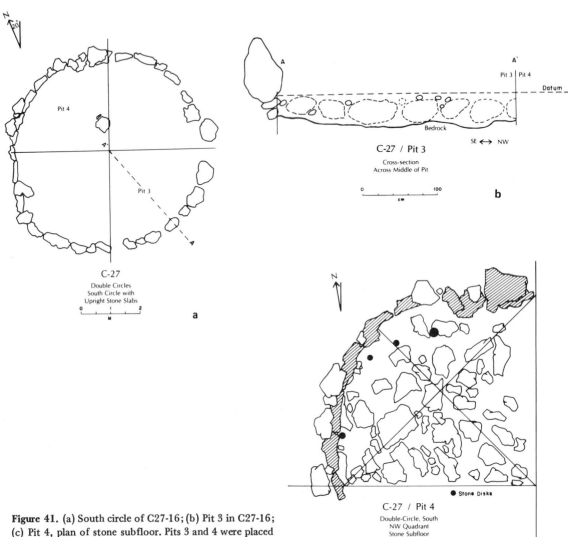

Figure 41. (a) South circle of C27-16; (b) Pit 3 in C27-16; (c) Pit 4, plan of stone subfloor. Pits 3 and 4 were placed in the south circle of the double stone circle (C27-16) (also see Plate 8). These excavations, as well as those in the north, showed that the upright slabs were set up on a crude foundation on bedrock. The floor was constructed by placing large stones on bedrock and then probably filling in with dirt to form a level surface. Sherds, shell fragments, and stone disks were among the materials uncovered by the excavation. In Pit 4, for example, four disks were found 20-25cm below datum. As discussed in the text, the function of the stone circles is a subject of much debate.

Plate 8 (a) C27-16; view of part of the wall, looking north from inside the south circle; (b) C27-16; looking east from inide the south circle at possible entryway; (c) C27-16; Pit 4; (d) C27-16; Pit 3.

The Wider Perspective

The importance of long-distance trade on Cozumel required a consideration of Agauda Grande in this light. Sabloff and Freidel (1975) have proposed that Aguada Grande served as a relay station for trade goods shipped overland from the northern lagoons into the interior. When viewed in terms of logical transaction places, such as San Miguel or San Gervasio, this route might appear to be very long and unnecessary. However, two factors make this route a viable one for long-distance commodities: (1) the need for defense and protection of stored commodities, and (2) the need for control of information concerning the quantity and quality of goods stored for future transshipment.

Because both these points are elaborated as discussion proceeds, they are only briefly introduced here. Cozumel's ideal location for storage facilities on a long-distance, maritime trade route is offset by the difficulties of defending any of the feasible port facilities at San Miguel and the northern and southern lagoons. The battlements and palisades surrounding the other coastal towns of Tulum, Xcaret, and Ichpaatun, to name a few, indicate that defense was an important consideration. There is no observation or description of such defensive works at the port of San Miguel, yet it was frequented by traders. The people of Cozumel probably defended facilities associated with trade by placing them inland, particularly along the eastern, windward coast, behind swamps, *aguadas*, sand bluffs, surf, and reefs (in that order). The effort of moving commodities overland on the island was offset by the security Cozumeleños could guarantee traders using their services. When faced with potentially hostile foreigners (such as the Spanish), the Cozumeleños' defense strategy was to retreat from the coastal settlements on the leeward side of the island. Any party foolhardy enough to venture inland along the narrow trails would find itself in deadly ambush before reaching its goal. The people of Cozumel could afford this strategy because in essence, the port facilities consisted of beaching areas, whereas the warehouses were safe in the interior.

With regard to information security, the dispersion of commodities in warehouses throughout the island made it difficult, if not impossible, for foreigners to gather more than a general idea of what was stored and in what quantities on the island at any one time. This information would have been the province of Cozumel's elite, the only people capable of engineering transactions on the island. In other commercial centers, traders maintained such security by living together in barrios, thus isolating their warehouses from the curious. Cozumel's traders maintained it by placing the warehouses inside their agricultural communities. If foreign traders lived on Cozumel, they must have lived in the port of San Miguel or in these widely distributed communities. In either case, they would have been dependent upon the native nobility of the island for not only their security but the administration of transport on the island as well.

The notion that Cozumel's intersite *sacbes* served as transport routes for commodities moving overland in no way contradicts their religious function. Not only were a substantial percentage of Cozumel's pilgrims long-distance traders (Scholes and Roys 1948), but such traders also habitually stopped at shrines along their routes. In a sense, perhaps the intersite *sacbes* on Cozumel were miniature replications of the long-distance routes traveled by these merchants.

Further evidence for the notion that Cozumel's inland communities contained warehousing facilities is presented in the following discussion of La Expedicion.

La Expedicion

La Expedicion (C25) is located approximately 4km south of Aguada Grande and about 1km inland from the northeast coast of Cozumel. The settlement zone, covering 9ha, is sharply delineated. This sharp delineation is evident in the distortion of the walls bordering the southern edge of the settlement; features outside the area given on the map (Figure 42) are rare and isolated. The settlement overall can be described as a compact-dispersed community because it contains elements of both dispersal and nucleation. There are approximately 400 structures per square hectare—somewhat more than the average for Tikal (Carr and Hazard 1961) and roughly half that at Mayapan (Jones 1952)—exhibiting no overall

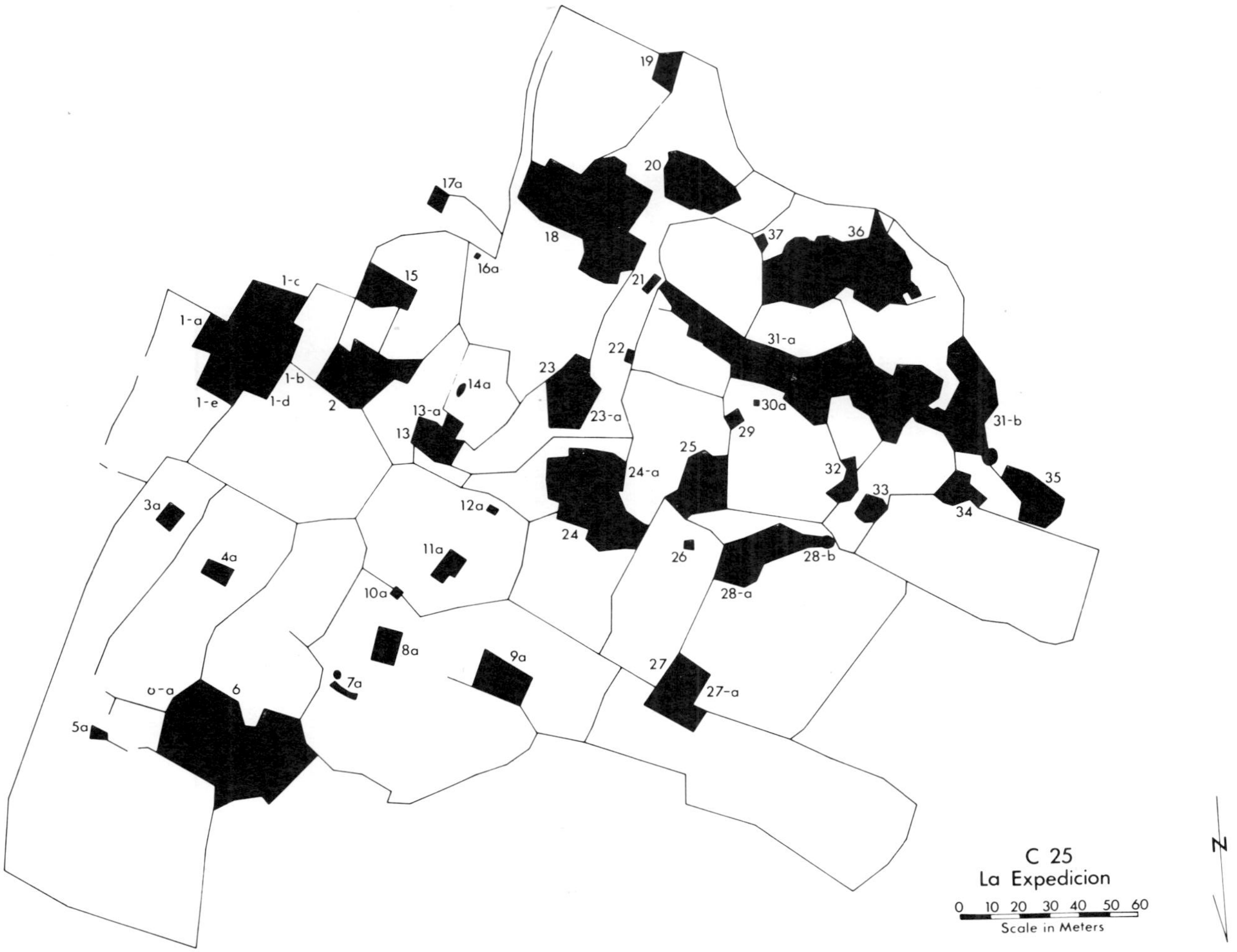

Figure 42. La Expedicion (C25) settlement.

plan. Like Aguada Grande and most other sites, the settlement was mapped with a Bruntun compass using both pace and chain measurement of distances.

La Expedicion is located on a shelf or rise inland from a series of seasonally inundated *aguadas*. Some of them contain water in the dry season. There is a second shelf or rise directly west of the site that is approximately 2m higher than the level of the site. This second rise is composed of level, well-drained, arable land that continues an indefinite distance inland, gradually dropping off to sea level as it approaches the swamps behind the northern lagoons.

The shelf on which La Expedicion is situated is densely pockmarked with ancient sinkholes and caves. The caves are usually shallow, with about 0.75m clearance. The larger ones have up to 2.0m clearance. All the larger caves, particularly those northwest and northeast of the settlement, showed evidence of use (in the form of sherds and broken stone tools) during the Decadent period. The sinkholes have deep accumulations of rich humus soils in them and, being much closer to the water table than to the surface, are a favorite location for large trees like the *ramon*.

Although it is possible that some of these sinkholes were active *cenotes* at the time of the occupation of La Expedicion, the majority of them were probably used in a manner analogous to practices noted on the peninsula of Yucatan at the time of the conquest and on Cozumel in the nineteenth century. In both cases, such sinkholes were prized locations of horticulture and arboriculture. In Yucatan they were used for growing small groves of cacao (Roys 1939) in regions otherwise unsuitable for the precious bean. On Cozumel sinkholes in the vicinity of Columbia plantation near El Cedral were used for planting a variety of fruits and vegetables, including avocado and pineapple (P. Sabloff 1975 and personal communication, 1973). At La Expedicion these sinkholes are particularly concentrated in an area extending approximately 1km north and south of the settlement and are confined to the shelf (varying from 500m to 1km in width) on which the site is located. Apparently the site was founded on the one section of this shelf where sinkholes are not abundant, because no sinkholes were found in the settlement zone proper. It should be noted that the wall network is distorted around

these sinkholes, producing a roughly circular wall around them here and elsewhere on the island.

La Expedicion is close enough to the northern lagoons and the sea for these to be considered potentially important resource areas. Economically important resources at La Expedicion may have included fish, shellfish, shell, salt, and commerical crops such as cacao, *mamom*, and other fruits. Honey, as elsewhere on the island, was probably also produced.

La Expedicion was first reported and named by Escalona-Ramos (1946:553-555). He only described the main plaza area of the site that we have termed *Complex I*. However, Spinden had actually visited the site in 1926 as part of the Mason-Spinden expedition. Spinden drew a plan of Complex I, which he termed *Santo Tomas*. Spinden also visited the northerly outlying shrine (C25-38-a), which was illustrated in Mason (1927: 276), as did Escalona-Ramos (1946) and Sanders (1955). Escalona-Ramos (1946:552-553) gave this shrine a separate site designation, calling it *Las Grecas* or *Cinco Manos*. It was extensively looted sometime between Sanders's visit in 1954 and our field research in 1972. Parts of La Expedicion also were looted sometime in the recent past.

The site was chosen as a second major focus of our 1972 surveys and limited excavations because it appeared to be connected with Aguada Grande, contained a more sizable settlement, and showed a wider array of elite architecture.

Date and Composition

Excavations carried out at La Expedicion indicate that the settlement was occupied from Florescent times through the Decadent period. Apparently the formal plaza group was a planned entity from its inception, undergoing several later rebuildings. Excavations in agglutinated substructures revealed buried retaining walls indicating that the substructures had been expanded during their use. The core substructures apparently predate the Decadent whereas the expansions may date to the Decadent.

Although necessarily subject to the final analysis of excavated materials, it seems that settlement modification through time was achieved primarily by horizontal rather than vertical growth of features as well as through the construction of

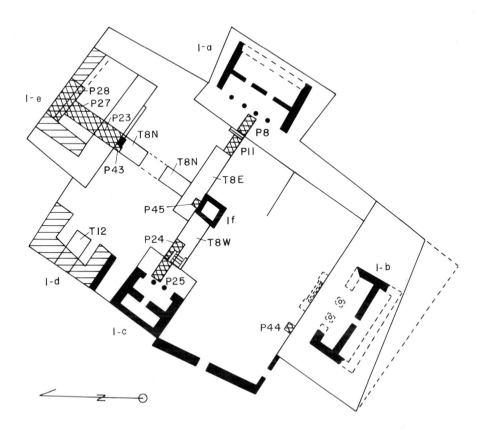

Figure 43. Location of excavation in C25-1.

entirely new features. The formal plaza group, C25-1 (Figures 24 and 43; Plates 1c, 1d, and 9), is the major exception to this generalization. In this case vertical modification by leveling existing structures and the consequent raising of the plaza level were revealed by excavation. The profiles of Pit 8 (Figure 44 and Plates 9b, 9d, and 10b) and Pit 11 (Figure 45 and Plate 10c), which were excavated in front of Structure C25-1-a, are illustrated here in order to show some indication of the nature of the vertical growth of Complex I. An earlier structure also was found in front of and underneath Structure C25-1-c. The small altar in the center of the plaza apparently was built at the time when the next to last plaza floor was laid down.

Given that processes of abandonment and reoccupation could not be detected, both surface

collections and the general pattern of growth within the settlement lead to the inference that the surface features mapped by the survey are roughly contemporaneous and reflect the community at its height during the Decadent period.

A single blue-glazed sherd, notched in a typical Precolumbian way, was found on the surface of C25-24. Thus at least part of the settlement was apparently still being used or occupied during the contact period.

La Expedicion is composed of the following features: (1) a residential formal plaza group (C25-1); (2) six agglutinated substructure complexes (C25-6, 18, 24, 28, 31, and 36); (3) seven relatively isolated dwellings (C25-3, 4, 8, 9, 11, and 27); (4) four possible multistructure household groups (C25-13, 20, 23, and 25); (5) a variety of smaller substructures that probably served as

Plate 9 (a) C25-1, looking east; (b) C25-1-a, showing Pit 8 in the foreground; (c) C25-1-a, showing Pits 8 and 11 in the foreground; (d) Pit 8, north profile, showing sequence of plaster floors.

outbuildings as well as several identifiable outbuildings (C25-5, 7, 10, 12, 14, 16, 19, 21, 22, 26, 29, 30, 32, and 33); and (6) several problematic substructures (C25-2, 15, 34, and 35).

The formal plaza group at La Expedicion is apparently the only planned plaza group at the settlement. Although some of the early plaza floors seem to run underneath the present main

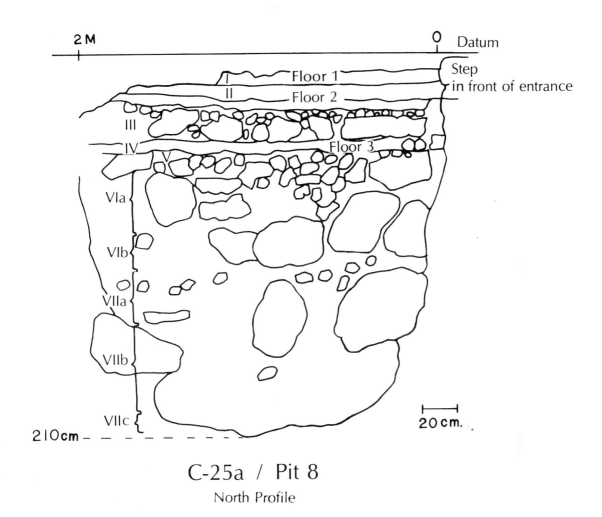

C-25a / Pit 8

North Profile

Figure 44. Pit 8 (1 x 2m) was placed in the platform in front of Structure C25-1-a. The excavations indicate that there were two building phases in the construction of the platform. The first consisted of the buildup of trash, large stones and rubble, Floor 3, and the large step at the base of the platform, whereas the second included the construction of the rubble layer on top of Floor 3, the building of Floor 2 and the little platform boundary, and the step in front of the columns. Floor 1 was then added at a later time. It is quite thick (about 8cm) and sits immediately on Floor 2. No sherds were found in Levels I, II, and IV. Sherds were found in the other levels, particularly in Level VII, which consists of a trash deposit. Bedrock was found immediately below this trash deposit.

dwelling (C25-1-e), excavation did not eliminate the possibility of other earlier dwellings (see Figure 46). Because C25-1-e rests on a northern extension of the plaza, the earlier floors underlying it may relate to earlier nonbenched versions of the dwelling. Nonetheless the basic plan of the group, including dwellings, was established early in the history of the site. How early is difficult

to determine without the final analysis of the ceramic inventory. Later raisings of the plaza utilized quantities of trash in the fill, indicating presence of an active residential area somewhere in the vicinity of the group.

In summary, La Expedicion was founded sometime prior to the Decadent, and from the beginning the community was made up of a formal

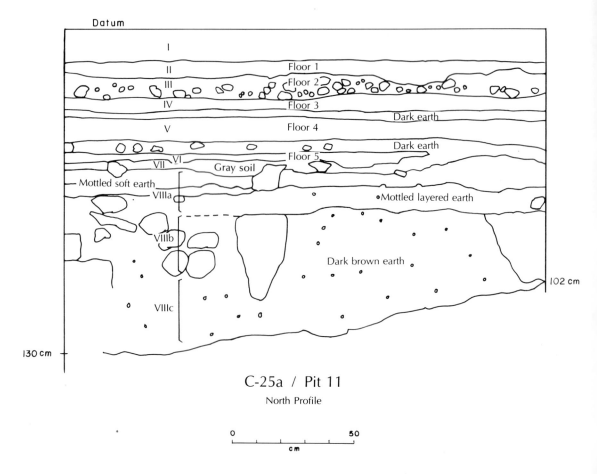

C-25a / Pit 11

North Profile

Figure 45. Pit 11 (1 x 2m) was placed in front of the platform of Structure C25-1-a. In effect it is a western extension of Pit 8. Five separate floors were uncovered, each associated with a limited number of sherds. A large trash deposit with numerous sherds, bone, and shell was found below Floor 5 (in Level VIII). Much animal bone also was found in Level I. The stones that make up the platform steps were laid down on Floor 2, with Floor 1 a later addition. It is not known how far under the steps Floor 2 extends. Bedrock was reached 1.10-1.30m below datum.

elite residential administrative center and dispersed residential substructures west and south of this center. Further chronological analysis of excavated ceramics may reveal whether or not there was a community at La Expedicion prior to the construction of the formal plaza group. At present the possibility that the settlement was indeed founded by a noble family is not out of the question. The founding of community centers and the gathering of people around them is a well-established process of community inception in the Postclassic on the Yucatan peninsula (Roys 1957, 1962). On the other hand, establishing a noble

family as rulers in existing communities is likewise well documented. The ultimate outcome of both processes is often the same, namely the incorporation of the community into a larger social sphere through the ties that bind the noble families of a region together. That social integration through the elite was well developed on Cozumel by Decadent times is documented by the presence of a *halach uinic* on the island (Roys 1957:156), the power of cacique Naum Pat (Chamberlain 1948: 46), and the evidence for coordinated leadership and policies concerning the first Spanish explorers (Wagner 1942b).

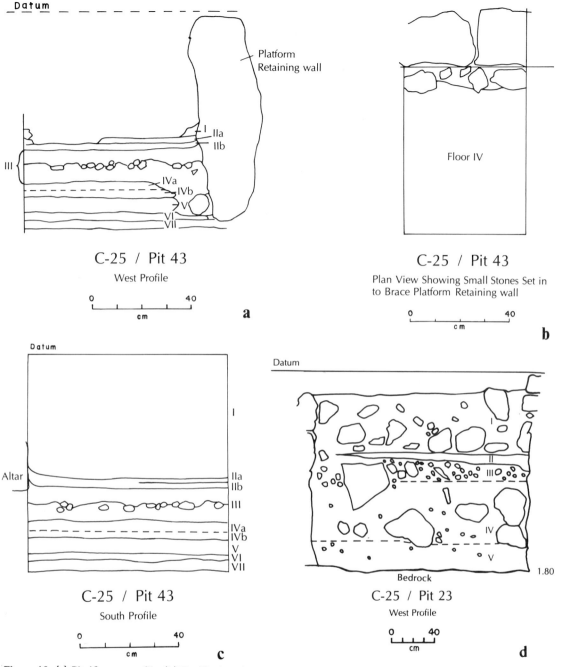

Figure 46. (a) Pit 43, west profile; (b) Pit 43, plan view at level of Floor IV; (c) Pit 43, south profile. Pit 43 (70 x 80cm) was placed at the base of the platform of Structure C25-1-e next to the altar. The excavation uncovered what appears to be the same sequence of floors as in Pit 11. In addition, the excavation revealed that the platform for the structure apparently was built at the time of construction of Floor III. At this time, the lower floors were cut into in order to set up the retaining stones for the platform. The altar also was constructed at this time because it is sitting in this floor. The fill continued underneath

Floor VI with no other apparent floors below.

(d) Pit 23 (1 x 2m) was placed in the front of Structure C25-1-e. The upper level (I) contained a medium to large rockfill. Only one floor, consisting of several layers of plaster, was uncovered in the pit (at .75m below datum). This floor ran under the large stones that form the edge of the platform and is lower than both floors around the altar in front. Level III contained bits of plaster, perhaps from an older, ripped-up floor, whereas Level IV revealed a trash deposit with sherds, bone, and shell.

C25-1

The regularities in the design of formal plaza groups on Cozumel, the presence of elite dwellings, the centrality of location, and the four-sided plaza arrangement in and of itself all indicate that these groups shared the substratum of prosaic functions associated with the everyday administrative and integrative needs of communities. From this perspective, the variations in formal composition reflect the special purposes or requisites of such plaza groups that functioned to integrate their respective communities into the whole that was Cozumel.

Given the identification of Type 6 masonry structures as community temples, the formal plaza group at La Expedicion, C25-1, which supports three Type 6 structures, reflects a particular concern for religious ritual. Factors such as the relative wealth, prestige, and status of the noble family administering La Expedicion may partially account for the form and number of religious structures here, but such factors are of limited explanatory utility. Because there are formal plaza groups on Cozumel that completely lack this type of building, the composition of C25-1 reflects not simply a difference in quantity but also a difference in kind.

Given the necessary wherewithal, such buildings probably were designed in anticipation of their most important, rather than their most common, function. Type 6 structures were most importantly used in conjunction with major periodic ceremonies involving participation of the entire community and representatives from other communities. As a theater for events, C25-1 is designed for festivals. The historical literature on the subject (e.g., Tozzer 1941) indicates that the integrative ramifications of periodic festivals were manifold and complex. The simplest proposition following from this identified specialty is that La Expedicion was the major religious central place on the northeast coast of Cozumel. Although this does not mean that festivals lasting several days could not have taken place, it implies that the center was designed for festivals of short duration, and that it was not designed to accommodate a continuous stream of activities involving the long-term presence of people without homes in the community. This reflects either the periodic nature

of ceremonial activity in the case of local participants, or the transient nature of participation by foreign pilgrims at the center. In either case, the composition of C25-1 complements rather than competes with the administrative center at San Gervasio. If festivals were a medium for the transmission of political and economic policy, festivals at La Expedicion could have provided an effective means of disseminating information from the capital of San Gervasio to the northeast coast communities, as well as a means of solidifying bonds between this subregion of the island and the capital on a much more frequent basis than that provided by festivals in the capital itself.

Given this interpretation of La Expedicion's formal plaza group, it is likely that the noble family administering the community also provided important religious leadership and was also specialized to some degree. The roles of religious and political leader are often combined in descriptions of political organization in Yucatec communities at the time of Conquest (Roys 1957).

Agglutinated Substructures

Of the agglutinated substructures at La Expedicion, only C25-18 seems a likely candidate for the process of household fission earlier conjectured to be reflected in this kind of feature. C25-18 consists of a large eastern rectangular platform with northwestern and southwestern extensions. All three of these areas, which are distinguished by variations in height, show some evidence of having supported superstructures. Unfortunately the cut-stone alignments on the surface are so fragmentary that no plans could be made. However, the impressions given by these alignments is that each of the three areas supported two or more structures arranged in a plazalike fashion. In this respect, C25-18 looks rather like a triple version of the other household groups (e.g., C25-23) found in the settlement.

The surface features on the other agglutinated substructures are more problematic. C25-36, which is divided up into seven areas of varying height defined by low retaining walls, supports one possible dwelling (C25-36-a) and a number of low rubble platforms of varying shapes and sizes, which are all smaller than identified dwellings in the settlement. These platforms show no particular organization into plaza areas. The presence of a single dwelling on a substructure approximately 1000m^2 in size indicates that the substructure was also built to support structures other than residences, specifically a variety of outbuildings. The effort required to build a feature of this size emphasizes the special importance of these outbuildings. These special outbuildings were probably warehouses for storing commodities. A consideration of other agglutinated substructures reflects the same situation.

C25-31 is the largest of the agglutinated substructures at La Expedicion. The single substantial dwelling, C25-31-a (see Plate 10a), is associated with a group altar, C25-30a (Plate 10d), and an outbuilding platform, C25-29, which may be a raised shrine. Together these features form a basic household group. However, the platform on which C25-31-a rests extends over 100m west of the dwellings and 40m in front of it. Like other agglutinated features, this massive substructure is divided into areas, but none of these areas shows any evidence of cut-stone or wall alignments. Consequently the material evidence for superstructures is lacking. Unless these raised areas were used for something other than supporting superstructures, the superstructures must have been made entirely of perishable materials. This certainly deviates from the material correlates established for dwellings on Cozumel. Whatever may have rested on these raised areas, their disposition off the ground was more important than the permanence of their foundations. This is demonstrably not the case with dwellings because several of them occur directly on the ground at La Expedicion. Again, the extensive raised areas around the one dwelling on C25-31 were probably built to support special outbuildings such as storage facilities.

As noted above, the agglutinated substructures show evidence for earlier retaining walls, and perhaps structures, beneath their surfaces. For example, excavations in front and just inside of Structure C25-31-a uncovered a wall in front and an earlier floor that might relate to the wall (Figure 47 and Plates 10b and 10c).

That C25-31-a was inhabited by a relatively wealthy family is indicated by the presence of a rich cache in the group altar, C25-30a. This cache included a variety of whole and broken exotics,

especially stone axes, laid on a bed of Florescent period sherds. Given the unobtrusive nature of the altar and the predilection of Decadent period peoples to rob or reopen earlier caches, this feature probably constituted a "safety deposit" box of readily available looted and otherwise acquired valuables. It is the kind of feature expected in the context of a household occasionally requiring ready capital on short notice, such as that of a merchant. That the household was likely a large one in permanent residence is indicated by the presence of a crudely vaulted tomb at the westernmost edge of the agglutinated substructure. This tomb had been robbed at the time of observation and contained only scattered bones. It was apparently entered from the side and was easily reopened. By analogy with other tombs found on Cozumel, this tomb appears to be the family crypt.

The irregular design of agglutinated substructures in general is dramatically illustrated by C25-31. Clearly this feature grew by accretion over a period of years. Given the relative lack of dwellings on it, it seems to have been modified sporadically as the need for more storage space increased.

The other three agglutinated substructures at La Expedicion, C25-6, 24, and 28 (Figures 33, 34, and 42), show the same pattern. They each have a dwelling and a massive extension of the substructure supporting the residential structure. Perhaps by coincidence, all these extensions support some wall fragments, but none can be identified as a dwelling.

In general, either the agglutinated substructures reflect the presence of a group of people at La Expedicion whose ideas concerning appropriate labor investment in household-related facilities strongly contrasted with their neighbors, or the families were investing in special facilities. As the types of structures and artifacts associated with households on agglutinated substructures do not differ from those found in households on the ground, we opt for the latter inference. Furthermore, the presence of small rubble substructures in the context of ground-level households distributed throughout the community supports the notion that the structures on top of agglutinated substructures were not the usual type of outbuildings (kitchens, corn cribs, turkey pens, etc). Lacking evidence for workshops or other special uses, the identification of these substructures as support areas for storage facilities is currently the best possible interpretation. Although it is possible that local commodities were stored on the substructures, it seems unlikely that local production was sufficiently great to warrant such extensive platform areas. Hence these features were most likely built for the storage of nonlocal commodities coming into the community in bulk.

Isolated Dwellings and Household Groups

The isolated dwellings and household groups at La Expedicion have already been discussed in some detail in Chapters 2 and 5. Their importance, aside from implications as to family organization, lies primarily in their contrast to agglutinated substructures. If formal similarity is a measure of contemporaneity, the dwellings associated with raised plazas and agglutinated substructures are contemporaneous with dwellings found on the ground. For example, C25-24-a, on an agglutinated substructure, C25-27-a, on a rectangular platform, and C25-3, on ground level, are all Type 2 perishable structures. Because the various types may have considerable time depth, an argument based on form is a hypothesis to be tested by independent data such as associated ceramics. Until the ceramic data are available, we proceed on the presumption that the superstructures are contemporaneous.

Given the variability in association of dwellings and other features, those families inhabiting isolated, ground-level dwellings or dwellings on ground level were probably not actively engaged in long-distance trade, although they may have been related to other families living on agglutinated substructures.

Socioreligious Boundaries

At La Expedicion, we have good control over the northern and eastern shrines and weak control over the southern and western ones. The northern shrine, C25-38-a, is an elaborate masonry structure on a raised substructure (Type 4). It is almost certainly the same structure identified by Escalona-Ramos (1946) as *Cinco Manos* or *Las Grecas*. The building faces east toward the sea and has a small Type 1 masonry shrine at the foot of its substructure north of the staircase. This arrangement is analogous to that found at Arrecife (C10). Thus technically C25-38 constitutes a shrine group. Fragments of a *sacbe* run between it and C25-1. This *sacbe* is about 1.5m wide and consists of a bedding of gravel with vertical slab borders. C25-38-a is not only the most elaborate of the outlying shrines at La Expedicion but is also closest to the settlement zone and the only one connected to the settlement by an observed *sacbe*. It was probably the major place of worship on the periphery.

C8-1-a and C2-a are shrines on the coastal side of La Expedicion. Despite their distance from the settlement, the location of these two shrines in front of the settlement argues for an association between them and La Expedicion. In Chapter 3 the high correlation of coastal shrines and inland settlements was noted and discussed.

A small shrine group half a kilometer south of La Expedicion was pointed out by a local ranch foreman. This group consists of two Type 1 masonry structures set on a single, low support platform. The structures face northwest, roughly the direction of the settlement zone. In form the group looks very much like C31-5, a peripheral shrine group at Zuuk, south of La Expedicion.

Figure 47. (a) Location of Pits 47 and 48 in front of and inside C25-31-a (also see Figure 31a); (b) Pit 47; (c) Pit 48. Pits 47 and 48 were placed just in front and just inside the open side of the house structure C-25-31-a, respectively. Pit 47 was excavated in four levels. The pit was discontinued in Level 4 as the large boulders became too difficult to remove. An earlier wall was found in Level 2. It showed much better construction than the surface walls. Part of this wall appears to be sitting directly on a very large boulder that begins 100cm below datum. Fragments of an earlier plaster floor appeared in the fill of Level 3.

Pit 48 revealed a number of large rocks just below the surface and a well-preserved plaster floor at 66cm. The floor was quite thick toward the south and thin toward the east. It stops on the east profile but was probably just broken up by roots and rocks. The floor goes under the bench (see Plate 10c) and may relate to the early wall of Pit 47. Many artifacts and sherds were found in the fill below the floor. A small plaster-floor fragment also was discovered 155cm below datum.

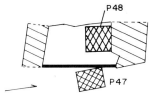

a

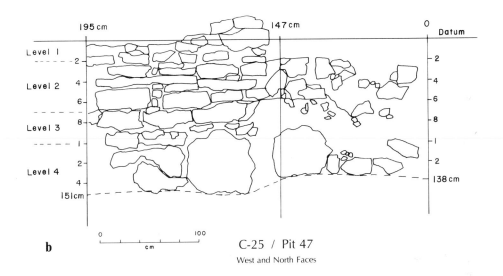

195 cm   147 cm   0 Datum

Level 1 — 2

Level 2 — 4 — 6

— 8

Level 3 — 1

— 2

Level 4 — 4

151 cm

2 — 4 — 6 — 8

1 — 2

138 cm

0   100
cm

b   **C-25 / Pit 47**

West and North Faces

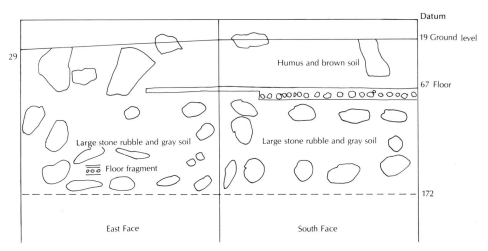

Datum

29

19 Ground level

Humus and brown soil

67 Floor

Large stone rubble and gray soil   Large stone rubble and gray soil

Floor fragment

172

East Face   South Face

C-25 / Pit 48

c

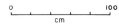

0   100
cm

Plate 10 (a) C25-31-a; (b) C25-31-a; Pit 42 reveals earlier wall; (c) C25-31-a; Pit 43 reveals earlier floor running under bench; (d) C25-30a; the stone in the center may have served as the core of an idol.

The same informant indicated that there is a large shrine west of the settlement zone. This structure was not, however, observed.

Thus, although control over the boundary shrines is tenuous, there are shrine groups north, east, and south of the settlement set roughly to the cardinal directions relative to La Expedicion and close enough to the site to be considered associated with it. It is possible that these shrines were placed on trails leading into the settlement zone and away from the shrines toward other settlements to the north and south. Fragments of a *sacbe* between La Expedicion and Aguada Grande offer some support for this view, as does the analogy with the modern placement of shrines in Maya communities discussed in Chapter 3.

Community Organization

From the prevalence of isolated dwellings and single dwelling households at La Expedicion, and by analogy with residential practices observed on the island early in the colonial period, extended families living under one roof appear to have been the norm in this community. The same residential pattern, in modified form, applies to the noble family inhabiting the formal plaza group, where there may have been a division of residence by sex. Although the varying associations of formal dwelling types with other features indicates that the community was culturally homogeneous (corroborated by artifact inventories), variation of formal types associated with raised substructures, shrines, and agglutinated substructures may well reflect social and economic differences within the community. By analogy with modern Maya residence practices, the extended family residence is appropriate to a local economic system offering a wide variety of income sources. The local economy reflects not only a wide variety of natural resources in the vicinity of La Expedicion but also a complex perception of local resources as valuable because the local economy was integrated into the wider realm of long-distance trade (Sabloff 1975).

The association of particular dwellings with agglutination as a process indicates that participation in commercial enterprise was carried out at the family level. In examining the layout of the settlement, the only constraint on growth of ag-

glutinated substructures appears to be in the general orientation of the wall network. Because there is no association of the agglutinated substructures with the central formal plaza group at La Expedicion, there is no indication that the planning or growth of these facilities were directly coordinated or administered by the political hierarchy. Political and economic policy involving long-distance trade was no doubt coordinated by the capital of San Gervasio through the social network binding the people of La Expedicion into a community and, at a higher level, binding the people of La Expedicion to the political leadership in the capital.

At this settlement participation in commercial enterprise was an outgrowth of the domestic unit of production (Sahlins 1972) or, in plain English, family business. No doubt merchants constituted something of a social institution, the *Ah Ppolom* (Roys 1939), in and of themselves, with special regulations and rituals. Yet the degree to which this institution administered the action of its membership is unclear in the literature. We tend to agree with Chapman (1957) that, on the whole, the administration of long-distance trade was carried out through a variety of social and political channels rather than through a distinct organization, as argued by Scholes and Roys (1948). Some students of the subject have argued that the merchant elite and the nobility were one and the same during the Decadent period (Scholes and Roys 1948; Thompson 1970; Rathje and Sabloff 1975b). Although there is good evidence that this was often the case, we now believe the relationship between nobility and merchants was variable and not one of complete identity.

At La Expedicion, for example, the clear spatial separation of the elite formal plaza and the agglutinated substructures implies that the traditional noble family of the community was participating only indirectly in commercial activities. Other settlements reflect different organization.

The formal plaza group at La Expedicion has been identified as an important religious center for periodic festivals drawing participants from other communities on the northeast coast and from San Gervasio via the intersite *sacbe*. The emphasis on religious activity in the group has, in turn, been considered a possible reflection of the special roles or offices held by the noble family of the community. The importance of La Expedicion as a religious center and the predilection of its administrative family in no way contradicts the importance of commerce reflected in the settlement pattern. On the contrary, these institutional foci complement each other. If the organization of commercial activity was a family-based enterprise, the value of periodic festivals as a means of transmitting policy (as in the case of the festival of the *nacom* [Tozzer 1941:122-123]) and enhancing solidarity between trading families at La Expedicion and those elsewhere on the island is apparent. In short, the ritual and social ties were a medium through which economic and political coordination could be maintained. These ties are concretely expressed in the shrine-punctuated *sacbe* linking San Gervasio with the northeast coast.

In the synchronic perspective, we have sketched a community in which social, economic, religious, and political institutions interdigitate via orientation to a system extending beyond the community, that of long-distance commerce and religiotourism. Without an examination of excavated materials it is difficult to determine how this state of affairs may have arisen. Given the probable establishment of La Expedicion's formal plaza prior to the Decadent, the probability that agglutination as a form of settlement growth was also established by Modified Florescent times (based on information from Chen Cedral), and the occurrence of agglutination at La Expedicion primarily during the Decadent, La Expedicion was most likely established as an important religious focus prior to its incorporation into the economic system servicing long-distance trade on the island. The development of special facilities in the community during the Decadent was a response to this incorporation as was the development of a previously existing ceremonial circuit connecting the settlements on the northeast with San Gervasio into an important commercial network. This perspective also helps explain the growth of Aguada Grande on this circuit. Unfortunately the *sacbes* and shrines associated with this circuit appear to date from Decadent times, and consequently do not establish the priority of ceremonial use of this route over economic use. However, they do not refute such a historical scheme, because one might expect to see the concrete expression of socioreligious ties along this

route increase as its economic importance to the capital increased.

Zuuk

The settlement of Zuuk is located approximately 4km south of La Expedicion. In contrast to La Expedicion, Zuuk is situated east of the *aguada*-bearing depression that runs intermittently along the northeast coast. It is parallel to that depression and inland of the beachhead. In terms of defense, Zuuk is much closer to the coast and lacks the protection that greater distance and the *aguada* swamps offer. On the other hand, the beachhead at Zuuk is substantially larger than the one at La Expedicion and forms a steep sand barrier about 15m high in front of the site. There is a large permanent *aguada-cenote* located on the western periphery of the settlement zone. The land base inland from Zuuk presently bears a thin but fertile topsoil, judging from the thick bush in the vicinity and the good stand of cattle fodder (termed *zuuk* in Maya) regularly cultivated in the settlement zone. Quantities of fishbone and small-mammal bone found in secondary middens indicate the people exploited marine resources and local game. Given the greater distance of this site from the northern lagoons, it is likely that fishing was carried out on the windward side of the beachhead. This indicates the windward coast was perceived as a feasible landing area for canoes that consequently necessitated some form of defense against unwelcome visitors. In this respect the location of one of Zuuk's peripheral shrines, C29-1a, on top of the beach ridge in front of the settlement is probably not coincidental. Locally available exploited resources seem confined to marine and terrestrial fauna and milpa land.

Data and Composition

The settlement is both larger and denser in features than Figure 48 indicates. This map includes only the features planned by the survey and some of the observed features known to exist at the site. Until a more comprehensive map is made, inferences concerning the community's organization must be regarded as tenuous. Known features

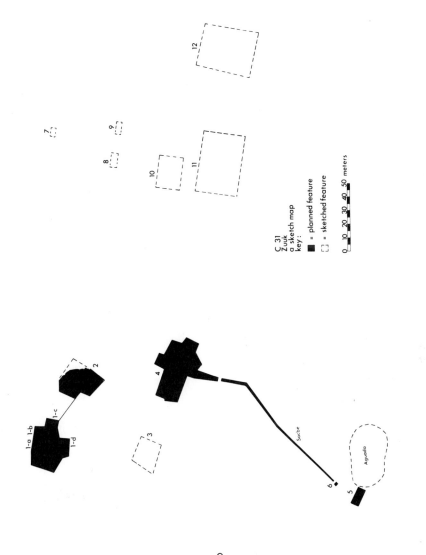

Figure 48. Zuuk (C31) settlement.

include a formal plaza group (C31-1), a large, formal dwelling on a small agglutinated substructure (C31-4), a possible household with associated Type 1 masonry shrine (C31-2), and a peripheral shrine group (C31-5). Observed but unplanned features include a group of low rubble platforms in the vicinity of C31-1, 2, and 4, a group of very large rectangular platforms south of the elite plaza group (C31-10 through 12), and two rectangular single-room masonry structures that may belong to Type 3 facing an open area that may be a plaza bordered on the east by low platforms (C31-7).

Test excavations in the plazas of C31-1 and C31-4 and into structures C31-1-e and C31-4-a yielded ceramics dating exclusively to the Decadent period. The rubble cores of both C31-1 and C31-4 were penetrated. Although it is possible that earlier materials underlie the exposures, there is no evidence from surface collections or excavations to indicate occupation of the settlement prior to the Decadent. Sherds from loot holes in C31-5 likewise seem to date to the Decadent. Given the presence of permanent water sources in the settlement and the histories of occupation elsewhere on the island, it seems likely that some people were living at Zuuk prior to the Decadent. However, on the basis of our information, major observable construction appears to date to Decadent times. In particular, the formal plaza group, C31-1, was apparently established in that time period and did not undergo a long sequence of rebuilding, as did C25-1 at La Expedicion.

The Analysis

The formal plaza group at Zuuk (Figure 24b) exhibits greater formal variability than the one at La Expedicion. In functional terms, the group has a community temple, public ritual house, and two dwellings, one of which may be a kitchen-women's quarters. A large nonbenched perishable structure may have stood against the northern edge of the plaza as well. By analogy with conquest period centers, this may have been an open-sided public building with perishable wooden columns, a proposition amenable to future testing by horizontal excavation.

Clearing above the plaster floor in C31-1-e yielded both plain and red-slipped sherds as well as fragments of obsidian and flint. In the middle

of the semicircle of cut stones set against the back wall identified as an altar, a finger from an effigy censer, a *Spondylus* shell-pendant fragment, and several obsidian blades were recovered. This material tentatively supports our identification of the structure as a dwelling.

In general, the formal plaza group at Zuuk fits the overall characteristics of such groups, as discussed in Chapter 5. It had a family in residence, possibly spatially separated on the basis of sex, and this family was intimately related to the administration of the community. The relatively wide variety of structure types in this group indicates that it was constructed to accommodate a variety of activities. In contrast to C25-1 at La Expedicion, it is a more flexible theater for events. Given the ceramic evidence for a Decadent period founding of C31-1 and the consequent probability that the various functional associations pertaining to these building types were already well established at the time of construction, C31-1 was probably unrestricted by the historical constraints found at other centers such as La Expedicion. It thus reflects the ideal of a well-rounded, all-purpose administrative center.

C31-4-a (Figure 31) is a large formal dwelling on a small agglutinated substructure. It is no less substantial in size and the quality of foundation features than the dwellings in the administrative group. The dwelling faces onto a lower plaza area that may have supported a second dwelling or another type of less-elaborate building. This inference is based purely upon the fact that the substructure distinctly juts out to the south. This kind of silhouette is characteristically associated with buildings. Unfortunately no surface remains were observed on the lower plaza area. It can only be positively asserted that C31-4 supported a group of structures. The fact that the single identified dwelling clearly dominates this group is tentative support of the hypothesis concerning single-dwelling residential organization proposed earlier. Alternatively there may have been additional light wooden dwellings inhabited by men serving their *haancab* (paying a bride price in work).

An examination of these two groups, C31-1 and C31-4, reveals a clear division of ritual responsibilities in the Zuuk community. Whereas the family in the administrative center is necessarily associated with the activities taking place there, the family of C31-4 is connected to the shrine group, C31-5 (Figure 27c), next to the *aguada-cenote* by a well-constructed *sacbe*. Although control over the northern and southern peripheries of the settlement is very weak, it seems likely that C31-5 was the most important boundary shrine group at Zuuk because it is next to the community water supply. From the perspective of ritual division of the community, C31-1-b, the public ritual house, has access off the formal plaza group to the east of the direction of C29-1a, the shrine on the coast.

The wealth and importance of the family inhabiting C31-4-a is supported by the discovery of a dual interment under the threshold leading to the northern plaza area on C31-4. One of the individuals, an elderly lady, had a string of gold-leaf pottery beads, a finely polished flat jade pendant, pieces of gold foil, and strings of *Spondylus* shell beads deposited underneath her. The burial cavity was paved with flagstones and filled with midden debris containing Decadent period ceramics. It seems unlikely that this furniture was deposited with future retrieval in mind. Given the predilection of Decadent period peoples for retrieving cached valuables, this family was apparently wealthy enough to sacrifice liquid capital permanently (see Sabloff and Rathje 1975b for an elaboration of this concept).

The ramifications of this ritual division of labor continued into other areas of community responsibility at Zuuk. The families probably were rather close in social status within the community and shared in certain administrative capacities. This sharing of responsibilities is documented in the rituals of the *uayeb* (Tozzer 1941:142), further discussed by Coe (1965), and reflected in the settlement patterns at the capital of San Gervasio. The fact that this organizational principle is found only in the settlement patterns of Zuuk and of the eastern district of San Gervasio (C22-1 through 30) and not in the patterns of other communities or districts at San Gervasio is consistent with the evidence that these settlement areas were founded during the Decadent period and were therefore not subject to the constraints of previous settlement growth patterns. In other words, there is some evidence of community planning at Zuuk and the eastern district of San Ger-

vasio.

At least one other household group at Zuuk, C31-2, may have ranked high socially. Here fragments of a large, nonbenched rectangular structure situated on the northwestern edge of the substructure facing east toward C31-2-a, a Type 1 masonry shrine, were found. The remains of a possible dwelling were too fragmentary to plan, but it is possible that clearing would reveal the remains more clearly. The presence of a masonry shrine as well as the location of the group next to the formal plaza center indicate that the family inhabiting it was of some importance.

There are a number of low rubble platforms in the vicinity of these three groups. These platforms are not agglutinated, unlike those at La Expedicion, and although they were examined only superficially, they may have supported other family groups.

With regard to the southern part of the settlement zone, we can offer no more than conjecture based upon the examination of the area after a burning at the end of the first field season. On the eastern side, there appears to be an open plaza area bordered by two single-room vaulted masonry structures on raised substructures on the west, and by low rubble platforms on the east. To the west of the plaza area, there are a number of massive, low rectangular platforms. These substructures are not of the agglutinated type and appear to have a single level area on top of them with a number of superstructural remains. These isolated rectangular platforms are much larger than the planned substructures in the northern part of the settlement zone and consequently probably supported more than a single household group.

Like the features in the northern zone, these platforms exhibit some planning not apparent in the agglutinated substructures at La Expedicion, for example. Nonetheless, these platforms may be comparable to agglutinated substructures in function. If these platforms were constructed at the same time the settlement was founded, as were the features in the northern zone, then they may be planned storage facilities constructed and maintained by the community as a whole. Thus the pattern would be comparable to that at La Expedicion, which became incorporated into a commodity transport route after it had been established for some time. Zuuk, on the other hand, was deliberately founded to service this route by a group of wealthy families. At Zuuk commercial enterprise would be a community rather than a family concern. From this point of view, the unique, open, ground-level plaza in the southern zone becomes particularly intriguing because it would be in the context of community enterprise that the more impersonal institutional exchange of a market place would be expected.

The peripheral shrines east and west of Zuuk are especially small, modest buildings relative to the masonry structures in the settlement zone proper. Although this is a matter of labor investment influenced by a variety of factors, the pattern contrasts with the relative quality of shrines and shrine groups acting as boundary markers at other settlements on Cozumel. Clearly the low labor investment does not reflect poverty in the community. Nor does it necessarily reflect the lack of control over the northern and southern peripheries if C31-5 is correctly assessed as an important religious focus for the community. These fragmentary data corroborate the general interpretation of Zuuk as a group of commercially oriented "pragmatic" (Sabloff and Rathje 1975b) families founding the settlement that would be expected to maximize property while minimizing actual costs. This interpretation might account for the peculiar combination of a rather substantial *sacbe*, symbolizing the ritual and hence political responsibility of a family, with a rather modest terminal religious focus. Using the general analogy for the concern with appearances exhibited by merchants (Sabloff and Rathje 1975b), certain appearances are stressed over others at Zuuk. Here the presence of a socioreligious boundary marker is less important than a particular family's association with it.

It is unlikely that the group of wealthy, perhaps noble, founding families could have been motivated to found a community at Zuuk simply because of its local natural resources. Although these resources are no worse than those found in many parts of the island, they are far more limited than those postulated for either Aguada Grande or La Expedicion. Certainly they are not of outstanding quality for purposes of either local consumption or commercial production. Thus the motivation for Zuuk's location appears to have been a perceived "non-natural" resource (Sabloff 1975),

namely the presence of an active commodity transport route down the ceremonial circuit from the northeast tip of the island to San Gervasio. From this inference, the peculiarities of the southern part of the settlement zone may reflect the nonresidential, commercial nature of the facilities there. A division of the community into a residential and a nonresidential commercial sector is commensurate with the evidence for planning in the settlement and ties in with the notion that commercial enterprise was carried out by the community rather than by individual families. Much of this overview follows more directly from the general proposition that the settlement patterns on the northeast coast reflect the integration of local and extralocal economic systems than from the facts at hand. This proposition, however, is compatible with the data.

Aguada Grande, La Expedicion, and Zuuk comprise the active Decadent period settlements known to be situated on the northeast coast. There may be two more, one behind El Real (C7) and one behind La Palma (C5). Local informants mentioned the presence of sites inland from these structures. Although further investigation of these settlements would undoubtedly qualify the general picture, an even higher density of communities along the coast would supply further support for the postulated ceremonial circuit and transport route.

Chen Cedral

Chen Cedral is located about 6km south of Zuuk and 2km inland from the northeast coast. It is situated to the west of a relatively large, permanent *cenote* (more than 10m in diameter) in a zone of arable land that continues inland toward San Gervasio. Today the soil cover between Chen Cedral and the coast is practically nonexistent, with surface flora consisting of low thorny scrub bush. The settlement was discovered late in the second season and was explored but not compass mapped. The core of the settlement seems to consist of a dense zone of massive agglutinated platforms covering at least 5ha. The scattered smaller platforms in the outer settlement zone bring the total settlement zone up to an area of 10 to 20ha (Figure 49).

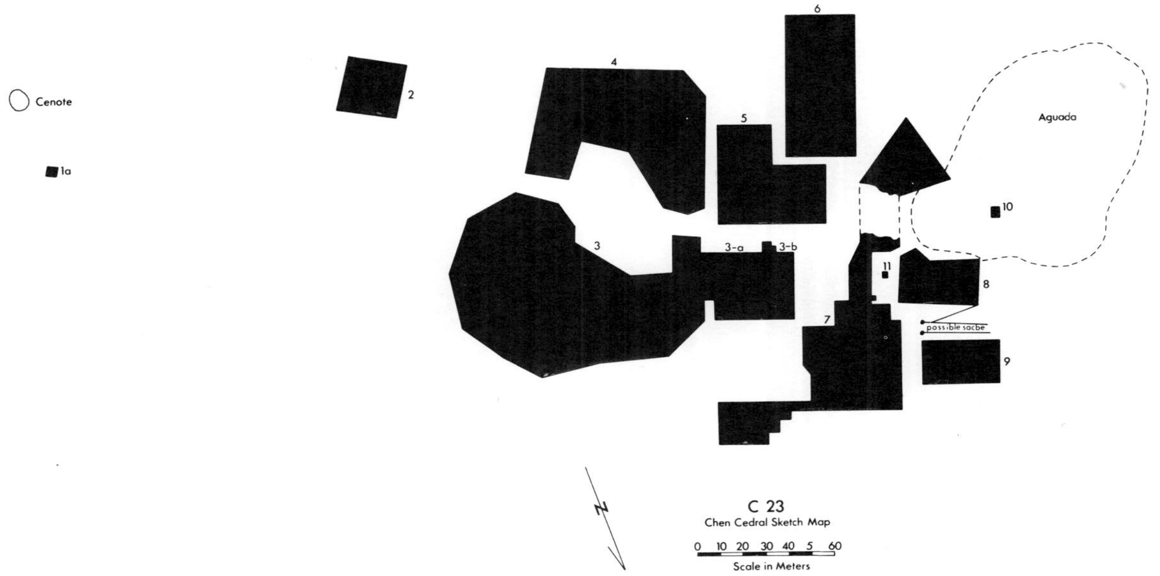

Figure 49. Chen Cedral (C23) settlement.

Date and Composition

In addition to the agglutinated platforms, observed features in the settlement zone include the raised substructure of a masonry shrine next to the *cenote* (C23-1-a, now completely destroyed by looting) and a second shrine (C23-3-b), a masonry-walled enclosure, at the center of the site.

The edges of the agglutinated substructures are so close together at Chen Cedral that they virtually define accessways and open plaza areas between them. Unlike those at other settlements, these substructures have well-preserved retaining walls in many places. The retaining walls are constructed of fairly well cut and squared to roughly dressed blocks (apparently dry laid) and are approximately 2m high. They are vertical and lack mouldings or sloping sections. Generally these walls look more like the well-preserved, well-constructed retaining walls found buried inside agglutinated platforms at La Expedicion and Buena Vista. In addition to being a result of preservation, this resemblance may also have chronological significance. Although ramps and fragmentary staircases allowing access onto some of the substructures were discovered, no discernable superstructural remains were observed, with the exception of one masonry shrine in the center of the settlement.

The shrine in the center of the settlement zone, C23-3-b, is a Type 1 masonry structure situated on the southern edge of the western extension of C23-3 (Figure 26a). C23-3-a is a miniature shrine situated in the center of the platform. Bordering the platform on its southern, eastern, and northern sides is a well-built masonry wall of cut and squared blocks laid without mortar, standing approximately 1m high, where preserved. This enclosure may house the elite formal plaza group, however humble, of Chen Cedral. Although clearing in several locations revealed no evidence of other superstructures within the enclosure, a more thorough investigation might produce such remains. For the present, we must conclude that the central plaza at Chen Cedral was a sacred enclosure and not an elite residential group as found at other sites on the northeast coast.

Both C23-3-a and C23-3-b were excavated to provide some modicum of chronological control over the settlement. Although the resulting evidence is not necessarily characteristic of the settlement as a whole, it is suggestive of possible chronological placement.

Excavation of C23-3-b produced abundant Decadent period censerware, including quantities of black-paste ware characteristic of Sanders's Aguada Grande complex (Connor 1975). These sherds were deposited in a matrix of fallen cut-stone blocks, marl, and dirt. The amount of cut stone in the room was insufficient to account for vaulting, but there was some fragmentary evidence for beam-and-mortar roofing. Therefore, either the roofing material was partially removed from the structure for use elsewhere or the roof was perishable. The former is more likely, because the deposition of censerware in, around, and under the few stones gives the appearance of postoccupational reuse of the building. This inference is supported by the fact that all sherds found under the sequence of floors in the structure, including some apparently intentional offerings of broken vessels, conch shells, and jade beads, dated to the Florescent or Modified Florescent. These sherds can only offer a *terminus ante quem* for the structure. However, in combination with the possible postoccupational deposition of Decadent period censerware exhibited by the discovery of broken whole censers more than 20cm above the first floor, the evidence points to construction of the shrine in Modified Florescent times or earlier and reuse in the Decadent period following abandonment.

Excavation in C23-3-a, the centrally located miniature shrine, produced a similar picture. Censerware, obsidian blades, utility ware, and other trash dating to the Decadent period were found above the plaster floor of the plaza in the vicinity of the shrine, especially in front of it. The miniature was built on a pavement of flagstones overlain by plaster flooring. A cache was found in the platform fill underlying the shrine. The cache consisted of several miniature vessels of "pseudo" Fine Orange ware, a Chichen Red slateware goblet, a necked jar of mottled grey slateware, two large whole blades of green obsidian and a third broken one, and a long lancet of banded grey obsidian. Unfortunately caches and burials on Cozumel have a tendency to contain materials dating to times other than those of interment (Connor 1975:

118; Rathje *et al.* 1973). Nevertheless, in addition to the fact that only Modified Florescent diagnostic ceramics are represented in the cache itself, the ceramics in the rather rich trash surrounding the cache also dated exclusively to the Florescent and Modified Florescent (based upon preliminary field examination). Thus this substructure and the miniature shrine above it were probably constructed and dedicated in Modified Florescent times. Although censerware dating to the Decadent was abundant near the miniature, none was found inside it, supporting the notion that the shrine had collapsed by the time of Decadent use.

These two test excavations indicate that the shrine group, enclosure, and the substructure supporting them were constructed during the Modified Florescent and were reused following abandonment during the Decadent period. The ramifications of this inference would be of less importance were it not for the facts that these shrines are the only standing masonry features at Chen Cedral and that they are located in the heart of the settlement zone. Although sections of the settlement might have been occupied during Decadent times, it seems unlikely that the central shrine group would have been used on the rather casual basis indicated if the Decadent period community was of the size and importance reflected in settlement features. It is more likely that the settlement was virtually abandoned in the Decadent period and that the ceremonial reuse of the central shrine group relates not to a local community but rather to the incorporation of this shrine group into a Decadent period ceremonial circuit.

Similarly, ceramics dating to the Modified Florescent period, including a rare sherd of plumbate tradeware, were found in a loot hole in the raised substructure of C23-1-a. The stone walls of the structure itself had been removed and used to construct a modern corral at the time of exploration.

The Analysis

An intersite *sacbe* enters the settlement zone from the west, and another possible *sacbe* in the form of a gateway and wall-lined path enters the settlement from the east. Thus Chen Cedral appears to have been connected with other sites via a cere-

monial circuit at some time in its history. It is impossible to determine the periods during which the circuit was active from the features we examined. It can only be noted that the informants familiar with the area say the intersite *sacbe* leaving San Gervasio connects with Chen Cedral. This circuit was probably established at the time of the founding of the community in the Modified Florescent. It lapsed into disuse or declined in importance during the transition from Modified Florescent to Decadent times when the settlement was abandoned, and was then reestablished as an important route during the Decadent period.

The presence of agglutinated substructures on Cozumel prior to the Decadent is further supported at Buena Vista. Extensive excavation at Buena Vista revealed that agglutination as a process of settlement growth was established by Modified Florescent times. Thus, agglutination is an expectable feature within the range of pre-Decadent settlement patterns. It should be noted that not all Chen Cedral's massive substructures are agglutinated. Some of them appear to be discrete rectangular features, with no defined variation in surface height, resembling the large substructures at Zuuk.

In order to place Chen Cedral, however tentatively, in the general historical and processual scheme on Cozumel, the problem of whether or not the agglutinated and massive substructures dating to the Modified and Pure Florescent functioned in the same way as those dating to the Decadent must be dealt with. The following general points can be made concerning pre-Decadent settlement patterns. First, both the dispersion and agglutination of features are extremes characterizing settlement organization. Second, defensibility does not appear to be the only factor necessitating the construction of agglutinated substructures. Both San Miguel and El Cedral, located on the leeward side of Cozumel, are dispersed communities despite their vulnerability to attack from the sea. Third, although the material inventories of dispersed and agglutinated features may vary as to quantity of typical artifacts, they do not reflect culturally distinctive groups. Finally environments do not vary enough to make agglutination a practical necessity. Thus the construction of agglutinated and massive substructures predating the Decadent can also be identified as supporting special facilities, as well as dwellings. Given the abundance of pre-Decadent trade wares, particularly slatewares, on Cozumel, it seems likely that these special facilities are also warehouses. It is significant that the cache associated with C23-3-a contained two whole green obsidian blades. Although a handful of green obsidian chips and broken blades were found in the course of excavations on Cozumel, these two blades are substantially larger than any of the rest. Because the only known source of green obsidian in Mesoamerica is the Pachuca outcrop in Hidalgo, Central Mexico, a cache containing exotics of this kind would be appropriate in a community oriented to long-distance commerce.

In summary, we have hypothesized that Chen Cedral was the major storage area on the northeast coast in Modified Florescent times. Given its greater proximity to San Gervasio than to other settlements on the northeast coast, and its lack of an elite residential administrative center, the community was probably under the direct control of San Gervasio. Commodities might have been brought in directly from the northern lagoons, down the circuit along the coast, or transported into Chen Cedral from San Gervasio for later retrieval. The abandonment of the settlement prior to the Decadent reflects its specialized function and dependency on Cozumel's involvement in long-distance trade. This trade probably suffered a sharp decline at the end of the Modified Florescent with the fall of Chichen Itza. This event is reflected at Chen Cedral.

A major theme in the treatment of the four settlements on the northeast coast is their relationship with San Gervasio. Empirically this region is the only one with a concrete link to the site believed to be the capital of the island from the Early period through the Decadent. In the next section, the history and organization of this complex settlement is considered in order to explain why its effects on settlement patterns elsewhere on the island were so pronounced.

San Gervasio

The settlement of San Gervasio is located in the north central region of Cozumel. The settlement zone, containing a high density of features, covers more than a square kilometer. Density within this zone is variable, however, and seems to form four distinct clusters of concentrations. These clusters are most likely significant units of organization within the overall community and are termed districts for purposes of analysis. All together 108 features were mapped using a combination of plane table, chain and compass, and aerial photographic sketch mapping. Full discussion of the fieldwork at San Gervasio will be published in the final report on this site. Only a brief discussion of selected aspects of the settlement of San Gervasio is included here. A large foldout map of the overall settlement zone was published in Sabloff and Rathje (1975b:Map 2) and is not reproduced here. (It also should be noted that the discussion below was written before work recently undertaken by Fernando Robles [Centro Regional Sureste, Instituto Nacional de Antropología e Historia] at San Gervasio).

The settlement zone is located on a ridge of high ground oriented approximately east to west (see Davidson 1975:Figure 6) in the immediate vicinity of the site. This ridge reaches a maximum height of approximately 15m above sea level. To the north, the ridge drops off gently toward the mangrove swamps bordering the northern lagoons, whereas to the south the ridge maintains elevation for a distance of several kilometers before beginning to drop off. This area is one of the highest and geologically oldest regions on the islands (de Chanenedes, personal communication, 1973). High elevation may partially account for the relatively high water table in the vicinity, whereas the great antiquity accounts for the relatively deep soils that result from prolonged exposure of the area to weathering processes. Soils seem especially deep south of the settlement zone. To the north, solid cover is more meager. As would be expected, exploration south of the settlement well populated at some point in San Gervasio's history.

Despite characterizations of San Gervasio in the literature as poor in arable land (Sabloff (1975), access to relatively well-drained, deep soils and abundant water are the only important natural resources attributable to this region. These resources, in addition to a perceived strategic or central location, must have been sufficient to inspire important occupations of San Gervasio during several periods in Cozumel's history. Although only two permanent *cenotes* within the settlement zone were observed, there are several earth-filled sinkholes that may have held water at the time of occupation given that the water table ranges from 2 to 4m below the surface. Some of these sinkholes may also have been planted with special crops.

Determining the periods of occupation and construction for various structures at San Gervasio is a complex problem that will be dealt with in detail in reports on the excavations and artifact inventories. Here we base our analysis upon a general familiarity with the results of excavations and the preliminary reports on these subjects (Connor 1975; Gregory 1975).

Structures in the San Gervasio settlement zone have been dated to the Florescent, Modified Florescent, and Decadent periods on the basis of primary and secondary ceramic deposits. On the basis of architectural style, one structure might be dated to the Early period. In terms of community organization, different parts of the zone were apparently the foci of intensive construction at different periods, although surface collections indicate that the entire zone was occupied during the Decadent. Because each of the four districts evinces a distinctive history, chronological details are supplied in the context of their individual analysis. By way of a preparatory overview, however, the western districts contained the major focus of the settlement in pre-Decadent times. Although there were several foci in the Decadent period, the eastern district appears to have been the most important.

District 2

Structures dating to the earliest observable construction phases are found in District 2 (C22-37 through 56). This district is dominated by a plaza group with structures on four sides (C22-49, 50, and 52 through 56) situated on the highest ground in the settlement zone of San Gervasio. The latest phase of construction on one of the substructures in this group is dated to the Florescent period by excavated ceramics. The lack of superstructural remains dating to the Decadent

and the ruined appearance of substructural retaining walls are additional support for dating the construction of this group to pre-Decadent times.

Ceramics dating to the Early period were sparse but present in excavated contexts. From the size, elevated location, and general layout of the plaza group, it seems likely that any monumental construction at San Gervasio dating to the Early period underlies Florescent construction in this group. Some support for the establishment of this center by the Early period is found in the construction and architectural style of C22-48a (Figure 17j). This two-roomed, tandem-plan structure has two widely spaced exterior doorways and two widely spaced interior doorways leading into the back room. This plan and its location on a low support substructure fit the descriptive criteria of a simple palace applied to buildings dating to the Classic period (Harrison 1970). The problem of identifying the function of Classic palaces are complex and tangential to the present discussion because we are more concerned with the temporal placement of the building. A description of diagnostic features for Early period architecture at Dzibilchaltun is virtually identical to C22-48a:

> The Early Period structures are characterized by true block masonry walls. The inner and outer courses touching or almost touching so as to leave no structurally significant core. The mass of the vault rested directly on the masonry blocks. It was a true corbeled vault, composed of superimposed flat slabs, projecting successively toward the center and counterweighted behind with heavy boulders. . . . Both medial and superior mouldings were rectangular and always consisted of a single member. Decoration was entirely in painted stucco carved in deep relief. (Andrews IV 1965a:52)

There are, however, some differences. Only one single-member rectangular moulding was found in place because the upper facade is partially destroyed. Directly above the medial molding is a facade of square thin-veneer stones carved with a stepped-fret motif. Other details include the facts that the vault steps are composed of double lines of finely dressed slabs, and the very well-cut blocks in the walls are made of a soft beachrock used exclusively for carved column drums during the Decadent period. Excavation of C22-48a produced Decadent period censer and utility ware lying directly on the well-preserved plaster floor. This situation probably represents reuse of the building during the Decadent while the vaults were still in place. The lack of a clear postoccupational buildup of trash in the room indicates that the structure was being kept clean during the Decadent period.

Apparently there was a major civil-religious precinct in District 2 that was established in the Early period and was built up and occupied during the Florescent period. We have no idea what was going on here during the Modified Florescent, but during the Decadent the precinct was used for worship. Prior to the Decadent there is nothing in the settlement zone that compares with this precinct in size or formal design. Thus it was probably the center of settlement during the Early period and the Florescent. The lack of clear evidence of use or construction during the Modified Florescent may be due more to the preliminary status of ceramic analysis than to the ephemeral nature of occupation during this period. From surface observation it is difficult to distinguish some of the features in the vicinity of the precinct as pre-Decadent because District 2 does show considerable Decadent period construction outside the precinct. The sloping ground around the precinct, for example, was terraced at some time. These terraces have low retaining walls of uncut rubble and, in some places, vertically set slabs of bedrock. The retention of soil and the creation of level space seem to have motivated the construction because the walls rarely rise above the level of the topsoil behind them. Alternatively this situation may have arisen from natural deposition behind the walls constructed to define space. The problematic function is compounded by the presence of field walls that cannot be easily dated as contemporary or later than the terrace walls. In some places these cross walls run up the slope and join the terrace walls at a higher level, and consequently seem to have been constructed after soil buildup behind the terraces. This tentatively implies that the terraces predate the wall system into which they are presently incorporated. As noted earlier in Chapter 4, terraces are dated to the Classic period in southern Quintana Roo.

The other surface features in District 2 south of the ceremonial precinct seem to date to the Decadent period on the basis of surface collections and architectural style. Excavation in C22-41-a, for example, indicated a Decadent period date for the final construction phase. These features consist of (1) a large, empty enclosure defined by walls made of monolithic, vertically set slabs of bedrock; (2) four agglutinated substructures (C22-42, 43, 45, and 46); (3) two household groups (C22-36 and 40); (4) a shrine group C22-37 and 38; Figure 27a); (5) a pyramidal substructure supporting a shrine (C22-41); and (6) scattered low substructures (C22-39 and 40). The district also includes several additional low substructures and a possible third household group southeast of the shrine group. These features were observed in the final days of work and were not mapped.

There are several descriptions of a walled enclosure associated with the shrine of Ix Chel located on the coast of Cozumel at San Miguel (Las Casas and Juan Diaz [in Wagner 1942a] and Lopez de Gomara [in Simpson 1966]). Las Casas apparently gets confused and gives a combined description of a town on Cozumel, Canpech, and possibly Ecab. The accounts of Juan Diaz, Lopez de Gomara, and others, on the other hand, are fairly consistent. Lopez de Gomara describes the enclosure in the following manner:

> At the base of this same tower [the temple of Ix Chel] there was a wall of stone and mortar, very well built, with battlements and at its center a plaster cross about ten spans high, which they held to be the god of rain and worshipped as such; and when water was scarce and the rains failed, they went to it in very devout processions and sacrificed partridges. (in Simpson 1966:36)

Several early accounts of the town of Canpech on the western side of the peninsula include descriptions of an enclosure. Thus there are two enclosures on record that were being used at the time of the Spanish contact. Another enclosure associated with a temple that may perhaps date to Decadent times is Feature 11 at Tancah on the coast opposite Cozumel (Lothrop 1924:Plate 26). Given the use of such features during the Decadent period and the association of the enclosure in District 2 with a shrine dating to the Decadent (C22-41-a), it seems likely that this enclosure was being actively used in Decadent times.

The numerous references in the literature to the importance of Cozumel as a pilgrimage center and the importance of the Ix Chel shrine in particular make it quite doubtful that the enclosure in front of the shrine was a focus of activities only in times of emergency. On the contrary, it seems likely that it was the scene of frequent, large-scale ritual. The nature of such ritual is not easily determined because, often, when authors like Landa describe rituals in the courtyards of temples, they do not indicate the presence or absence of structures bounding the other three sides. In one instance, Landa (Tozzer 1941:115) describes "great beams standing erect and ornamented with sculpture" situated in a temple courtyard. This observation is part of a description of sacrificial activities, one form involving shooting arrows into victims tied to a "stake." Although Landa mentions a stone column in the courtyard that might have been used to secure the victim, it seems possible that Tozzer misinterpreted the passage in that he identifies the beams as possible stelae, and that the victim was tied to one of the beams. The question arises because Landa's description resembles others (Juan Diaz, Las Casas, and Oviedo in Wagner 1942a) given of the sacrificial platform within the enclosure at Canpech in many respects. There the platform supported three large wooden beams covered with blood and many arrows, as well as several large sculptures, including a serpent devouring a jaguar or puma. No doubt stelae were erected during the Decadent period (Proskouriakoff 1962), making Tozzer's interpretation plausible. Nevertheless Tozzer notes that Landa was probably familiar with the works of Oveido and Las Casas. Consequently Landa has probably included a gloss of this description along with information from other sources.

If Landa's general synthesis is more or less in order, it seems likely that the enclosures on Cozumel associated with pyramidal temples were places of sacrifice. He gives the following description:

> Besides the festivals in which they sacrificed persons in accordance with their solemnity, the priest or *Chilan*, on account of some misfortune or necessity, ordered them to sacrifice human beings, and everyone contributed to this, that slaves should be bought or some in their devotion gave their little children, who were made much of, and feasted up to the day

> (of the festival), and they were well guarded . . . And in the meanwhile they led them from town to town with dancing, while the priests, Chilans and other officers fasted. (in Tozzer 1941:117)

The notion that sacrificial victims were paraded through the towns correlates with the identification of intercommunity ceremonial circuits on Cozumel. Perhaps it is noteworthy that movement of victims through the towns culminated with festivals focusing on the sacrifice. Although it is difficult to determine how important human sacrifice might have been on Cozumel, Landa (in Tozzer 1941:109) seems to think it was comparable to that at Chichen Itza.

C22-41-a (Figure 15) has already been identified as a possible predecessor to the Ix Chel temple observed by the Spanish on the coast in the port of San Miguel. Because C22-41-a is connected to the enclosure by a *sacbe*, this temple enclosure at San Gervasio is probably comparable to the one observed on the coast. Although there may have been other variations on the theme of talking idol shrines on Cozumel, the location of this particular one in the vicinity of the ancient ceremonial center of District 2 indicates that this is the original temple of the oracle. Although the latest construction phase on this structure dates to the Decadent, deterioration of the substructure has revealed the presence of several earlier construction phases.

Interpretations of the other features in District 2 follow from the identification of it as the original center of the oracle cult. East of the great enclosure there are four agglutinated substructures. One of these is built against the wall of the enclosure, demonstrating that it postdates the construction of the enclosure. Like other features of this type on Cozumel, these substructures probably relate to storage facilities that were expanded over a period of years. The difference between these features and those at La Expedicion is that the District 2 substructures yielded no observable superstructures. Although this may be the result of poor preservation, it may also be due to the lack of household groups on them. The absence of household groups is not in conflict with the identification of these substructures as warehouses because these particular storage facilities had a function rather distinct from those elsewhere on the island. Our arguments hinge on the nature of offerings brought to the oracle by pilgrims.

Landa makes several references to the offerings brought to the oracle on Cozumel:

> And they held Cozumel and the well of Chichen Itza in the same veneration as we have for pilgrimages to Jerusalem and Rome, and so they used to go to visit these places and to offer presents there, especially to Cozumel, as we do to holy places; and if they did not go themselves, they always sent their offerings, and those who went there were in the habit of entering the abandoned temples also, as they passed by them, to offer prayers there and to burn copal. (in Tozzer 1941:110)

He uses the gloss *present* in another context:

> They also joined together for hunting in companies of fifty more or less, and they roast the flesh of the deer on gridirons, so that it shall not be wasted, and when they reach the town, they make their presents to their lord and distribute the rest as among friends. . . . The Indians in making visits always take with them a present to give, according to their rank; and the person visited gives another gift in return. (in Tozzer 1941:97)

Although Tozzer interprets *present* here as tribute to the lord, reciprocal gift is implied in the second use of the term. Although the word *present* in some contexts may not have the connotation of tribute or gift in addition to that of sacrificial offering, it seems to be a reasonable possibility in other contexts. Herrera sheds additional light on the problem: "And there were some idols that gave replies (on Cozumel). In other places, the priests invented them, deceiving the people in order to get the presents from them" (in Tozzer 1941:109-110). Here presents are clearly not destined for sacrifice but rather are gifts to the priests. In another description of the high priest of Mayapan, Landa indicates that neither offerings or presents were sacrificially destroyed but rather were consumed by the priest or used to support the cult at Mayapan: "He was very much respected by the lords and had no repartimiento of Indians, but besides the offerings, the lords made him presents and all the priests of the towns brought contributions to him" (in Tozzer 1941:

27). Finally, a *relacion* quoted by Roys *et al.* (1940) states that pilgrims coming from Xicalango, Potonchan, and other known ports of trade brought as offerings some of the products of their lands.

These bits and pieces of evidence seem to indicate that the cult of the oracle was largely supported by offerings and presents brought by merchants and other pilgrims. Granted the identification of District 2 as the original center of the cult, the four agglutinated substructures directly associated with the great enclosure probably supported storage facilities for the offerings and presents brought to the oracle.

Compared to the agglutinated substructures, the single-dwelling household groups in District 2 (C22-36-a and 40-a) are on relatively small, well-built substructures. Although the dwellings are not the largest and most elaborate, C22-36-a has a well-defined straight C-shaped bench area within it and is generally comparable in size and formal layout to dwellings found in elite central plaza groups elsewhere on Cozumel. C22-40-a is nonbenched, but is situated on a substantial support substructure with a small *sacbe* running from it in the direction of the enclosure. The third, unmapped, household group south of the *cenote* shrine group is of similar proportions. These features might be the residences of priests administering the cult center. Their proximity to the enclosure and temple indicate positions of high prestige and their spatial disassociation from the agglutinated substructures reflects not only the public nature of these storage areas, but also removes any implications that the priests trafficked in goods, as did the merchants who lived on the platforms supporting their storage areas.

These dwellings surround a shrine group (C22-37-a and 38-a) situated adjacent to a *cenote*. The shrines are connected to each other by a short *sacbe* that curves around the edge of the *cenote*. The platform of C22-38-a has a staircase down to the *cenote*, which is presently filled with dirt except for a small pool of water under a ledge on the western site. No doubt this *cenote* played an important role in activities at the center.

In summary, District 2 was the major ceremonial center on Cozumel in Early period and Florescent times. The tradition of this center as a sacred place of some renown may date back this early (Rathje *et al.* 1973). Perhaps this is the *Tantun* Cozumel mentioned in the Maya prophecies (Roys 1957:155). The lack of Modified Florescent material is puzzling but may simply reflect the limited temporal control over features in the main plaza group of the precinct. Certainly a strong tradition of sanctity in this precinct would explain the presence of the Decadent period cult of the talking idol combined with a complete lack of construction activity in the precinct itself. The location of buildings dating to the Decadent period, including some elaborate household groups, some distance from the precinct is further support for the sacred nature of all the facilities within it. It may also reflect the organization of the cult as an institution distinct from the political institutions administering the island, analogous to the organization of Cholula (Bernal Diaz in Maudslay 1910:18).

District 3

District 3 is a zone of large rectilinear substructures located west of the cult center and between it and the port of San Miguel. The settlement zone of 10ha is presently situated in a field of cattle fodder of about 25ha in extent. This field had just been burned when we observed it for the first time at the end of the first season. During the second season the field was under dense *zacate* grass. Due to limitations in time, most of the features were not mapped. Their proportions on the settlement map represent a sketch made from field sketches and aerial photographs. Two of the features were mapped as well as excavated and several of the structures were surface collected during the first season. The rest of the information concerning the layout of mounds and surface features comes from field notes made in the course of exploration.

District 3 is probably the largest and possibly the most complex part of the San Gervasio settlement zone. It is composed of an identified elite residence group (C22-90), a temple group (C22-95), three, possibly four, single-dwelling households (C22-91, 93, 94, and 97), a colonnaded structure (C22-89), a mortuary platform (C22-99), and a variety of other substructures (C22-96, 98, and 99 through 109).

The elite residence group is apparently a single-

dwelling household (Figure 29b). Although the support platform extends east away from the two structures (C22-90-a and b) and group altar (C22-90-c) making up the group, no additional remains of perishable superstructures were observed at the eastern end. Furthermore a line of vertically set slabs distinguishes the eastern and the western parts of the substructure. Hence the group at the western end is defined as a distinct unit.

This group is probably elite because the dwelling, C22-90-a, is one of the largest and most elaborate houses identified on Cozumel. It combines attributes of a single-room dwelling with the colonnade of a public structure. Two of the columns bore elaborate sculptures, which are weathered beyond recognition. No doubt this dwelling was often used as a place of public audience, comparable to dwellings found in administrative plaza groups elsewhere on the island. The oratory associated with this house is similarly elaborate and well built. The block-C bench within the oratory indicates that it was also designed to accommodate relatively public ritual. In short, although the group lacks the public buildings characteristic of administrative centers on Cozumel, C22-90-a appears to have been designed with frequent important public use in mind. The central location of the group between the rest of District 3 and the cult center of District 2 supports the notion that the family inhabiting C22-90 was one of the most important in the area and likely functioned in official capacities. Excavated ceramics date this household to the Decadent period.

The temple group, C22-95, consists of a perishable religious structure, a perishable structure (C22-95-c) identified as a public building, and a platform altar that covers a large vaulted tomb in the plaza between them. The pyramidal substructure has a running stucco facade on the northern side of its balustraded staircase that apparently covered all four sides of the structure at one time. The one figure now discernible is a leaping monkey with a ball in its hand. The monkey is among the many attributes of Ix Chel (Tozzer 1941:10) and Juan Diaz (in Wagner 1942a) describes images of apes and bears at the main temple of San Miguel.

The large colonnaded structure, C22-89, is unusual in several respects. It is actually a group consisting of a massive, low rectangular substructure with a secondary elevated substructure along the southern edge. This secondary substructure supports a square building lined with at least four rows of composite drum columns. It is apparently open at the sides. Remains of several perishable superstructures are in front of this building to the north. This raised colonnade is unique on Cozumel and is quite distinct from the other colonnades identified as public buildings serving a variety of functions. Although Arnold and Frost (1909:151) note raised rectangular colonnades at Cancuen Island, we can find no reference in the literature on Decadent period architecture that mentions a raised square colonnade of this kind. In some respects the building resembles the Temple of the Warriors at Chichen Itza and may represent a crude replica of that structure. Such replication of Modified Florescent structures during the Decadent period is well attested at Mayapan (Proskouriakoff 1962). In any case, C22-89 is presumably a public building associated with a plaza group of perishable structures. As a group it is quite unlike the other central administrative plazas on the island and seems more comparable to C22-95 where again a public building dominates a perishable structure.

Between C22-90 and C22-95 there are several probable household groups. Only one of these, C22-91, was examined in any detail. It supported a single large straight C-shaped benched structure comparable to C22-36-a. Given the patterns on Cozumel, it seems likely that this is a single-dwelling household group. The other substructures, C22-93, 94, and 97, are of familiar size and proportions and probably served the same function.

North of these structures are massive rectilinear substructures and a few smaller rectangular substructures of a size appropriate for household groups. Although fragments of superstructures appear on several of them, we are essentially ignorant of their function. We do have pertinent information on two of them. C22-96 is an L-shaped structure standing approximately 4m high. The surface of this mound has remains of a single non-benched rectangular perishable building, probably a dwelling, situated in the southeast corner. No doubt the substructure supported other perishable substructures dating to its final occupation phase, but it seems highly unlikely that the feature was designed simply to support isolated perishable

dwellings. Whatever its additional functions may have been in the last occupation phase, its L-shaped design and centralized location indicate that C22-96 was originally built as a massive colonnade comparable to the smaller L-shaped colonnade in District 1 (C22-5-a:Figure 22). If this is the case, it is possible that District 3 once contained far more impressive public architecture than it did during the Decadent period. Perhaps structures C22-95, 96, 97, 104, and 105 formed a very large and imposing plaza group at some time predating the Decadent.

If the ceremonial center in District 2 was still actively occupied during the Florescent period and was the major interior center on the island, then it seems reasonable to suppose that a Modified Florescent occupation would be found in its vicinity. A shrine group, C22-33, 34, and 35, northeast of District 2 dates to the Modified Florescent, indicating that people were in the area at that time. Furthermore, a *sacbe* running from this group in the direction of District 2 is dated to the Modified Florescent by an associated shrine, C22-35. This *sacbe* was deliberately cut off some time after its construction. It seems highly probable that it once ran to District 2 and from there on to District 3. Although shrine groups do occur at considerable distances from settlements, they are usually found on the periphery of communities on Cozumel. Thus there is some circumstantial evidence to support the notion that the transition from Florescent to Modified Florescent is marked by a shift of the community center from District 2 to District 3. Such a shift is commensurate with settlement reorganization observed at Chichen Itza during this transition. Surface sherds in District 3, particularly those from iguana holes, included some slatewares that might support the notion of a Modified Florescent occupation. This posited state of affairs might help explain the general paucity of Modified Florescent materials at San Gervasio, which is perplexing because the most elaborate shrine group, C22-34, dates to this period and is found within the settlement zone.

In the Decadent period, District 3 exhibits all the elements of a centralized administrative center, including elite residences, temples, and colonnades, but these facilities are dispersed throughout the district and do not occur in the characteristic forms found in Decadent period administrative centers elsewhere in the San Gervasio zone and on the island. It is quite clear that the major Decadent period administrative center was located in District 1, more than a kilometer southeast of District 3. During the Decadent, District 3 was the most important residential area at San Gervasio, housing a number of well-to-do families. It was also an important area for religious and commercial activities. Although the cult center was initially located in District 2 and may have been moved to San Miguel later, District 3 was the sector of the community that serviced the pilgrims coming to worship the talking idol. As such it was the focus of various services and facilities required to deal with the resulting influx of foreigners.

District 4

District 4, south and west of District 3, is a compact zone of roughly rectangular (C22-84 and 86) and agglutinated (C22-85 and 88) substructures surrounding a residential administrative center (C22-87). Like the one at Zuuk, the composition of the central group reflects a variety of functions (Figure 23a). Here, however, a colonnaded public building and a small Type 1 shrine replace the community temple and public ritual house, indicating different functions were being stressed at C22-87. The semiresidential function associated with colonnaded public buildings in historical descriptions relate to both social and religious activities. Especially in light of the possibility of a second public building in the group, C22-87-d, the combination of a colonnade with a diminutive religious building makes it unlikely that this colonnade on C22-87 functioned primarily for religious observances within the group. On the other hand, District 4 appears to be too small to require a public residence for unmarried men or men observing ritual purification, especially because the much larger community of La Expedicion lacks such a facility.

Although it is possible that C22-87 was an administrative center for a large dispersed population south and west of the district, a second possibility fits the overall assessment of this district better. In keeping with the general interpretation of agglutinated substructures, C22-85 and 88 probably supported warehouses. Each of these massive features has a single, straight, C-shaped benched perishable structure identified as dwellings (only C22-88-a was planned). Both of these dwellings are smaller and less substantial than C22-87-c, the dwelling in the center. The two roughly rectangular substructures, C22-84 and 86, lack discernible superstructural remains, but have very curious piles of uncut stone on them. These piles, approximately 1m in diameter and 30cm high, seem to form rows or parts of rows across the substructures. They may be the remains of wooden pillar supports inside very large perishable structures. If this were the case, the structures would cover between 400 and 600m^2, well outside the range for dwellings on Cozumel. Three of the substructures in this district, C22-85, 86, and 87, abut one another or are connected by a short *sacbe*. The other two are very close by.

District 4 represents the holdings of an extended family heavily committed to commerce. The small dwellings outside the center represent the homes of lesser members of the family, surrounded by storage facilities for commodities. It follows that C22-87 is not the administrative center of a community as such, but rather the administrative center of a substantial family enterprise. This perspective helps explain the disposition of structures in the central group. Rather than servicing a surrounding community, the two large public buildings were hostels for housing visiting merchants, their porters, and goods. The diminutive nature of the shrine reflects the fact that this facility was used primarily by a family and not by a community. Unlike the household group in District 1, it was not politically important for this family to maintain a large and impressive religious facility.

District 1

Excavated ceramics indicate that District 1 at San Gervasio was founded in the Decadent period. It is the largest assemblage of functionally identified structures covered in this report and as all of the structures and groups have been subjected to analysis in this and previous chapters, we concern ourselves here with qualifications of these analyses and a synthesis of the district as a functional whole.

The main formal plaza group is surrounded by four elite residential complexes. Three of these are attached to the center by *sacbes*. The other is too close to the center to warrant a *sacbe*. These groups are located to the north, east, south, and west of the center. The location of C22-29 through 30 to the northeast rather than to true north is the only imperfection in this spatial order. C22-29 to 30 was planned so that its *sacbe* intersected the *sacbe* connecting the center to the northeast coast. The ritual significance of participating in this intersection apparently overrode the ritual value of being located directly north of the center in the minds of the builders. It is clear that District 1 is a planned center from the layout and its establishment away from the rest of the settlement in the Decadent. As previously discussed, the arrangement of residences around a purely public plaza group makes this district comparable to, but at a higher order than, the formal plaza groups found in other communities on Cozumel.

The ritual significance of quadrapartite organization is manifest in the literature on the Maya. Coe (1965) argues that this kind of organization, combined with concepts of cyclical events, ramified throughout the social and political structure of Maya politics. Coe is clearly presenting an ideal model with ideal ramifications when he argues for a four-part division of Maya society and a rotation of power among the divisions. Roys (1957) has noted that the fundamental sociopolitical structure found throughout the Maya area at the time of contact was overlain with considerable variability in institutional expression. Insofar as District 1 exhibits a clear quadrapartite organization, Coe's ideal model is confirmed empirically. This seems reasonable in light of the fact that District 1 was founded in an area of previously sparse occupation and consequently was not restricted by previous settlement growth. However, the ramifications of Coe's elaborate analogy are more difficult to discern, for, just as Roys notes historical variation in actual practice, so District 1 deviates from Coe's ideal in several respects. For example, Coe postulates that the center will be the focus of residential areas, a reasonable suggestion in light of both described and normative patterns given in the literature. District 1, however, is located some distance from the residential areas of the settlement. Coe also postulates that the

ritual routes from the periphery to the center will pass through the household compounds. At San Gervasio the elite residences are end points for the *sacbes* running to the center. These criticisms are not meant to denigrate Coe's contribution. On the contrary, we support the notions that, at the time of Spanish contact, the Maya regarded all space as ritual space; that social, political, and economic integration were reinforced and even structured by ritual ties expressed in the ceremonial movements of people in, around, and between communities; and that these movements in real space and time reflect the temporal and spatial structure of the Maya cosmos to a large degree.

This interpretive framework, however, should not be applied uncritically. In examining the mechanics of institutions expressed spatially, the fact that any given empirical instance is going to be a variation on a general theme should be anticipated. Thus the ideal analogy is not an ideal at all, but rather the postulated range of variation in the relationship between culture and its material expression. The real hypothesis concerns the structural principles expressing themselves in such variation. In this respect, Coe has made a good case for the operation of quadrapartite-based structural principles in sixteenth century Maya society. The planning of District 1 reflects their expression. This congruence in turn encourages an interpretation of the pattern in terms of the possible ramifications of such principles.

The major point of contrast between the administrative center of District 1 and the other administrative centers on Cozumel is that no one family inhabits the main plaza. Instead four families are in close association with the center. Granted that the most elaborate political organization at the time of contact was hierarchical, a higher order of magnitude expressed in a multiplicity of smaller elite residential administrative centers surrounding a larger center might logically be expected. This administrative center would also have served as a residence for the highest political authority. This expectation may be partially realized in District 1 although the lack of a dwelling in the main administrative plaza reflects an incomplete or truncated pyramidal organization.

This pattern might be interpreted in several ways. The model offered seems to integrate the bulk of the information. Presumably the lack of a central residence reflects the relatively equal status of the four family groups. No doubt there are nuances of power and authority, but their spatial distribution reflects an official equality in their status. Thus, Cozumel was officially governed by a confederation of four families residing in District 1. The actual power of these families, however, was probably not equal due to the manner in which this capital was founded.

A strong association with Mayapan is clearly expressed in the elite residences surrounding the formal plaza group. In fact there is a Mayapan-style elite residence and oratory in each of the groups. Moreover this particular dwelling type is not found elsewhere on Cozumel. The remains of one of these, C22-12, are poorly preserved, but because this group is nearly an exact replica of C22-1 through 3 and C22-30, with the exception of foundation walls, it can be identified as a Mayapan-style residence as well.

A formal seriation of features based upon deduced changes in the patterning of the district and the structure types follows. This is analogous to the earlier treatment of the shrines of talking idols. In this case, formal control is stronger and there is at least a potential for independently testing the hypothesis through temporally diagnostic ceramics.

As noted above, three of the Mayapan-style elite residential groups are almost identical with regard to size, composition, layout, and cardinal orientation. These groups probably express a specific official residential type adopted in the district during the course of its development. Two of the groups, C22-13 and C22-26 through 28, however, deviate from this pattern in significant ways that reflect the establishment of the center and its political growth. In contrast to the official type, the dwellings in these groups face south rather than east. Further, although they presently differ in formal plan, it is likely that they both began as variations on single-roomed, nonbenched rectangular structures with wide doorways on the front. This is probably the basic dwelling type prior to Mayapan influence on Cozumel. It is important to emphasize that neither of these elite residences began with the characteristic Mayapan tandem plan or group layout.

Other evidence, particularly the planning of

the district, indicates that groups C22-13 and C22-26 through 28 predate the other residences and represent the original founders of the center. If a point is chosen between these two groups so that processional routes emanating from them and oriented to the cardinal directions converge, the central altar of the main administrative plaza, C22-10 sits on one of the two alternatives. Furthermore, the distances from the centers of these two residential groups to the group altar on C22-10 are almost exactly the same. Perhaps coincidentally, this distance is 180m which in Maya units of measure equals 9 *kaans* (the *kaan* is one of the basic units of land measurement that survived the conquest in the form of the *mecate* [Tozzer 1941:96]). Finally, these are the only two groups that have *sacbes* leading directly into the central plaza. Thus the main plaza and groups C22-13 and C22-26 through 28 were probably established at the same time and prior to the building of the other residences. Given the disposition of these two elite residences, the capital seems to have been founded by two important extended families, neither of which was initially affiliated with Mayapan. Using this postulate, the earliest ceramic material found in primary contexts in these groups should predate the period of Mayapan's hegemony on the peninsula and fall somewhere between the Modified Florescent and Decadent periods. Preliminary analysis of such ceramics seems to confirm these expectations. Connor (1975) is somewhat mystified by the recovery of a Sihlo Fine Orange bowl in conjunction with several diagnostic Decadent period vessels from a burial under the group altar in C22-26 through 28. Gregory (1975), however, notes that this burial is secondary because not all bones are present nor do they exhibit primary articulation. Perhaps this is not a secondary burial at all but merely a disturbed one that was originally interred at the close of the Modified Florescent period. It could have been reopened during the Decadent, at which time a cache of Mayapan-style vessels were placed with it. Connor (1975) also notes that the dating of the dedicatory cache in front of C22-4-b is tentatively placed in the Decadent because the vessels conform to Decadent period shapes but are unslipped. Although unslipped wares occur during the Decadent, the fact that these vessels lack the characteristic red slip of the pervasive Mayapan

Red and Tulum Red complexes may be due to their manufacture prior to the introduction of these slips on the East Coast.

The organization of features within the main plaza indicates the family residing in C22-26 through 28 was more powerful than the one at C22-13. Not only is the eastern entrance into the plaza marked by a wide staircase, but the central altar in C22-4 through 10 is oriented toward C22-26 through 28, which in turn is directly aligned with C22-4-b, the main temple in the central plaza. Nevertheless, the fact that neither of these founding families inhabits C22-4 through 10, coupled with similarities in their formal relationship to the center, indicates that the spatial expression of an alliance rather than a sovereign-vassal relationship is represented.

In the formal seriation, the next transformation of District 1 is uncertain. Either Mayapan-style residential plan and quadrapartite organization were introduced simultaneously over a short period of time, or there was a more gradual transition during which C22-26 through 28 initially established an alliance with Mayapan and affiliated centers. Through this contact, Mayapan's conception of quadrapartite organization was gradually asserted. The latter model is preferred because it entails a transition resulting from processes other than outright takeover by Mayapan and because it explains the information somewhat better.

The first clear indication of an alliance with Mayapan is in the transformation of C22-25-a into a "palace." As argued previously, this building begins as a single-roomed dwelling and is subsequently modified to include an interior shrine and a colonnaded front room.

The resulting plan of C22-25-a, though within the range of variation for Mayapan, is quite different from the other three Mayapan-style residences that lack shrines in the back room, beam-and-mortar roofing, and masonry columns in the front room. The final plan actually looks more like the palaces at Tulum that, with one exception, include a masonry shrine at the back (Lothrop 1924:Plate 25). Because Sanders (1960) has identified Tulum as a Decadent period center, the greater affinity between C22-25-a and the palaces there does not reflect a major chronological disparity between C22-25-a and the other elite residences in District 1. Nevertheless this affinity and the other unusual

features of C22-25-a may indicate that this group was established as the first Mayapan-style residence in the district. Presumably its builders took their model from Mayapan at about the same time as did the builders of Tulum's palaces.

Thus the transformation of C22-25-a reflects the first alliance between the Decadent period government at San Gervasio and the Mayapan confederacy. C22-13, however, does not follow suit and resists modification of its main dwelling to the end, indicating that this alliance was not accepted with equal enthusiasm by all members of Cozumel's ruling elite. Following the transformation of C22-25-a, the three official Mayapan dwellings were built and the quadrapartite organization was established. These three new residences are so similar that they appear to have been built on the same basic plan. They reflect a rigidity in design not seen at Mayapan itself and might be viewed as a provincial variant built by people not totally familiar with the Mayapan idea of domestic architecture.

Differences in the quality of construction and labor investment in the three official Mayapan-style residences may reflect varying commitment on the part of inhabitants to the new regime. Both C22-1 through 3 and C22-29 and 30 are considerably more substantial than C22-12. The building of C22-12 by the family of C22-13 may express a reluctant acceptance of the new order and the material facilities necessitated by it.

The final quadrapartite organization of residences around the main plaza does not imply that Coe's hypothesized structuring principle was not operating when the district was founded. The placement of the first residences at right angles to each other relative to the main plaza and the four-sided arrangement of the main plaza itself are indications that the principle was operative prior to the development of the final pattern. Thus, given the pervasiveness of the quadrapartite principle in sociopolitical organization as outlined by Coe, it seems likely that the center was, from its inception, operating in terms of a four-part political division of the island.

Presumably then the two original founding families were fully committed to the establishment of a new island-wide government at the beginning of the Decadent period. There was nonresidential participation in the administrative center by two other political sectors. With the establishment of a strong alliance with Mayapan (see Roys 1962:32-33 for a suggestion that Mayapan may have been founded by people from or associated with Cozumel), this central government became powerful enough to inspire or require the leadership of the other two divisions to establish residences in the new capital. From this perspective, Mayapan primarily assisted in the final consolidation of a central government in the Decadent period on Cozumel.

In pointing to the sparsity of occupation in the vicinity of District 1 as evidence for its function as a supracommunity center, an analogy to the "empty" center type of settlement organization found in modern Chiapas and Guatemala has been implicitly drawn. There is, however, some evidence of residential occupation other than the elite households. Not surprisingly these other residences occur in the vicinity of the first two elite residential groups, C22-13 and C22-25 though 28. This situation probably reflects the fact that the inhabitants of C22-13 and C22-25 through 28 were permanent inhabitants of the district, whereas the inhabitants of the other elite residences maintained dwellings among their support communities elsewhere on the island. Sabloff and Rathje (1975a) have argued that the elite dwellings at District 1 were showcases for large gatherings or other public activities. If District 1 was an empty administrative capital, it seems likely that these residences were the focus of a wide variety of activities relating to the coordination of policy on the island and its integration into a functioning whole. In this respect, the elite residences in District 1 functioned in the same way as those in the formal plaza groups elsewhere on Cozumel. The presence of Mayapan-style dwellings as the theater for such activities emphasizes the importance of the alliance between Cozumel and the confederacy. Returning to Coe's analogy, it seems likely that some form of administrative rotation was taking place between the four elite families in the district and the communities they represented.

One of the best lines of evidence supporting the characterization of District 1 as a supracommunity capital is the intersite *sacbe* 1 connecting it with the northeast coast. This *sacbe* enters the main plaza from the east even though it originates in the north, indicating it was constructed after

the main plaza had reached its final form. This eastern entrance of S-1 may also reflect the particular importance of C22-25 through 28 and C22-29 and 30 at the time of its construction.

In addition to the evidence and inferences given in previous chapters on the northeast coast communities, there is another aspect of the special relationship between this part of the island and San Gervasio's District 1 that must be presented. C22-4 through 10 contain three large colonnaded public buildings. These types of structures are described in the historical literature as semiresidential in function. Among other things, they are used as *popolna* by participants whose dwellings are not in the immediate vicinity during times of important religious ritual and political gatherings. If District 1 was the capital of the island, participants would come here from all over the island. The formal plaza groups at Buena Vista and El Cedral in the southern sector of the island have their own colonnaded structures, whereas none of the northeast coast settlements has them. (La Expedicion contains Type 6 masonry buildings with colonnade doorways, but these are quite distinct from perishable structure Types 12 and 13, which are colonnades.) Although the inhabitants of northeast coast communities were probably able to improvise when required to do so, their centers were not designed to house the functions particularly associated with colonnades. The colonnades at District 1 seem to have supplied these facilities for the northeast coast settlements. Presumably people from the northeast coast frequented the capital on a more regular basis than did people from other communities on the island, and ceremonial occasions demanding the use of such facilities were relegated to the capital. Thus the northeast coast communities were more dependent on and more closely tied to the capital than were other communities on Cozumel.

The general economic underpinnings of the central government at District 1 can be viewed from the same perspective. If agglutinated substructures accommodated long-distance trade, one might expect to find such facilities in close association with an island capital exhibiting close ties to distant places like Mayapan. The lack of storage facilities in the immediate vicinity of District 1, their presence on the northeast coast, and the close affiliation between the northeast coast and

District 1 are probably interrelated systemic phenomena. If political alliance was based on social ties (Roys 1957) in Decadent period Yucatan, then the families committed to commercial enterprise on the northeast coast were probably closely tied to some of the elite families in the capital. In other words, the commercial interests of C22-25 through 28 and C22-29 and 30 may be expressed in communities on the northeast coast. Of the other two communities with colonnades of their own, El Cedral shows no investment in such facilities despite a substantial resident population, whereas Buena Vista exhibits extensive development of such facilities in the form of agglutinated substructures.

Of course, the presence of colonnades in communities located in the southern part of the island may simply be a reflection of the greater distance and consequent greater political and religious independence from the capital. This perspective is not in conflict with previous considerations.

Dispersed Substructures

East of District 4 and south of Districts 2 and 3 there are a number of dispersed substructures. These features, generally smaller than those in the districts discussed, are located in two large, open fields. Although no excavation was carried out in these substructures, surface collections yielded quantities of utility wares, some luxury wares, and obsidian blades. Such debris may generally be characterized as domestic and lends plausibility to a residential function for these features.

These areas of the settlement zone are lacking in features with high potential for functional identification, such as elite residences and standing masonry architecture, but some of the substructures themselves may provide clues to functions other than residential. C22-80, 92, and 109 are small, square substructures with vertical retaining walls of well-cut stone. From the size and quality of construction, these platforms probably supported perishable religious structures. These little platforms are the only indications of some defined socioreligious boundaries around any of the districts at San Gervasio. Similar platforms were located on the eastern and southern peripheries of District 4 but were not mapped. C22-114, near

District 1, is a pyramidal substructure that probably supported some kind of religious building. A *sacbe* (S-7), leaving C22-114 in the general direction of the western districts, implies some ritually important connections between District 1 and the rest of the settlement, but it disappears long before reaching that area. The wall system is clearly operative in the San Gervasio zone. The walls mapped in the two fields are merely illustrative of the system that is found throughout the settlement zone except in the immediate vicinity of the main formal plaza group in District 1.

The bulk of the settlement is in the western part of the zone, leaving the civil-administrative capital located in District 1 virtually isolated from the rest of the settlement. The shrine group comprising C22-33, 34, and 35 is the only prominent group between District 1 and District 2. This group has been discussed in passing on several occasions. Here it is significant that only one structure was added to the group during the Decadent, although the other structures exhibit use during that period. Like *sacbe* 5, *sacbe* 6, heading in the direction of Laguna Ciega on the north coast, was apparently constructed during Modified Florescent times. This is inferred from the ceramic material found in the platform altar terminating the *sacbe* next to the shrine group. There is a third *sacbe*, crossing a shallow *aguada*, that heads in the general direction of District 1. This *sacbe*, the perishable temple C22-34-e, and a few Decadent period sherds on the surface are the only indication of occupation. Although the route up the northeast coast was established prior to the Decadent period, perhaps *sacbe* 1, connecting District 1 to the northeastern coast, eclipsed the importance of the route to Laguna Ciega by Decadent times.

Additionally, this shrine group demonstrates the presence of a functional assemblage composed of community temple, public ritual house, and shrine prior to the Decadent on Cozumel.

Summary

Throughout the history of Cozumel, San Gervasio was the major interior settlement. During the Early period, the original center was located in District 2. This precinct was further elaborated during the Florescent. The focus of settlement shifted west to District 3 in Modified Florescent times. In the transition from Modified Florescent to Decadent times, District 2 became the focus for the cult of the oracle and a new island capital was founded in District 1, approximately a kilometer away. During the Decadent period, District 3 remained the most important residential area in the settlement and probably housed facilities directly related to the commercial and religious activities surrounding the pilgrimage center in District 2. Although District 2 may have roots in Decadent times, this complex of features most likely represents the domestic and commerical facilities of a merchant family in the Decadent period. From this perspective, District 4 was not a traditional focus but rather was probably one of several such complexes on the eastern and western sides of District 3.

The Decadent period settlement consists of an administrative center isolated from the influx of religious tourists coming to the oracle, the cult center for the oracle, and a residential-commercial district near the oracle. On the periphery of the residential-commercial district are scattered residences and facilities of particular merchant families operating out of the capital. Although the elite families in the administrative capital probably also had strong commercial interests, these were located in their support communities rather than in the capital. Thus, in terms of both residential and commercial facilities, District 1 is an empty center, tied to its support communities by a network of ceremonial circuits running around and through the island.

San Miguel

Both the Grijalva and Cortes expeditions stopped at a port on the northwest coast of Cozumel (Pagden 1971:11). Ironically this coastal port is the best-described but worst-preserved contact settlement. Descriptions of the ruins in the vicinity of the modern town of San Miguel left by Holmes (1895-1897) indicate that the bulk of this settlement lay to the north of the modern port. Much of this settlement was probably destroyed when the airport was built because informants remember a number of standing buildings being torn down at that time. Unfortunately, such destruction creates a difficult interpretive situation

for modern researchers. Clearly, the site was a coastal port of some importance. But the nature of this importance is unknown. As Haselgrove (1976:161) has noted, the negative evidence from San Miguel weakens our general arguments about the organization of trade on Cozumel. However, no matter how significant San Miguel was, it definitely was not the sole center of trade on the island. As we shall argue below, it was part of an island-wide system.

Not surprisingly, the remnants of this ancient settlement are located between the airbase and the town of San Miguel. This concentration of features lies behind a ridge running parallel to the beach for the entire length of the modern town. The features presently consist of large 100-400m^2 low rectilinear platforms and a few small pyramidal substructures. A similar concentration of features lies behind the ridge at the southern end of San Miguel. Cortes (Pagden 1971) stated that the town he called San Juan Porta Latina lay a crossbow shot inland from the beach, implying that most of the settlement was originally strung out behind this ridge. This might have been a defensive measure as well as protection against winter storms (nortes) that move in from the northwest.

Surface collections and excavations revealed a high proportion of exotic ceramics and other materials. Occupation apparently extended back to the Formative period. Thus, it seems likely that this settlement housed an important community throughout most of Cozumel's history.

The descriptions include references to pyramidal temple mounds, colonnaded structures, shrines, houses along roads, houses with stone foundation walls, and sacbes. Roads connected San Miguel to other settlements on the island. All the various attributes of settlements elsewhere on the island are represented at San Miguel with the exception of formal plaza groups and agglutinated complexes. With regard to formal plazas, the early explorers may have failed to mention that colonnades and other buildings were arranged in this way. Alternatively the settlement may have been organized without a single administrative center like District 3 at San Gervasio. Agglutinated substructures would not be expected features in a coastal port. Juan Diaz (in Wagner 1942a), however, notes that some of the men with Grijalva traveled inland along one of the paths and saw country estates of great beauty. These might have been agglutinated substructures supporting storage facilities, although this is sheer speculation.

As noted in Chapter 3, descriptions of the main coastal pyramidal structure observed by members of the Grijalva and Cortes expeditions conflict. Oviedo (in Wagner 1942a:93) describes a building that sounds like a Caracol with a spiral staircase inside it. Lopez de Gomara (in Simpson 1966:35), on the other hand, describes a temple housing the talking idol, presumably Ix Chel. There are few ways to resolve this conflict. El Cedral has a large pyramidal substructure on its periphery that is nearer the sea than the town. San Miguel apparently had one (possibly C11; Escalona-Ramos 1946) and it is quite possible that San Gervasio had one somewhere on the northern coast. Hence the potential for confusion is considerable. Here we follow Lopez de Gomara in placing the talking idol he describes on the coast, specifically at San Miguel. San Miguel is the only settlement of any size directly on the coast and shows a high percentage of exotics in surface refuse as well as a long period of habitation. Thus it is the best candidate for a port on Cozumel. The descriptions are fairly consistent in situating the pyramid temple near the port. Finally, if the Temple of the Talking Idol was located on the coast, it seems likely it would be in the settlement closest to the disembarkation of pilgrims coming from the mainland. San Miguel is a more appropriate point of disembarkation than the other settlements. Thus, from the limited evidence, San Miguel appears to have been a port town catering to the needs of pilgrims and merchants stopping on Cozumel.

The formal seriation of talking-idol temples entails the removal of the focus of the Ix Chel cult from San Gervasio to San Miguel sometime during the Decadent period. It seems likely that the oracle at San Gervasio remained operative but became a more exclusive center. Given that the talking idol was an important concern at the time of contact and that it developed out of ceramic idols that occurred relatively late at Mayapan, the transfer probably occurred after the fall of the Mayapan Confederacy. If this is the case, then there are two complementary motivations for removing the cult center to the coast. As a trading center, Cozumel would have been operating in cooperation with a large number of polities during the confederacy

and commerce would have been assured. With the collapse of the confederacy, Cozumel may well have been left to its own devices, competing as best it could with rival ports on the northeast coast of Quintana Roo. From this perspective, the creation of a bigger and better talking idol may be seen as a competitive response, amplifying the image of Cozumel as a cult center and attracting pilgrims and traders to the island's facilities. Second, the period following the sacking of Mayapan was surely one characterized by greater caution and distrust at centers servicing foreigners. Removal of the idol to the coastal port may have functioned as an effective screening device, keeping those whom the local leaders distrusted at the port and allowing only a select few of the important foreigners into the sanctuary at San Gervasio. This arrangement would also have weeded out the mundane pilgrims from the active traders.

El Cedral

The other important settlement on the western coast of Cozumel is El Cedral, probably ancient Santa Maria Oycib (Roys 1957). Located about 4km inland on the southern part of the coast, El Cedral is situated on flat, well-drained land that has been used for milpa and commercial agriculture since the resettling of the island in the past century. There are a number of fruit orchards in the community today and wild *zapote* grows in abundance south of it. The conch beds on this section of the western coast were, until very recently, quite rich and there is evidence that the ancient inhabitants fished these beds, using the shell for implements. Relative to other parts of the island, El Cedral is rich in local resources.

Although it might be more extensive, the ancient settlement seems to cover about 40ha and may be generally characterized as dispersed. Unfortunately, much of the ancient settlement is on privately owned land and many features have been robbed of stone for construction or looted for the tourist trade despite the protective attitude of some members of the community.

Chronologically, both excavated remains and looted objects reveal an occupation of the settlement beginning in the Formative period. A large fragment of a Sierra Red mammiform tetrapod bowl indicates possible contact between Cozumel and Protoclassic sites to the south at this time. Florescent and Modified Florescent ceramics are relatively abundant and Decadent period wares are well represented.

Despite the settlement's dispersed pattern (Figure 50) many of the typical assemblages found elsewhere on the island are found here, including a formal plaza group (C15-5), two shrine groups (C15-1 and 14), isolated shrines (C15-10 and 11), and household groups (C15-8, 9, 12, and 13). Although one large substructure, C15-6, was not divided into levels like agglutinated substructures, it may have served a similar purpose and was located south of the formal plaza group.

In addition to the types and assemblages above, El Cedral has features that make it an unusual settlement by Cozumel standards. These features are small, narrow rectangular colonnades on raised substructures (C15-4 and 5), single-room nonbenched structures with colonnaded doorways (C15-5-a and possibly C15-9), and a two-level, tandem-plan benched dwelling (C15-12-a).

Because few of the structures were actually planned or dated by excavation, it is difficult to explain these peculiarities. Nevertheless, the evidence indicates that El Cedral was a very conservative settlement during the Decadent period despite the presence of glass beads from the time of Spanish contact and other exotics, indicating some indirect participation in long-distance trade. Additionally, references by early explorers and colonists describe a community located in this area. Some of the structures, however, appear to have been built during the Florescent or Modified Florescent periods.

Sanders (1955) thought that shrines C15-1 and C15-14-a might have been built in Classic times because of the quality construction and despite the fact that he indicated the presence of stepped vaulting rather than beveled vaulting in the rooms. Holmes (1895-1897) and Fernandez (1945), however, correctly noted the characteristics of Florescent construction in these buildings as did E.W. Andrews V and A. Andrews (personal communications, 1973). In addition to having beveled, boot-shaped vault stones, these structures have false stone offsets along the end walls (Pollock 1970:81) as well as real ones under the vault. The retaining walls are constructed of blocks that are well squared off on their outer faces, but

are beveled on three of the interior sides to form a long tenon. These blocks are coursed in a grouting of mortar, sand, and small rock. Here, the hearting, as in later Decadent structures, plays a secondary role to the retainers in supporting the roof of the structure. In combination with the other Florescent traits, this method of wall construction compares well with Florescent period architecture found by Andrews and Stuart (1968:80) at Ikil, Yucatan. These investigators believe that such wall construction is also characteristic of Chichen Itza during the Florescent and that the architecture of the two sites constitutes a distinct subtradition within the general Puuc style.

The ramifications of these shared characteristics are complex and it is perhaps too soon to conclude that Cozumel and the Chichen Itza region share an architectural tradition prior to the Decadent, although this would not be surprising given the other indications of contact. Excavation in the plaza of the platform supporting C15-14-a produced Decadent censerware on the surface of the sealed plaster floor. A mixed lot of Florescent and Modified Florescent sherds were under it. However tenuous, these data indicate a Modified Florescent, as opposed to a Pure Florescent, date for the structure. Furthermore, the exterior of C15-14-a has a medial and superior three-member moulding, characteristic of Decadent period structures. C15-14-a and C15-1-a were probably constructed prior to the Decadent. It follows that we generally support Andrews's (1965b) suggestion that the shrine form and architectural style found on the East Coast has considerable time depth before the Decadent period.

The only other structure tested at the site is C15-5-a, a single-roomed, nonbenched rectangular perishable structure with two columns in its doorway. Here excavation produced a small sample of Florescent period ceramics under four sealed plaster floors. Like those from C15-14-a, these sherds offer only a *terminus ante quem* for the building. In combination with C15-15-b, the beveled vault arch, however, they imply that this plaza group may have been constructed prior to the Decadent period.

A large dwelling on C15-12 and a tomb on C15-9 yielded excavated remains dating to the Decadent. Although this dwelling has been characterized as Mayapan style, it is quite different from

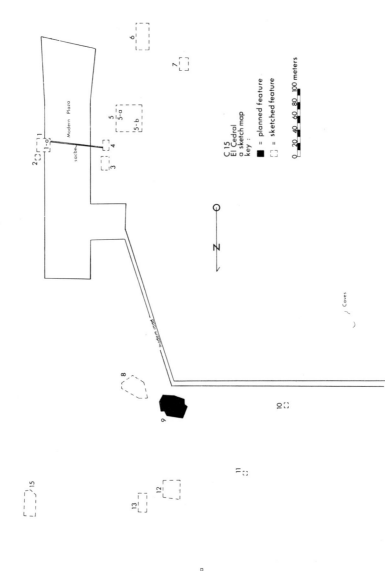

Figure 50. El Cedral (C15) settlement.

the structures in District 1 at San Gervasio and looks more like the early phases of a Decadent period structure at Nohmul, Belize (Hammond 1973:47) or Haviland's (1963) Late Classic Cluster C structures at Tikal. Like these structures, C15-12 is basically a two-level rectangular platform. The tomb had been looted in antiquity but contained shell, jade, gold and glass beads, and red-slipped wares. The tomb has a stepped entrance and may well have been for multiple secondary burials, as was Feature 7 at Buena Vista (Rathje and Phillips 1975:85).

In functional terms, El Cedral seems to be composed of dispersed substructures supporting household groups. C15-9, for example, has remains of several rectangular nonbenched structures on it, one of which has a colonnaded doorway. C15-12, in addition to the planned dwelling, has remains of other perishable structures on it. C15-7 supports remains of a rectangular perishable structure with a colonnaded doorway.

A distinctive feature of the settlement is the fact that the observed shrines occur either in shrine groups (C15-1 and 14) or on isolated elevated platforms (C15-10 and 11) but not in the context of household groups. These dispersed structures surround two plaza areas, the formal plaza group (C15-5), and another formed by features C15-1, 2, 3, and 4.

There is a large pyramidal substructure approximately half a kilometer west of the settlement zone. This substructure has remains of a *sacbe* running from it toward the coast. This pyramid may be one of the religious boundary structures for El Cedral. C15-14, a shrine group consisting of two Type 1 masonry religious structures and a public ritual house, may be another boundary marker. However, given the location of a shrine group, C15-1, in the center of the settlement near the formal plaza group, and the dispersed nature of the settlement, it is possible that the boundary structures are farther out.

In summary, El Cedral was probably a conservative community in which pre-Decadent structures as well as pre-Decadent architectural traditions were actively maintained during the intensification of long-distance ties on Cozumel in the Decadent period. Although the community no doubt participated in the outward-oriented island economy in some way, we suspect that the people

here, as they do today, dealt exclusively in local products.

Harking back to the analysis of Chen Cedral, El Cedral is probably not typical of pre-Decadent patterns. Rather it represents one aspect of a range in settlement variation that was established prior to but persisted into the Decadent.

Buena Vista

The settlement of Buena Vista is located on high ground about 1.5km inland from the southeastern coast of Cozumel. A massive complex of agglutinated substructures, covering an area of 5 to 7ha, dominates the settlement (Figure 51). Although there are dispersed substructures and masonry religious buildings in the vicinity of this complex, Buena Vista, in contrast to El Cedral, is predominately nucleated. Full discussion of fieldwork at Buena Vista will be published in the final report on this site now being prepared by William L. Rathje and David A. Phillips. Only a brief discussion of selected aspects of the settlement of Buena Vista is included here. A map of the central part of the site was published in Sabloff and Rathje (1975b:Map 1).

The settlement is situated at the southern end of an area of high ground that extends north and west for several kilometers toward the central interior. Davidson (1975:Figure 6) illustrates this area as the largest section of high land on the island and further implies higher rainfall for the area when he characterizes its vegetation as *rain forest*. Sabloff (1975:40) notes that until recently this region was considered one of the highest in agricultural potential on the island. Thus the location of the site appears to be a compromise between accessibility to local land-based resources and the lagoons to the south, which are not only a marine resource area but also are a potential beaching area for trading canoes. Today wild fruit trees are common in the vicinity and may indicate the potential for arboriculture (that was a speciality of Cozumel at the time of the conquest).

Date and Composition

Although the dating of construction phases at Buena Vista must await analysis of the excavated materials, there are some preliminary indications

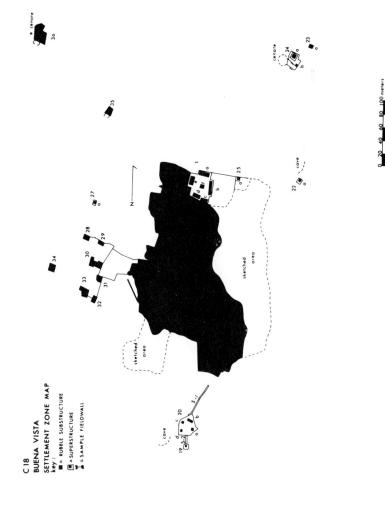

Figure 51. Buena Vista (C18) settlement zone (also see Sabloff and Rathje 1975b:Map 1).

of the site's history. Early period, Florescent, and Modified Florescent ceramics occur in mixed lots with Decadent sherds on the main complex of substructures (Connor 1975). Clearly the settlement zone was extensively occupied during the Decadent period and it is likely that most superstructural features were built then. Nevertheless there are some indications that the observed pattern of substructural features was established prior to the Decadent. A burial was found on the western periphery of the main complex that contained several Puuc Slate bowls. If these can be assessed as a primary deposit, the boundary of the main complex was apparently established by Florescent times and was not superseded by later development. Sherd samples from loot holes in all the outlying substructures supporting masonry religious structures contained high percentages of Florescent and Modified Florescent wares. These substructures also showed several major modifications throughout their histories. A diagnostic boot-shaped vault stone, for example, was found in the fill of C18-20, indicating the presence of beveled vaulting at the site at some point in its development. There seems to have been a heavy and extensive occupation of the settlement zone in Florescent and Modified Florescent times.

The settlement is composed of a main complex of agglutinated substructures that supports a variety of perishable superstructural remains and a Type 1 masonry religious structure (C18-7-a), a formal plaza group (C18-1), two outlying shrine groups (C18-20 and C18-23 and 24), five outlying shrines (C18-18, 21, 22, 25, and 27), and a zone of isolated rubble substructures (C18-20 through 36). Interspersed among the outlying features given on the map are small low platforms and the fieldwall network. These low platforms continue in moderate densities east, south, and west of the main complex. Beyond the outlying shrines and proximate substructures, the wall network incorporates a number of massive wall sections discussed in Chapter 4.

The main complex shows evidence of modification over a long period of time, expressing emphasis on horizontal growth as noted at La Expedicion. There is little planning in the organization of surface platform units that might indicate an overall design. Instead, the nucleus of the site reflects more or less what La Expedicion might

have looked like if its growth had not been terminated by the conquest. As noted above, the nucleus may have reached its present dimensions prior to the Decadent. Further modification during that period appears to have been primarily vertical.

There are two clear western accessways off the main complex. Several of the lower, narrower areas on the complex have also been tentatively identified as accessways or lanes running between postulated superstructural groups (Rathje and Phillips 1975). This notion receives some empirical corroboration from the patterns at Chen Cedral where clear accessways are formed by the proximity of substructures resting directly on the ground level.

Despite these postulated accessways, it is difficult to discern discrete groups of associated platform areas on the main complex. There is some reason to believe structures C18-14-a, C18-17-a, and the large rectilinear substructure next to them are all part of a single group. These structures are surrounded by a more or less rectangular wall with a gap in its eastern edge. Although the large rectilinear substructure does not show surface evidence of superstructures, it does have an extension along its eastern side, typically made to support superstructures. If this supposed group is any indication of the size of other units on the main complex, such units must have incorporated several different elevations similar to the disposition of compound or agglutinated substructures at La Expedicion. On the other hand, the large open area just south of the formal plaza group has little defined variation in elevation and yet seems to form a discrete unit. This open area incorporates C18-7-a, a shrine, and the fragmentary remains of several individual superstructures.

Superstructural remains are equally confounding. In Chapter 2 functional identifications for those features that can be dealt with as discrete units were offered. These identifications, however, are no more than extrapolations from more certain contexts on the island.

Round Structures

The most unusual and best-represented superstructures on the main complex are the circular ones. The Motul Dictionary translates round houses as *vovoloc che* (Wauchope 1938:20) and Tozzer

(1928) describes representations of round thatched buildings in frescoes at Chichen Itza. None of the early historical observations, however, makes any reference to round buildings except obvious masonry religious structures. Thus there is no easy way of assigning a function to these structures.

The etymology of *vovoloc che* may provide a lead. The common word for dwelling throughout the Maya area is *na. Che,* meaning "wood or wooden," is incorporated into words referring to structures that did not serve as dwellings, like *zooyche* in the Ticul Dictionaries and *ucoycheil ulum* in the Motul Dictionary, which are glossed as "chicken coop" (Wauchope 1938:132). This information tentatively implies that round buildings were not used as dwellings at the time of the conquest. This is commensurate with historical observations that describe rectangular dwellings. It is also possible that the word *che* is used in words that refer primarily to perishable nondwellings. Roy's (1957:150) statement that "Ecab c'octoche" literally translates "Ecab is our house" may qualify the statement.

The Modified Florescent illustrations of round structures at Chichen Itza appear to be dwellings. Tozzer (1928) has argued that these are the dwellings of foreign, presumably Mexican, invaders. Given the distribution of round structures in Mesoamerica (Pollock 1936), it seems likely that the general architectural concept was introduced at the time of foreign incursions on the peninsula despite the considerable time depth of apsidal structures there (Andrews 1965b).

The general rarity of round perishable structures even at Chichen Itza seems to indicate that the invaders coming into the area with this house type quickly discarded it in favor of local rectilinear types. Nevertheless, the round form may have persisted into the Decadent as a sacred form in association with religious activities. Synthesizing the lines of evidence above, we arrive at the tentative conclusion that perishable round structures were a type of sacred outbuilding in the Decadent period. This functional identification appears to be supported by the association of these features with others at La Expedicion and San Gervasio as discussed in Chapter 2. The other round structures scattered throughout the island and on the main complex at Buena Vista are more problematic. Nonetheless, in the absence of more substantial

evidence, the same argument applies to them. However, as discussed earlier, this argument is just one of several that deserve further refinement in field testing.

With regard to Buena Vista, the dating of superstructural features is the important question. If these buildings date to the Modified Florescent, then they might be more easily thought of as dwellings. On the other hand, if they date to the Decadent period, round structures must represent a conservative tradition in the face of change elsewhere, or a kind of special outbuilding. Given that these round structures are well constructed and have plaster floors and are unquestionably the most common type of structure on the main complex of Buena Vista, the notion that they were some kind of special facility implies that dwellings on the complex were more perishable. This alone would be quite peculiar. Thus, in the last analysis, we are mystified by these structures.

Rectilinear Features

The rectilinear features, such as they are, have been identified as dwellings, with the exception of C18-3-a, which was probably a ritual meeting house. In addition to these structures, there is an agglutinated circular structure on the west central periphery and a possible rectilinear agglutinated structure at the southeastern edge of the mapped area. Other fragmentary wall alignments and the low rubble walls on the main complex may pertain to superstructures, but simply identifying their forms would necessitate an unwarranted imposition of imagination on the data. The small amount of level area covered by observable superstructures lends some weight to the notion that many superstructures here have left no trace. Excavation indicates that the platform surfaces were plastered over, making it unlikely that the now open space was used for agricultural purposes.

The low number of observable superstructural features is true of agglutinated substructures elsewhere and is not easily explained by the processes of natural decay because those observable superstructures on top of agglutinated substructures are generally no worse for wear than superstructures in other contexts. Thus, the number of dwellings on agglutinated substructures is probably indicated by the number of identifiable superstructures and, as has been argued before, the largest portion of the platform surface was prepared to support relatively light, perishable structures that served as warehouses. Moreover a relatively small number of extended families lived in the main complex, whereas the majority of the local population was dispersed in the vicnity.

Like agglutinated substructures elsewhere on Cozumel, the main complex at Buena Vista occurs in the context of dispersed structures. Exploration around the site revealed a higher density of these dispersed features here than elsewhere on the island, indicating that nucleation is not a characteristic type of settlement on Cozumel, but rather is an aspect of settlement pattern that is emphasized in varying degrees.

The idea that nucleation was a defensive response to attacks by hostile groups makes some sense for the Decadent period on the peninsula. However, defensibility per se does not explain the variable expression of nucleation on Cozumel. There is no reason to expect, for example, that some people at La Expedicion or Buena Vista would feel a need for defensive nucleation whereas the majority did not. Furthermore, El Cedral, which is one of the more accessible settlements, shows very little evidence of such nucleation. Defensibility, on the other hand, makes good sense if there is something especially attractive, such as warehouses full of commodities on top of these substructures. At Buena Vista there is potential defensive utility in the massive walls in its vicinity as well as for the unique multiroomed masonry structure (C2-1-a) in front of the site on the southwestern coast. Similarly its nucleated form, coupled with a high density of dispersed settlement between the main complex and the coast, related to the special function of the platforms there.

The notion that nucleation might be a response to local resource utilization or environmental factors like seasonal inundation is controverted by the presence of nucleation in a wide variety of microenvironments as well as in the context of variable superstructure location that includes ground level.

Given Cozumel's established association with long-distance trade and the noted presence of warehousing in other participating centers, agglutinated substructures are most likely storage areas. Those at Buena Vista are particularly extensive and are the only ones known in the southern part of the island. Thus, this site appears to have been the major storage area and commercial center of southern Cozumel.

C18-7-a, the only masonry structure on the agglutinated substructures, has been badly looted in recent times. It apparently was a Type 1 masonry shrine that faced west and rested on a low support platform. Because this building is not associated with any other observable structures, its status was more likely public than private. This status and its centralized location makes C18-7-a somewhat like the centralized shrine group at Chen Cedral. Unlike Chen Cedral, however, there is a formal plaza group attached to the northern edge of the agglutinated complex.

The formal plaza group at Buena Vista (C18-1) is an extreme variant of this assemblage type on Cozumel in that there are three possible perishable dwellings and no masonry religious structures in the group. C18-1-a and C18-1-e are two identified dwellings found together on the northwest side of the plaza. This arrangement generally conforms to the pattern of dwellings in other formal plaza groups containing dwellings. C18-1-c, however, is located in the southeast corner of the plaza between two colonnaded public buildings. It presents a problem. On the one hand, the presence of three dwellings is not in concert with the proposition of dual residence by sex in such groups. On the other hand, the identification of C18-1-c as a nondwelling qualifies the generalizations that perishable nonbenched structures in formal plaza groups are dwellings. We choose to identify C18-1-c as a public building because it is disassociated from the two dwellings that otherwise conform spatially to the patterns found elsewhere and is positively associated with two colonnaded public buildings. Thus, in terms of arrangement within the group, it seems likely that C18-1-c is a public building. Furthermore, only one other Type 10 structure was discovered. This was C22-95-c. C22-95-c, on the plaza of a pyramidal temple mound, is found in a location outside the range of variation for dwellings. The combination of deviant location and shared plan provide a basis for identifying them both as public structures. Finally, although both these structures are found in locations where masonry religious buildings might be expected, in both instances this expectation is not realized.

The elaborate pyramidal substructure, C22-95, supports a perishable religious structure, C22-95-a, and the formal plaza group at Buena Vista completely lacks masonry religious structures. Hence in terms of formal plan and construction materials, the identification of C18-1-c as a public building is more consistent with the patterns of associated features than is its identification as a dwelling.

With regard to other buildings in the group, the two colonnaded public buildings, C18-1-b and d, are quite substantial and indicate the importance of activities related to such structures. C18-1-b has a unique, elaborate, constricted accessway on the southern side. This doorway probably opens on to a staircase descending off the plaza group to ground level. It is matched by a constricted accessway on the north side of the structure that leads into the plaza. Apparently access onto the group from the ground level went through the structure. Although a similar situation might exist at C18-1-d, there is no clear evidence for it.

C18-1-e is a side-benched dwelling like C31-1-e on the formal plaza group at Zuuk. It is a particularly large example of a nonbenched dwelling with constricted access. The carved square columns, believed to be doorjambs, are uniqe iconographically on the East Coast and bear a vague resemblance to the style found at Coztumalhuapa in Guatemala (Parsons 1967). It is perhaps significant that perishable structures with colonnaded or jambed, constricted doorways are found in the two observed formal plaza groups at the southern end of the island. In the north, this type is found only in C22-13, the conservative elite household group in District 1 at San Gervasio.

The lack of masonry religious structures in C18-1 is compensated for by the large number of such structures on the periphery of the settlement. This particular pattern may help qualify the function of C18-1 in general and its colonnaded public buildings in particular. Many of the observations pertaining to the organization of settlements in conquest period Yucatan note the central location of important religious buildings. Although this pattern is found at some settlements on Cozumel, it is clearly not at C18-1. Apparently the activities associated with masonry religious structures were not being carried out in this group, but rather were performed on the periphery of the settlement.

The resulting separation of colonnades from masonry temples leads to the inference that the former were foci for activities on the more secular end of the historically observed range, including men's houses, boys' houses, barracks, arsenals, guest houses, and markets. Any or all of these possibilities might apply. They follow from the fact that C18-1 is designed to house people on a semiresidential basis and not as a focus for religious ritual. This deemphasis of the center as a religious focus parallels the pattern at C22-87, which is also identified as a commercial, warehousing center.

Peripheral Religious Structures

Control over the boundary religious buildings at Buena Vista is better than at any other site on Cozumel. The shrine groups to the north and south are particularly important. Both of these are located next to sources of water that may have been the major sources for the settlement. Although neither of these areas holds water today, its presence in antiquity can be reasonably inferred. The southern source is a large, deep rockshelter. At the back of this shelter the differential weathering caused by a small underground lake is clearly evident, and there are several water lines at different heights. The northern source is a deep, refuse-filled *cenote* partially surrounded by a masonry wall to the north and the shrine group platform (C18-24) to the east.

The southern shrine group (C18-20) is composed of three shrines and a public ritual house. The substructure probably supported a fourth shrine between C18-20-a and b, 90 percent of which has been removed by looters. C18-20-c is perishable. C18-20-d may also have been perishable but it is too far gone to say more. A tomb in the plaza has also been exposed by looters. Despite the wholesale destruction of the group, enough remains to say with certainty that it strongly emphasizes small, Type 1 masonry structures. C18-19-a may be another shrine associated with this group because it is connected to C18-20 by a short, wide *sacbe*. It is situated on its own elevated substructure and, judging from size alone, may have been a single-room structure.

This proliferation of small religious structures may reflect the representation of several social groups or deities at C18-20. This type of group may have been one of several ways of marking the major entrance into a settlement or region, the others being pyramidal substructures and arches. A similar multiplicity of small shrines characterize the groups at Xcaret (ancient Ppole), the point of embarkation for Cozumel (A. Andrews, personal communication, 1973). Moreover a group of three small shrines was situated on the trail between the sea and the town of Ecab on the northeast coast (Roys 1957:150) and a similar group may have stood in front of Champoton near a *cenote* (Bernal Diaz del Castillo in Maudslay 1908:21). Thus it seems possible that C18-20 not only marks the southern periphery of the main settlement zone but also a major entrance into the settlement from the south. The presence of another masonry shrine south of C18-20, C18-18, which might lie on a trail connecting to the southern shrine group and ultimately to the main settlement, provides additional support for this notion.

The northern shrine group, C18-23 and 24, contains two Type 1 masonry shrines and the only Type 6 masonry community temple in the settlement zone. C18-24 is clearly oriented toward the formal plaza group and there may have been a route connecting the two. In contrast to the southern shrine group, elevation of the structure and elaboration of its formal plan emphasize the importance of this focus to the community. Although C18-23 is close enough to C18-24 to be considered associated with it, it faces east away from the group rather than toward it. It probably faces a trail leading away from the group to the north. This supposition, combined with the inferences based on the southern pattern of shrines, leads to the proposition that the importance of the northern and southern shrines lies not only in the fact that they mark the major water sources in the community, but also in their marking of a major north-south route running through the community. To the south lie the southern lagoons and the small community containing the arch described in Chapter 3, and the important shrine group of Caracol (C1-1 and 2). To the north, there is a zone of particularly fertile land that more than likely was farmed by people of the settlement zone. Moreover, the natural ridge on which Buena Vista is situated, and which runs north-south parallel to the coast, is artificially widened and leveled in several places north of the settlement. This may also relate to a route. Finally, there are reliable reports (Carlos Vivas, personal communication, 1973) of several more settlements on this ridge north of Buena Vista and south of the cross-island highway. These probably lie behind C19 and C3. At present all we can say about these settlements is that they are described as having formal plaza groups.

The eastern and western shrines, C18-21 and C18-27, appear to be substantial Type 1 masonry structures. Unfortunately C18-27 has been damaged almost beyond recognition. Both of these shrines face the main complex of agglutinated substructures. In terms of formal layout and plan, C18-21 may have been a third, but secondary, way of marking an important boundary. It is not only larger, but it also has a four-way vaulted roof and medial and superior three-part mouldings, as well as a cupola on top. Therefore C18-21 lies somewhere between the multiple, small, simple shrines of C18-20 and the elaborate Type 6 masonry temple of C18-24.

There are two masonry religious structures, C18-22 and 25, that deviate from the ideal pattern presented above. C18-22-a is situated on top of an elevated substructure next to a cave. Although the structure is badly damaged by looters, it shows evidence of having a concentric two-room plan and is oriented toward the main complex. Given the elaborate form and raised location this shrine is clearly an important focus for the community, but it is placed at an intercardinal point. In this case, the location of the shrine appears to be dictated less by ideal spatial relationships than by the location of the cave next to it. This cave is a deep rockshelter that shows substantial human modification. A staircase leading from the mouth down onto the floor area was carved into the rock and several tall columns were left to support the cap-rock roof. These columns are roughly arranged in rows. Along the back wall, a bench area was carved out of the soft rock underlying the cap. Unlike other *sascaberas* in the vicinity, this one shows clear indications of important ritual use.

C18-25, a Type 1 masonry structure, is peculiar in that it is located near the main formal plaza group and yet faces east away from it. This may be the only private masonry shrine at Buena Vista, facing a household group of particular importance in the community. Unfortunately, while in the field we erroneously supposed that the main house of this group was situated over a *chultun* discovered on the eastern extension of the main complex. It is clear to us in hindsight that the dwelling, a large and rather elaborate one, lay south of the area we so carefully cleared and mapped (Figure 18b). This cleared area was probably the plaza of the group. All that we can say about this dwelling on the basis of casual observation is that it is a large, rectangular, two-level tandem-plan structure with side benches in the plaza-level front room. It resembles C15-14-a at El Cedral.

In contrast to other sites, like La Expedicion, that exhibit boundaries marked by religious structures, the shrines at Buena Vista do not define the periphery of the settlement zone per se. Even the small sample of platforms recorded along the western side of the main complex indiciates that dispersed occupation continues unabated beyond the shrines. A more thorough survey of the support area would probably produce evidence of a high-density occupation for at least a square kilometer around the site nucleus. Hence the boundary shrines at Buena Vista mark the territory of the main complex of agglutinated substructures and associated features and define the center of the settlement rather than its entirety. Lacking good chronological control over the outlying rubble substructures, it cannot be ascertained whether this inner boundary was established before or after the development of the dispersed settlement area. In the Decadent period, however, it seems possible that the boundary demarcated the nucleus of the settlement as a special precinct. This could be commensurate with the special facilities supported on the agglutinated substructures.

Summary

Buena Vista is a large, dispersed community with a nucleated core. Like Chen Cedral, it shows evidence of having been nucleated in the fashion characteristic on Cozumel prior to the Decadent period. Today it contrasts with Chen Cedral in that the lower areas at Buena Vista are artificially

raised whereas those at Chen Cedral are on ground level. This appears to be the result of vertical modification at Buena Vista during the Decadent period. It is possible that the analysis of excavated remains will indicate that Buena Vista was continuously occupied from Modified Florescent times through the Decadent. Rathje and Phillips (1975:84) imply this when they observe that a tomb on the agglutinated substructure complex was used throughout the Postclassic. Such continuity in use lends some credence to the proposition that the functions associated with agglutinated substructures were established prior to, and persisted into, the Decadent period.

It has been argued that only a few extended families occupied the core of the settlement at any one time, leaving much of the area occupied by various kinds of storage facilities used in long-distance commerce. In terms of the social organization of this nucleus, we offer some very tenuous speculations that are too weak at present to support additional generalization, but might be of use to future investigators. A substantial household group has been identified at the southern extremity of the mapped area. Another household group and associated shrine (C18-25) are situated east of the formal plaza group. The formal plaza group itself constitutes a third. These household groups are situated on extensions of the main complex as it was mapped and sketched. We predict that future research will reveal the presence of a fourth elaborate household on the southwestern extremity of the nucleus, indicating that the nucleus of the settlement was occupied by these four families and their servants, retainers, and slaves during the Decadent period. The rest of the local community probably was dispersed around the nucleus. This seemingly radical interpretation is actually in keeping with the inferences concerning agglutination at La Expedicion and San Gervasio where substantial agglutinated areas were associated with individual extended families. If there were four families at Buena Vista, the area associated with any given family would not be greater than that found with families elsewhere on Cozumel.

As Cozumel was noted for various kinds of local produce, particularly honey and wax, the dispersed population probably brought goods to the center of the settlement for exchange and as tribute. It follows that the leaders of Buena Vista were coordinators of a local production center as well as middlemen moving commodities from the Yucatan Peninsula and other areas.

The ritual boundary at Buena Vista is the best recorded for the island and provides a good model of what such community boundary systems looked like. No doubt Buena Vista was somehow connected to other communities on the island by trails. A major north-south trail running along the western ridge of the island has been identified, connecting Buena Vista to the southern lagoons and communities on the western coast. A route might ultimately be found that connects with the north-south trail along the northeast coast. Each community of Cozumel most likely related to a number of ceremonial circuits making up the information-transportation network on the island. Thus, Buena Vista may have been identified with shrines in front of it on the southwest coast as well as with the shrines along the southern coast.

CHAPTER 7

SETTLEMENT PATTERNS ON COZUMEL: A SUMMARY

Sites and Settlements

The eight sites discussed in the foregoing chapters are the foci of distinct communities on Cozumel. Of the remaining sites shown on the map of the island (Figure 3), only C14 is known to be a community. This site was briefly visited twice, but no plans or maps were made of it. It consists of a cluster of rubble substructures surrounding a small formal plaza group. No standing masonry structures or remains of perishable foundations were observed. The site, however, was explored for only a few hours. The location of C14 corresponds to that of a village explored by members of the Cortes expedition prior to Cortes's arrival on the island (Bernal Diaz del Castillo in Maudslay 1908: 91). The other sites, with the exception of C20 (historic Columbia Plantation), mark the location of shrines and shrine groups. No doubt in some cases, such as C16 and C17, careful exploration would reveal the presence of small communities in the vicinity of these shrines, similar in organization to Aguada Grande. C30 marks the location of an isolated homestead consisting of two rubble substructures covering approximately 240m^2. Other isolated homesteads of this kind were noted in the vicinity of Buena Vista and there are probably many of them scattered throughout the island.

It is difficult to arrive at any general conclusions concerning demographic patterns on Cozumel given the information at hand. The location of known shrines and communities shows a high correlation with trails established since the reoccupation of the island in the last century. The major settlement of San Gervasio, for example,

lies on what was the main cross-island trail prior to the construction of the modern road. San Francisco cave (C32) lies on what used to be the main trail from San Miguel to El Cedral. Several more structures were reported by informants in the vicinity of this trail but they were never located by the survey. In short, local knowledge of ancient ruins, which provided the main source of information for our survey and those of previous professionals, is best concerning the areas of modern occupation. Cattle ranchers and hunters, however, reported numerous well-preserved structures and other features that they had stumbled on in the dense bush. Inevitably, attempts to follow up on these reports proved disappointing. In the last analysis, the blank areas on the map, particularly the south central region, represent territory that is unknown archaeologically.

Demographic Patterns

If only as a guide to future research on the island, it is worthwhile to offer a tentative extrapolation of general demographic patterns on Cozumel despite the rather limited data base discussed above. All reliable informants agreed that there are several more settlements along the windward, eastern coast of the island between C18 and C23. These are reported to lie behind C19, C3, and C5. Because known settlements lie behind coastal shrines, these settlements probably can be found within 2 or 3km of the coast. Certain details of these reported settlements are intriguing. The site behind Punta Morena (C3) supposedly contains numerous large sculptures of rabbits and a masonry structure surrounded by a circular stone enclosure that sounds like the ruins explored by Prince William of Sweden (Lothrop 1924:158-159). As discussed in the previous chapter, these east coast settlements are probably situated to take advantage of the relatively high ground in the vicinity of the fossil coral formations and beach ridges that form a large ridge 500m to 2km inland from the present coast. Not only is this land relatively well drained, but the higher ground is made more attractive by a higher incidence of accessible ground water in *cenotes*. A main trail most likely ran down this coast through the settlements, ultimately turning inland to connect with San Gervasio along the major intersite *sacbe* discovered by the survey. The implication that settlements were linked in this fashion is an extrapolation from the notion that religious foci were serially linked to form ceremonial circuits circumscribing settlements and the island as a whole.

The lack of reported settlements north and east of El Cedral is rather surprising. This is good land by local accounts and has been the location of small homesteads for many decades. Even William Davidson (personal communication, 1973) who explored this region for many days reported no major settlements. Perhaps, as is the case today, this area was occupied by homesteads affiliated with El Cedral. The lack of major coastal settlements between El Cedral (C15) and C14 may be partially explained by the presence of extensive mangrove swamps bordering this coast. The old trail from San Miguel to El Cedral runs inland several kilometers to avoid these swamps, and it is possible that the ancient transport-communication line did so as well.

A modern trail runs between El Cedral and Buena Vista, but it traverses very rough and uneven terrain. Although we received reports of a large isolated shrine somewhere along this trail, we were unable to locate it; it is possible that these settlements were connected by this trail in the past. It is also possible that they were linked by a trail that ran south of this rough terrain, incorporating small settlements near the southern lagoons.

The region north of San Miguel and between San Miguel and San Gervasio is virtually unknown. It is possible that Miramar (C11) is a settlement though this area was not explored by the survey.

It is just as likely that Miramar is the northernmost extension of the settlement of San Miguel which was dispersed along this relatively high area of the leeward coast.

Thus, the pattern of presently known or reported sites consists of a series of settlements located within 2 or 3km of the coast circumscribing the island. Given the reliance of the ancient inhabitants on both marine and terrestrial resources, this location of communities is rational. San Gervasio, the postulated capital of the island, is centrally located in the northern interior, however. It is interesting that until the modern road was built across the island and an accurate survey of the interior was provided by aerial photography, San Gervasio was perceived and mapped as lying in the center of the island (Escalona-Ramos 1946: 573). Although it might be reasonable to postulate a second major settlement comparable to San Gervasio in the south central sector of the island, it might well be that San Gervasio was the only capital. Although it is not ideally located for coordinating the activities of settlements encircling the island if these settlements are individually linked to a central place, San Gervasio is reasonably located if these settlements are serially linked by a trail running around the island. Furthermore, San Gervasio is more or less centrally located between the populated east coast and the main port settlement of San Miguel.

In terms of gross size and importance, there are two major sites in the north, San Gervasio and San Miguel, and two in the south, El Cedral and Buena Vista. It would be nice to think that these sites are the four communities represented in the residences of District 1 at San Gervasio. This must, however, be tentative until the island has been subjected to systematic exploration. La Expedicion, Zuuk, and possibly C14 seem to represent secondary communities. The elite residence formal plaza groups give these communities the appearance of being formally "chartered" and incorporated into the overall organization of the island as centers of political and economic importance. The settlements reported along the east coast probably had a similar status as they apparently contain formal plaza groups. Aguada Grande represents a tertiary center with a small resident population surrounding some shrines on a major ceremonial circuit. Another example of this type of community was observed at the southern tip of the island by Spanish explorers (Juan Diaz in Wagner 1942a). Lower-order settlements that were virtually homesteads were observed in the course of exploration in the vicinity of Buena Vista, between La Expedicion and Aguada Grande, and at C28 near Punta Morena. Juan Diaz (in Wagner 1942a) describes such rural estates along the trails leading away from San Miguel. It seems reasonable to assume that primary and secondary centers were extended boundary communities with jurisdiction over larger scattered rural populations as was the case in highland Guatemala at the time of the conquest (Miles 1957).

Population Estimates

It is traditional in settlement pattern analyses to offer some gross estimates of population. Given the state of the art used to identify dwellings and the questionable use of analogy based on estimates from a few communities in Yucatan to determine the number of individuals inhabiting dwellings in the Maya area in general, we are wary of all such estimates. Lopez de Gomara (in Simpson 1966:34) estimates there were 3000 inhabitants in Cozumel's three major towns (presumably San Miguel, San Gervasio, and El Cedral). This is the only available estimate from the expeditions prior to the introduction of smallpox on the island in 1520 by members of the Narvaez expedition (Edwards 1957: 130). Presumably Lopez de Gomara's estimate is based on eyewitness reports and is probably a reasonable indication of general magnitude. Because several additional communities observed by the survey were probably occupied at the time of contact but were not observed by the Spanish, and there are probably more to be discovered, it is likely that the total population of the island was considerably larger than 3000 people. The secondary centers like La Expedicion probably had a maximum of 200-300 residents. Smaller centers like Aguada Grande probably had fewer than 50 residents. Approximately eight of the known and reported secondary centers may have been occupied at the time of the conquest, giving a total

population of about 2000 people. Moreover the substantial number of homesteads affiliated with these centers provides an additional 3000 or so people living outside the primary and secondary centers. This would give an estimated total of about 8000 inhabitants for the island, which is more or less in concert with Edwards (1957), who gives an estimate of about 9000 based on historical documents and a postulated mortality rate of approximately 90% following the first wave of epidemics prior to the conquest of the peninsula.

These figures are significant as a general indication of magnitude. Basically the information available from the colonial period and the exploration of the remains on the island indicate that Cozumel was well populated. There is no reason to believe, however, that the island was overpopulated or that population pressure ever strained the local resource base. Even using a more generous estimate of 10,000 inhabitants and a conservative estimate of $241 km^2$ of arable land (Davidson 1975), there were only 41 people per km^2. This is well below carrying capacity estimates given for other parts of the Maya area (Cowgill 1962; Sanders 1963) where only terrestrial resources are taken into consideration. The people of Cozumel exploited a variety of marine resources for subsistence as well. No doubt its fame as a pilgrimage center and participation in long-distance trade placed a premium on local resources amenable to commercial exploitation.

As we discuss in Chapter 8, there is some evidence that the location of settlements on Cozumel was conservative through time. The known size and location of settlements at their maximum extent implies that a well-developed hierarchy of communities was present by the time of the Spanish Conquest. Furthermore, the routes binding these communities into a functional whole were likewise well established by this time. Several of the institutions expressed in the location of settlements and their internal organization have been discussed in the context of individual settlements. In Chapter 8, the spatial organization of Cozumel as a whole is considered.

CHAPTER 8

COZUMEL DURING THE DECADENT PERIOD: A FUNCTIONAL SYNTHESIS

Introduction

From the inception of the Cozumel Archaeological Project, one of its major goals has been to test the hypothesis that the island was a long-distance trading center in Precolumbian times, particularly during the Decadent period. Although Cozumel's role as a pilgrimage shrine is made quite clear in the ethnohistoric literature, its role as a trading center is more ambiguous. However, there are at least strong hints in sources such as Scholes and Roys (1948:3, 33-34) and Roys (1943:56) that Cozumel also functioned as a trading center.

If it was a trading center, we believed that we should be able to find material correlates of the trading activities that took place there. Because we could not turn to other reports on archaeological research at trading centers in the Maya area in particular or in Mesoamerica in general, we decided that one significant aspect of our field research would be to undertake a basic pattern recognition study. Were there settlement and architectural patterns that were similar to or different from published patterns for large multifunctional sites? Could we convincingly relate such patterns to trading activities on Cozumel? In other words, could we correlate the material patterns with behavioral patterns? If these preliminary goals were achieved, then the Project would be in a position to fully test our general hypothesis. Moreover, we hopefully would have begun to lay the groundwork for future studies of more general regularities in the cultural roles of trade and trading centers in complex societies.

On the basis of our initial surveys on the island and our more intensive research at Aguada Grande (C27) and La Expedicion (C25) in 1972, we were able to observe a number of striking features in the archaeological record of the Decadent period and begin to piece together some preliminary patterning in these features. Among these features (many of which first had been observed by other scholars) were numerous dry-land fieldwalls, large agglutinated rubble platforms, fragments of *sacbes*, stone circles, a shell tool industry, close architectural ties to Mayapan, lack of elaborate Decadent period caches and burials, the size and importance of the San Gervasio zone (C22), and a Decadent period dating for most of the archaeological features visible on the surface. As our work progressed, we began to see some larger-scale patterns, including an island-wide system of stone walls, a coastal shrine system, a probable system of *sacbes*, nucleated settlements with outlying shrines, community rather than family shrines, and a variety of patterns related to inferred building functions.

Another interesting result of our initial analysis of the settlement survey data was the apparent high degree of political integration on Cozumel during the Decadent period. Instead of a single port on the coast, or a series of separate trading zones being the focus of Precolumbian development on the island, the island as a whole appears to have functioned as an integrated unit with economic and political control maintained by the elite residing in the administrative center at San Gervasio. With this initial interpretation in mind, we tried as much as possible to look for intersite, island-wide patterns and not just intrasite ones. In other words, to understand Cozumel's potential as a trading center, as well as the nature of the island's Decadent period occupation, we found that we had to search for relations among the island's 35+ sites. Fortunately, we did not have to face the boundary problems confronting some multisite surveys.

Most of the patterns we found have been discussed at some length in Chapters 2-4 and particularly in Chapters 5-7. We believe that our interpretations of these patterns in terms of the organization and control of traders and traded materials by the rulers of Cozumel are plausible and testable. Additionally, we have been unable to come up with alternative interpretations that better fit the data. Moreover, recent research elsewhere in southern Mesoamerica also lends very preliminary support to some of our interpretations. For example, John Henderson's (Henderson *et al.* 1979:173-174) work at the well-identified trading center of Naco in Honduras has uncovered a large platform with no superstructure, which is similar to those found on Cozumel. This structure is identified as a possible storage platform. At Xcaret, the coastal embarkation point for Cozumel, Andrews and Andrews (1975:60) report the presence of platforms that appear to be similar to those on the island. They also describe other features, including a field wall system, that closely resemble ones found on Cozumel.

A second major goal of the Project was to elucidate further the nature of Decadent period society in the northern Maya lowlands. With the exception of the very important, well-published research of the Carnegie Institution of Washington at Mayapan (Pollock *et al.* 1962; Smith 1971; the *Current Reports* series), Lothrop's (1924) early work at Tulum, Sanders's (1955, 1960) important East Coast survey, and the recent report on Xcaret (Andrews and Andrews 1975), there have been relatively few large-scale, published reports on sites occupied during the Decadent period. Generally speaking, the basic archaeological conception of the Decadent period is derived from Mayapan. As careful as the research at Mayapan was, fieldwork at the largest Decadent period center in the northern lowlands cannot substitute for research at a number of varied sites throughout the area.

Are certain settlement features at Mayapan related to peculiar local conditions or do they reflect more general conditions in the northern lowlands? Are they related to Mayapan's position as a major political capital?

We believe that our settlement research on Cozumel adds a useful new dimension to archaeological perspectives on Decadent period lifeways. The publication of the whole series of Cozumel reports will provide a much richer comparison to the Mayapan data. After these reports, as well as other pending reports (such as that of Arthur Miller's Tancah project and the final Dzibilchaltun report), are published, scholars will be in a better position to see the variety of Decadent period settlements and relate such variety to the differing environmental and cultural conditons in various regions of the northern lowlands.

To summarize our settlement data in relation to the two goals noted above, we present brief discussions of our interpretations of social, political, religious, and economic organization on Cozumel. These discussions summarize our arguments why certain features and patterns observed on the island are best interpreted as related to trade and indicate how the Cozumel data have expanded our understandings of the Decadent period in the northern lowlands. In regard to economic organization, we also try to relate our findings to some broader, Mesoamerica-wide considerations.

Social Organization

The extended family single-dwelling household characteristic of Cozumel in the early Colonial period is apparently an institution dating back into the Decadent. This inference, which is based on the associations of dwellings with other types of buildings, may explain some of the variability within the domain of dwellings. Formal variability occurs primarily in size and the presence and location of permanent furniture. A perusal of the types shows that size and formal layout seem to vary independently in many cases. This independent variation may be attributed to different factors. It has been postulated that formal plan is dependent upon the degree of important ritual activity carried out in the context of the home. Such activity, of course, is closely linked to the social, political, and religious status of particular families. In this respect, the Mayapan-style dwellings, and perhaps other styles not yet affiliated with areas on the mainland, are as much expressions of political status as of economic status. Wealth per se probably does not play a very important role in generating such variability because the investment of effort in superstructures across the board is quite modest on Cozumel. This attitude ties in with Rathje and Sabloff's notions (1975a; also see Rathje 1975) of pragmatism among merchants and finds some support in modern Maya practices. At Chan Kom, for example, the masonry dwelling is a symbol of that village's status as a pueblo (Redfield and Villa Rojas 1971:28). Although wealth is necessarily invested in such buildings, Redfield and Villa Rojas (1971:33) state "the masonry house is an innovation and a luxury for the progressive and the ambitious; the thatched house is a necessity for everybody." The masonry dwelling is thus less an outward display of wealth than a statement of political commitment to the community. It is an appropriate channel for transferring the fruits of incentive into legitimate prestige, but is perceived as such because the masonry house is a concrete contribution to the status and prestige of the community as a whole.

Dwelling size is another matter. A recent study of dwelling size and household composition in a Maya village in northern Belize (D. Birdwell, personal communication, 1975) indicates that size is determined by the size of the family building the structure. Certainly, where much community-related activity takes place in the home (which is not the case in this particular village), size might relate to such activities. Nonetheless, household size may also be a general contributing factor. In this respect, it may be significant that the majority of dwellings on Cozumel during the Decadent period fall into the upper end of the modern range of dwelling size and are between 40 and 60m^2. If extended families were occupying them, a relatively large dwelling on the average would be appropriate.

When considering location and general elaborateness of dwellings, there are some indications that the more prestigious dwellings are associated either with important religious and/or political foci or with commercial facilities. C25-31-a, for example, located on an agglutinated substructure far from the formal plaza group, is as elaborate as most of the dwellings found in formal plaza

groups, and C22-87, as a group, has been identified as the estate of a merchant family.

Some of the general ramifications of large families living under one roof have been considered earlier. Certainly it is a residential pattern amenable to economically diversified domestic units of production. Such organization of the basic unit of the economy is, in turn, appropriate to a trading center with its multiplicity of services and opportunities for the commercial exploitation of local resources. Although Roys (1957) mentions possible multiple-family dwellings in towns with no apparent commercial interest like Chancenote, such organization seems to have characterized the great trading center of Chauaca on the northern coast.

If the distribution of clan or lineage names is any indication, Cozumel's elite apparently had strong social ties with centers on the northeast coast, particularly Tulum, Ecab, and Cachi (Roys 1957). According to early descriptions, the latter two centers were oriented to commerce. Naum Pat, a prominent cacique and possibly *halach uinic* on Cozumel in 1526, was on his way to a wedding on the mainland with 400 followers when Montejo met him (Chamberlain 1948; Roys 1957). The Pat clan, rarely found beyond the northeast coast, was well represented in the province of Cochuah, which controlled the port facilities at Acension Bay, and in Mani, ancient heartland of the Mayapan confederacy. The maintenance of social ties between Cozumel and known commercial centers on the northeast coast is perhaps indicative of economic and political coordination among the centers of the region involved in trade.

Political Organization

Five of the settlements on Cozumel contain plaza groups that have been identified as administrative centers. However, only the pattern at District 1, San Gervasio finds clear corroboration in the historical literature. Its composition is comparable to other remains on the East Coast like Cancuen Island (Lothrop 1924). Because the composition of C22-4 through 10 is virtually identical to the center of Potonchan described by Bernal Diaz (Maudslay 1908), the pattern may have had a very broad distribution in the Decadent period. No doubt some of the structures in such groups served as *Popolna*, town council chambers, whereas the colonnades served a variety of functions related to the carrying out of policy.

The combination of elite residence and administrative center is not reported in either the historical or archaeological literature to our knowledge. This is not surprising because, on the one hand, the early explorers were primarily concerned with regional capitals adhering to the District 1 type. On the other hand, investigators of remains dating to the Decadent, with the outstanding exception of the work at Mayapan (Pollock *et al.* 1962), have shown little interest in the remains of perishable structures. Thus, more examples of this pattern may be discovered by a careful examination of perishable structures in groups containing masonry buildings.

The combination of administrative centers inhabited by the ruler in local communities and administrative centers surrounded by the dwellings of rulers in the regional capital has some interesting ramifications. We have argued for the presence of a joint government of *multepal* on Cozumel (Roys 1957:3), ruled by several leaders representing different parts of the island during the Decadent period. Because District 1 appears to be an "empty" center, it is likely that at least some of these rulers maintained dual residences, with second homes in their main support communities. This is essentially a replication of Mayapan at a lower order of magnitude. As is the case at Mayapan, it is possible that one of the rulers bore the title of *halach uinic* (Roys 1957) whereas the others were *batabs* in their own towns.

Mayapan might represent, on the other hand, the application of an old and well-established principle of elite organization at a higher level. The gathering of people into communities mentioned in the Maya historical and legendary literature could have been efficiently carried out by dual residence on the part of local leadership in outlying centers (P.L.W. Sabloff, personal communication, 1974). Unfortunately, as mentioned before, the literature is lacking in information relating to lower-order communities. Both Peter Martyr (MacNutt 1912:35) and Lopez de Gomara (Simpson 1966:52), however, mention the fact that there were people in Potonchan who maintained dual residence, and that the country homes were magnificent multichambered affairs situated on courts. Although Lopez de Gomara surmises that these were maintained for pleasure, it is possible that they were the formal administrative centers of outlying communities.

Certainly any political system integrating a number of widely spread communities into a polity would have required an efficient communication-transportation network, as well as institutions encouraging the movement of people between outlying communities and the capital. On Cozumel there are remnants of possible ceremonial circuits that may have been involved in the ritually sanctioned circulation of people between major and minor centers for a variety of purposes including the dissemination of policy decisions. The importance of ritual in the Decadent political structure is well attested in the historical literature (Coe 1965; Roys 1933, 1939; Tozzer 1941). We see no reason to demarcate "secular" political ritual from "sacred" religious ritual in this time period. No doubt the Yucatecan Maya were fully aware of the political or economic ramifications of certain kinds of ritual, but the religious and social sanctions still formed the fundamental matrix of thought and action among these people.

This is not to say that the precontact Maya were rugged individualists living in a state of social anarchy or that their social system was in any sense "simple" relative to states as defined by social theorists. The integrative forces of sanctions embedded in thought and action are as powerful and pervasive as the reified rules and regulations of institutionalized bureaucracy.

Customs determining the ownership and use of land on Cozumel, for example, may have had strong political ramifications. The wall system on the island implies a rather rigorous control of land use and a degree of cooperation among communities in determining their jurisdictions. This situation can perhaps be reconciled with what is known of modern and historical Maya practices in the following way. In addition to the established allusions to common ownership of land in the Colonial period (in Tozzer 1941:230), there are various references to the ownership of villages and towns (Roys 1962:61). The apparent contradiction in these observations is resolved if land was technically owned by noble families, but in actual practice this ownership allowed them the right and obligation to arbitrate disputes over land use, to prevent infringement on the rights of individual families in their communities, and to protect their community lands from encroachment by others. Theoretically, land could be "owned" by individual families who used it, by nobles residing in communities in cases of internal dispute, and by regional lords in cases of intercommunity dispute without any contradiction. Again, technically, tribute was rent paid to the noble owners for the use of resources by communities in the Maya area (e.g., for salt at Chauaca), but in actuality was payment for services rendered in a system in which rights and obligations flowed both ways. This perspective is in concert with the general impression given in historical documents (Roys 1939; Chi in Tozzer 1941:230) that although the resources were public property, improvements on resources and the fruits of individual incentive were privately owned. Disputes over access to prime natural resources could be resolved if in fact ownership was invested in the people responsible for arbitrating them.

No doubt this system of arbitration was highly politicized in actual practice. This would be particularly true in the vicinity of trading centers where incentive for commercial exploitation of resources was strong. Given this incentive, the presence of a complex and relatively permanent definition of the landscape is appropriate on Cozumel and the East Coast generally. The regularity of the fieldwall network on Cozumel and the lack of divisions between communities imply that ultimate responsiblity for access to land and other resources lay in the hands of a powerful few who had centralized control of the island.

There are allusions in the literature to the fact that members of the nobility had privileged access to certain valued resources, such as prime cotton and corn land, or hollows suitable for growing cacao. It is easy to envision a normatively egalitarian system of arbitration that was politically abused, resulting in actual control of commercial resources concentrated in the hands of the nobility in some areas. Thus the most successful merchants may well have been members of the nobility. Nonetheless there is no a priori reason to believe that ambitious members of the commoner class could not rise to positions of political power through successful commercial enterprise.

Religious Organization

The degree to which *ideology* (the body of articulated sanctions promoting integrated and co-ordinated behavior in society) was dependent upon religious reinforcement or expression through symbols relating the social to the cosmic order is far from resolved. Many students of the Maya have identified a trend toward an ideology more independent of religious reinforcement in the era following the collapse of the Classic centers, particularly in the Decadent period (Pollock 1962:16-17; Proskouriakoff 1962:136; Tozzer 1941). This is an issue of immense complexity. Here we merely offer additional data and some thoughts on the subject.

The Decadent period is a time marked by a relative decrease in the importance of centralized religious architecture and a relative increase in dispersed religious structures. It should be stressed from the outset of this discussion, however, that centralized edifices and presumably the institutions housed in them are still very much apparent at this time. This emphasis is necessary because some investigators have viewed this trend as a gradual replacement of centralized with dispersed religious foci, whereas we view them as functionally interdependent phenomena.

At Mayapan, for example, where a large number of shrines and oratories occur in the context of households, this situation has been interpreted as a reflection of the breakdown of control over religious activities by the organized priesthood and an increase in the importance of nonspecialists in ceremonial and has been labeled "secularization." At the same time, the Mayapan pattern shows a general rise in private worship over public worship. The proliferation of idols, found in almost every conceivable context, is added support for the idea that religion was "vulgarized" in the Decadent.

On the other hand, some of the most imposing public architecture dating to the Decadent is found at Mayapan, and Chi (in Tozzer 1941:230) notes that the inhabitants spent much of their time tending the temples of the cult of Kukulcan. Although this informant may have been prejudiced by his claim of descent from a high priest at Mayapan, clearly centralized community ceremonial and the organized priesthood were far from defunct at this capital.

Outside of Mayapan, on the East Coast and especially on Cozumel, dispersed diminutive religious edifices are not as strongly associated with households. On the contrary, the majority of such structures appear to be nodes on community and supracommunity ceremonial circuits. Ethnohistoric information confirms that this pattern of dispersed religious structures disassociated from residences is present at other coastal settlements in the Conquest period. Thus, the particular emphasis on religious foci in residential contexts at Mayapan appears to be an extreme in the range of location for dispersed shrines and temples. The settlement of Buena Vista on Cozumel is probably close to the other end of the range because only one of the dispersed shrines can be tentatively associated with a household. The correlation of a movement from centralized to dispersed religious structures with a change from public to private worship is not supported outside the confines of Mayapan. When the peninsula is viewed as a whole, a rather more complicated set of dynamics seems to be operating.

During the Decadent period the Maya cosmos was populated with a bewildering variety of deities and aspects of deities. These entities were physically rendered in the form of idols and virtually every kind of social grouping from the family to the state operated under the aegis of one or more of them. Cosmic symbols were probably used to reinforce the distinctiveness of different groups with presumably overlapping membership. Although hierarchical order or structure relating the cosmic forces to each other was present, it appears to have been superseded to a large extent by dyadic relations between deities that replicated those between members of the groups identified with these forces. On the one hand, religious symbolism reinforced the heterogeneity of Decadent society. On the other, it provided a medium for expressing relationships between social groups in basically nonhierarchical terms.

Diminutive religious structures were commissioned by the membership of particular social groups and were dedicated principally to the deities associated with such groups. In this way, the proliferation of shrines, temples, and idols tended to emphasize the heterogeneous, frag-

menting processes operating in society. This perspective ties into the idea that, on Cozumel, variability in masonry religious structures was generated as much by available economic resources as by the appropriateness of the desired product for a given ritual purpose.

If the patterns identified in relation to dispersed religious structures have some basis in fact, it is apparent that religion must have reinforced integrative mechanisms as well. For although these structures may have been edifying particular components of society, they were clustered together or linked by ceremonial circuits bounding and interrelating communities. In this way, religious structures contributed to the definition of social, political, and economic spaces and networks integrating communities, regions, and ultimately the peninsula with regions beyond it.

Although the role of the organized priesthood in this scheme is easy to explicate, the actual relationship between centralized and peripheral ceremonials probably goes beyond the mechanical scheme proposed here. Contrary to Tozzer, religious specialists apparently had a hand in all but the most private of ritual: "The office of the priest was to discuss and to teach their sciences, to make known their needs and the remedies for them, to preach and to publish the festival days, to order sacrifices and to administer their sacraments" (Landa in Tozzer 1941:111-112). From Landa's discussion of festivals, it seems that processional activities were often, if not always, an intrinsic part of them. With possible exceptions, such as the festival of Kukulcan, priests played an active part in preparing and administering festivals that had centralized temples and public buildings as their ultimate focus. From analogy with historical and modern pilgrimage practices in Mesoamerica (V. Turner 1974), feast days were particularly important to the circulation of people outside their communities. In regulating festivals and publishing their days, the priesthood was in fact responsible for regulating the movement of large numbers of people on ceremonial circuits. Because the majority of aboriginal holidays were movable feasts, such regulation must have been crucial.

Festivals and the processions associated with them provided an important structural balance that countered the trends toward an anarchic cosmos and a fragmenting social order in the Decadent. The Classic period transcendent idea of a cohesive, hierarchical cosmos in which everything has its place was successfully replaced in the Postclassic by the transcendent event of moving from shrine to shrine, weaving a fabric of unity over the dispersed symbols of heterogeneity.

Thus religion, at the local level on Cozumel, provided a vital matrix for the expression of multiple social identities of any given individual, as well as the expression of cohesion, transcendent unity, and coordinated effort on the part of the island's inhabitants as a whole. No doubt it also provided a way of regulating the circulation of foreigners on the island by scheduling their appearance in numbers and by directing their movements along set paths.

The mechanical, inflexible quality of this scheme is offset by the demonstrable importance of personal mediation and interpretation of the cosmic forces by *chilanes*. Prophets, oracles, and sorcerers, the mouthpieces of the gods, provided a vital "antistructure" (V. Turner 1974), balancing the fatalistic cycles of cosmic events that were the structural underpinning of Maya ideology. The ability to respond to natural or social crises in a coordinated way must have been important at all times in Maya culture history. It must have been particularly important to the inhabitants of Decadent period Cozumel who serviced interactions between far-flung and often hostile groups (Freidel 1975; Sabloff and Rathje 1975b).

The religious sanctions permitting and even encouraging the movement of people over long distances through traditionally hostile territory must have been quite strong. In 1535 the lords of Mani attempted to go on pilgrimage to the sacred *cenote* of Chichen Itza to ward off severe drought. Traveling under sanction, they delivered themselves into the hands of their enemies, the Cocom, who, after greeting and housing them with all due hospitality, murdered them. Despite such gross abuse, traveling under ritual sanction in time of warfare and mistrust must have been the only feasible manner of moving peacefully over long distances and through the territory of independent polities.

It has been noted that pilgrims, thought to be traders by Roys (1957), traveled from the Tabasco region to the shrine of Ix Chel on Cozu-

mel. The argument can probably be couched in stronger terms. All traders were in fact "pilgrims" traveling under divine sanction for the ostensible purpose of visiting shrines and participating in festivals. Even the Mexica *pochteca* traveled under heavy sanction, stopping regularly at shrines along their routes and worshipping nightly their particular god at improvised altars, thereby creating a string of improvised shrines along the route. Peaceful economic intercourse in the Decadent period cannot be understood apart from the religious sanctions that permitted it. If the last phase in the culture history of Mesoamerica is characterized by heterogeneity in the cosmic and social orders, these sanctions may have been much stronger in earlier periods that were marked by greater internal cohesiveness on both counts, or they may not have been necessary at all.

From this perspective, it seems quite reasonable to suppose that Cozumel, documented as one of the three major pilgrimage sanctuaries on the Yucatan peninsula in the Decadent and located on the coast at a time when canoe trade was ascendent, was also a major commercial center. The correlations between pilgrimage centers and commercial centers is strong (V. Turner 1974). Furthermore, it is well documented at known pilgrimage centers in Mesoamerica at the time of the conquest. The example of Cholula is particularly outstanding. This center, sacred to Quetzalcoatl and a pilgrimage terminus of great renown, remained a very active commercial marketing town even after its incorporation into the Mexica empire (Lopez de Gomara in Simpson 1966:123-131; Bernal Diaz del Castillo in Maudslay 1910:1-24).

Economic Organization

The institutionalized exchange of goods and services has formed a prominent theme in the discussion of Cozumel's settlement patterns. Although we clearly have not proved that Cozumel was a major Decadent period trading center, we hope that the foundation for such an argument, which will be carried further in future reports, has been started. Rather than reiterate points made in earlier chapters, two major propositions pervading our analysis are considered. First, long-distance trade and local economies are significantly interrelated, especially at nodes on the long-distance networks. Second, warehousing facilities on Cozumel, and perhaps elsewhere during the Post-classic, are nucleated but not necessarily located at centralized port facilities.

Anne Chapman's (1957) seminal article on Aztec and Maya long-distance trade has had a profound effect on subsequent thinking on the subject. Her salient point is that long-distance trade as an institution is generally distinct and independent of market institutions servicing local or regional needs. This is a theoretical position that follows from a theme established by Polanyi to some degree. Highly organized long-distance commerce can exist outside the matrix of the western conception of free market.

Chapman takes the position that Mexica long-distance trade was the exclusive province of the *pochteca* and that the dealings of long-distance traders in local markets were casual and incidental. Most transactions were in the form of direct exchange between merchants in ports of trade. We believe that the first position does not agree with certain facts about the Mexica imperial economy. The descriptions left by Bernal Diaz del Castillo (in Maudslay 1910:70-73), Cortes (in Pagden 1971:102-103), and Lopez de Gomara (in Simpson 1966:160-163) note the abundance of exotic luxury goods in the markets of Tlateloco and other central valley cities. Virtually all the commodities exchanged by the *pochteca* in ports of trade are also found in the markets, in addition to some such as cacao that these merchants apparently did not move in quantity. Interestingly enough, Chapman (1957:125) notes that the kinds of commodities exported by the *pochteca* were found in the markets and admits in passing the possibility that these merchants acquired some of the exports in markets. At the same time, she seemingly ignores the fact that similar imports were moved by the *pochteca* and were also found in the markets. Thus, the relationship between marketing and long-distance trade seems to have been rather more complicated than that proposed by Chapman.

In the first place, the Mexica empire incorporated a large number of non-Mexica merchants such as the Cholulans into their economic network. The fact that the markets and fairs of Cholula were filled with salt, cotton, gold, featherwork,

and other exotics is clearly implied in the accounts of writers such as Lopez de Gomara (in Simpson 1966:127-131). Presumably the goods were reaching these markets via the home-based traders there, as well as through merchants traveling there from elsewhere. How the Cholulans obtained such goods is unknown, but they may have maintained their own expeditions beyond the borders of the empire because they definitely had such long-distance connections prior to their incorporation by the Mexica.

Second, a mechanism for exchange in long-distance ports of trade (aside from direct negotiation between merchants) was the fair. Drawing on the famous Texcocan chronicler Ixtlilxochitl, Chapman (1957:140) mentions that fairs occurred at Xicalango but summarily brushes them aside. Fairs are also mentioned at Cholula and Lopez de Gomara specifically states:

> In the land of Acalan, so they say, the people have the custom of choosing as their lord the most prosperous merchant, which is why Apoxpalon had been chosen, for he enjoyed a large land trade in cotton, cacao, slaves, salt and gold . . . in colored shells . . . in resin and other incense for the temples; in pigments and dyes . . . and many other articles of merchandise, luxuries and necessities. *For this purpose he held fairs in many towns, such as Nito,* where he had agents and separate districts for his own vassals and traders. (Lopez de Gomara in Simpson 1966: 354; emphasis ours)

The idea that these fairs were a common means of exchanging goods is further implied by an account given to Cortes of Spanish incursions into the port areas of Honduras:

> Among the seven men was one from Acalan, a merchant, who had dwelt a long time in Nito, where the Spaniards were. He said that many bearded men . . . had entered the town a year since and sacked it, mistreating the citizens and merchants, causing the flight of the brother of Aquiahuilquin (who had a storehouse there) and all the other merchants. Many of them had asked Aquiahuilquin's permission to settle and trade in his country, *for the fairs had been destroyed and the merchants ruined by the foreigners.* (Lopez de Gomara in Simpson 1966:364; emphasis ours)

The importance of fairs held in conjunction with religious festivals is well attested in the Conquest period of Highland Guatemala (Borhegyi 1965; Miles 1957). There fairs were held by the rulers of towns or merchants who taxed the participants.

If they were such an important institution, it might well be asked why so few fairs were actually described. The Spanish were describing things as they saw them and were not scheduling their arrival in any given place to coincide conveniently with social phenomena of interest to later scholars. An observer arriving at the famous highland-lowland wholesaling market of San Francisco El Alto in Highland Guatemala would see a scatter of houses on an off-day (McBryde 1947). On a market day, the same scene would be filled with thousands of people and rows of improvised stalls stocked with exotic goods. Similarly, someone attending the yearly market of Eight Monkeys in Momostenango or the festival of El Señor de Equipulas in his Guatemalan sanctuary would be greatly impressed with the throng of merchants and customers. The same scenes are relatively unobtrusive during the rest of the year. Thus even though eyewitness corroboration from the Spanish is lacking in many cases, it does not seem unreasonable to accept the statements of the merchants themselves that fairs were an important means of exchange in trading centers.

If fairs, rather than or in addition to direct exchange, were the major form of exchange in ports of trade (and San Francisco El Alto is certainly analogous to such ports in terms of location and function), this might help account for the exotics in the market systems of Central Mexico. There is also some evidence that the Mexica themselves maintained ports of trade within the borders of the empire at frontier locations. Chapman (1957:137) specifically discusses the example of the trading center of Tochtepec in Oaxaca. Aside from the fact that this center is located within the confines of the Empire, it is difficult to distinguish it from other trading centers defined as ports. Like ports of trade, it has a colony of *pochteca*, and presumably was inhabited by merchants from other areas if it was indeed a trading center. It is also located in a border region like ports on the Gulf Coast. The assumption is that such border towns operated in a significantly different way

from trading towns located in weak borderland polities. It is difficult to understand how such differences would affect the mode of exchange. It seems simpler and more reasonable to presume that the fair, as well as direct exchange between foreign merchants, operated in towns within the confines of the Empire in the same way they did outside it.

Chapman points out that there are similarities in the way trade was carried out in the Gulf of Honduras and Tabasco-Veracruz areas. She states (1957:146): "There are references stemming from the conquistadores testifying to the existence of factors and warehouses, *both of which were notably lacking within the Aztec Empire proper as well as in Yucatan.*" However, the San Juan de Ulua region, under Mexica domination for over 100 years at the time of the conquest, was a trading area very much like the rest of the Gulf Coast east of it. San Juan de Ulua caught the attention of each of the first three expeditions to Mesoamerica because here the Spaniards found people willing to engage in a lively exchange of gold, precious featherwork, and other items for the trinkets of Spain. Adjacent to this region was Isla de Sacrificios, described as more than a league from the mainland, with its shrines and sacrificial altars. This place was sacred to canoe-using people and there is no reason to think that it was less frequented by traders than the more diminutive shrines near Potonchan. Excavation on the island by Nuttal (1910) produced Fine Orange, Plumbate, and Mixteca-Puebla wares, as well as exotics such as *teocalli* vases. Thus the people using this sacred island probably had a history of long-distance contacts.

In terms of facilities, there is a much more important description. Cortes and some of his men made a foray in from the beach in the general direction of Cotaxtla, a regional center of some importance. Lopez de Gomara gives the following account:

> Immediately beyond the river they came upon a deserted village, whose inhabitants had fled at the approach of our men. Cortes entered a large house, which must have belonged to the lord, made of adobes and timber, with floors that had been raised more than a fathom from the ground, and a roof covered with straw, of a strange and handsome

appearance viewed from below. *The house had many rooms, some filled with jars of honey, centli, and other grains which they eat and keep in storage all the year, and other rooms filled with cotton garments and featherwork decorated with gold and silver. A great deal of the same was found in the other houses, which were built in the same style.* . . . The village had a temple, resembling a house in its living quarters, with a low but massive tower at its summit and on top of the tower a kind of chapel. . . . From this village they proceeded to three or four others, none of which had more than two hundred houses, all abandoned but full of provisions . . . like the first. (in Simpson 1966:64-65; emphasis ours)

The goods described are typical long-distance trade commodities and the facilities are clearly warehouses. There is reason to believe that in this particular instance the trade was administered to some degree by agents of the Mexica government. These may have been *pochteca* like those at Tochtepec, because Teudilli (Teuhtilli) and the other Nahuatl speaking leaders of Cotaxtla and the surrounding area are consistently described as ambassadors of Moctezuma. They negotiate in his name and are in direct communication with the capital. This contrasts with other leaders such as the Cholulans who are considered allies or vassals of the Mexica. Other Mexica operating in the region of Cempoala are identified as tax gatherers or garrisoned warriors, but Teudilli is called governor by the Spanish.

Support for the notion that this trade was partially administered by agents of the government is given by Bernal Diaz when describing employees of Moctezuma: "Let us go on to the Indian women who did the weaving and the washing [of cloth], who made such wonderful featherwork designs; the greater part of [these goods?] was brought daily from some towns of the province on the north coast near Vera Cruz called Cotaxtla" (in Maudslay 1910:68). Nonetheless, the fact that much trade in small luxury items, gold, and cloth was carried on between local natives and the Spanish rank and file implies that trade was not the exclusive province of the emperor's agents.

From descriptions of their canoes, the people of San Juan de Ulua region were as adept at canoe transport as their eastern neighbors. They were in communication with other coastal peoples, as demonstrated by their foreknowledge of Cortes's arrival. The news had traveled up into the territory of the Totonacs along the coast. They maintained warehouses and moved salt, cotton, honey, and other commodities into the empire. Cholula apparently was one of several intermediary trading centers for such goods moving toward the Basin of Mexico. The details of such communication-transportation networks are no doubt more complicated than the sketch given here. It seems reasonable to propose, however, that the simple model of trading ports in neutral territory is an inadequate perspective on the situation (contra the earlier papers of the Cozumel Archaeological Project, such as Rathje and Sabloff [1973]).

The great importance of long-distance trade lies not so much in supplying important status-significant luxuries to the elites as it does in the stimulation of local demand for exotics and local production for commercial export (Flannery 1968). Perhaps it is by investigating trading institutions at the time of Spanish contact that we may come to understand how localized economies were integrated into regional and interregional economies. Unless there was total self-sufficiency at the level of the local economy, any model offered at that level must take into consideration the way local economies articulate with regional and interregional networks (a point well made by Rathje 1972).

The notion that long-distance trade operated as an open system articulated with the local and regional economies does justice to the information presented by Sabloff and Rathje (1975b) and others. At the time of Spanish contact the commodities moving in bulk over long-distances were not simply luxuries but were also necessities of everyday life for the common folk. Even the *pochteca*, the outstanding example of administered traders, carried utilitarian items such as flint knives and combs along with their fancy wares. The case of the Mexica trade embargo against Tlaxcala (Lopez de Gomara in Simpson 1966:122) is even more significant because the principal items blocked by the Mexica were salt and cotton. Hundreds of merchants from Tlaxcala accompanied Cortes to Cholula to obtain these commodities, and it was salt and cotton that the Tlaxcalan authorities took as booty in their sack of the city.

Finally, Chapman (1957:120) has proposed that long-distance trade must have been distinct from market economies because its disintegration through neglect and disruption in the Colonial period resulted in no great economic turbulence. Although particular routes, transport systems, and commodities surely fell by the wayside, others were actively maintained. Thus, in the years following the initial incursions, while places like Itzamkanac, Xicalango, and Cozumel were quickly declining in wealth and importance, over a quarter of a million pounds of salt were culled annually from the beds of northwestern Yucatan (Roys 1957) for export to Mexico and elsewhere by the towns of Canul province, which used the old canoe transport system (pointed out to us by R. Thompson, personal communication, 1973; see also Andrews 1980). These beds constitute only a fraction of the total that were actively exploited for regional and long-distance commerce during the Colonial period. With regard to the use of aboriginal long-distance trading institutions, A.C. Maudslay wrote in 1899 that:

> The great festival of the year is held in January, and then for a week or more the usually half-deserted little town of Esquipulas swarms with pilgrims. In old days its fame was so great that it attracted worshippers all the way from Mexico and Panama and the fair which was carried out at the same time was the great commercial event of the year. Thither the English merchants from Belize brought their wares and carried on what was practically the whole of the foreign business of Honduras, Salvador and Guatemala, taking in exchange the native grown indigo. (McBryde 1947:83)

Similarly, commercial production for long-distance export of indigenous products like cochineal dyes were not only maintained but were expanded under Spanish rule. The very fact that the Colonial period is marked not by the intense isolation of regions in Mesoamerica but rather by their total incorporation into a much larger economic sphere maintained by the Spanish argues for a previous articulation of long-distance trade and market economies.

This does not imply that the ports of trade defined by Chapman did not exist. The importance of her article is undeniable because it clearly isolates one of the crucial aspects of long-distance trade in Mesoamerica, the administration of bulk exchange between foreigners. Yet goods must be initially gathered and ultimately consumed. The kinds of goods moving long distances at the time of contact were important to societies as a whole and were, for the most part, subject to piecemeal production and consumption. Thus, at least some of the trading centers situated on long-distance routes must have been administering the collection of commodities into bulk shipments and the distribution of commodities into smaller retail or short-distance wholesale units. These are the functions of the *entrepot*, as defined by Vance (1970). Ports of trade and entrepots were probably not mutually exclusive places. They probably did not encompass the total range of trading centers on long-distance routes, as once a year the festival of Esquipulas is just as much the scene of a major trading center as any of the ports of trade in Tabasco or Honduras were. On the contrary, it seems more likely that these functions were usually combined in some way. The degree of foreign transshipment or local commodity production may have depended largely on what was locally exploitable.

The local economies found in the vicinity of Postclassic ports of trade and other trading centers in Mesoamerica make some sense from this perspective. In spite of all the exotics flowing through the Bay of Honduras, for example, it was still a major production center for cacao, a crucial commodity. Similarly, Itzamkanac was surrounded by cacao groves. The Chetumal region produced honey, wax, and cacao, among other things. Potonchan had potentially enormous grain production in the ridged fields surrounding it. Such fields are described in detail by Lopez de Gomara in the battle of Cintla near Potonchan in Tabasco: "The meeting place of the two armies was cultivated land, cut up by many ditches and deep streams, difficult to cross, among which our men became confused and disorganized . . . the foot went to the right, crossing ditches at every step" (in Simpson 1966:46). Corn and other grains were important trade items in central Mexico, and cotton pollen has recently been reported from ridged fields in Belize (B. Dahlin, personal communication, 1975) so this commodity may have been grown in such places. Chauaca, a large trading center on the northern coast of Yucatan, not only had its vast salt beds but also had diversified production into groves of copal incense trees. Finally, Cozumel was producing substantial quantities of honey and wax, well-established commerical commodities (Roys 1957:162; Simpson 1966:34). Presumably they were also for export. Thus, far from being a distinct entity, long-distance trade was apparently stimulating the development of local economies. Roys's (1943) observation that the markets near the coast in Yucatan were apparently larger and more diversified than those of the interior makes sense if in fact water transport was the order of the day.

Qualifying the nodes on long-distance trade routes as entrepots as well as transshipment centers makes the theoretical argument for Cozumel as a trading center virtually complete. The island is strategically located on the water route around the peninsula and a sanctuary of interregional renown, and, from the perspective of canoe transportation, it is centrally located on the East Coast. In short, it is the ideal location for an entrepot servicing the production centers on the coast in front of it.

Methodologically, the notion that long-distance trade was effectively interrelated with the local economy on Cozumel has necessitated viewing the ramifications of this factor throughout the totality of settlement patterns rather than searching for the separate and distinct remains of a special port facility. Consequently, as noted earlier, several features of the total settlement pattern have been interpreted from this perspective. The settlement component most specifically related to trade on Cozumel is nucleation, and, as with other aspects dealt with so far, there is some evidence that it is not peculiar to Cozumel.

The agglutinated and massive single-unit rubble substructures, identified as warehousing facilities, are dispersed on the island and are disassociated from the beaching areas that might be considered the logical location of warehouses in a coastal trading center. The location of warehousing facilities in the San Juan de Ulua region described by Lopez de Gomara (in Simpson 1966) confirms that this arrangement is within the range of locations for similar facilities at the time of the conquest. Other shared features are the absence of fortifications, the relatively small size of the

communities specializing in such facilities, and the nucleation of storage areas, represented here by superstructures rather than substructures. It is possible that the substructures in the San Juan region are also comparable to those on Cozumel because Escalona-Ramos (1946) reports the presence of massive, low (2m) earthen platforms in settlements near the coast just south of Vera Cruz. However, the chronological placement of these settlements is undetermined.

The particular form of nucleation on Cozumel is posited to be single-unit warehouses on agglutinated platforms. There is some possible corroboration for this pattern in the Bay of Honduras region. In one of the towns located on a river near the sea, apparently not Nito or Naco but one of many communities in the region specializing in warehousing facilities, Lopez de Gomara gives the following description of Cortes's exploration:

> They slept in the open but (were awakened by a loud alarm), at which they rushed into the square, while the citizens fled. In the morning they searched the houses and found a great deal of raw cotton, mantles and other clothing, and a quantity of dry maize and salt—this last being the principle object of their search, for they had had none for many days. They also found a store of cacao, chili, fruit, and other provisions, such as turkeys, many pheasants, quail, and dogs in coops. (in Simpson 1966:368)

Although it is unfortunately unclear whether or not the superstructures or substructures are nucleated in this instance, the description implies that the facilities were situated near the main square of the town. In other words, the warehouses were more or less centralized. As noted above, Henderson *et al.* (1979) also report the presence of a large platform at Naco, which they infer was used for storage.

In the course of their survey of northwestern Honduras, Strong *et al.* (1938) carried out some settlement pattern analysis and excavation at the known trading center of Naco. They give the following description of the center of town:

> To judge from our test cuts, these long, low mounds (15-20 meters by 60-70 meters) north of the central pyramid complex consist of rows of house floors. Owing to the curve of mounds 2 and 14 they en-

close a crescentic area which may have been the old plaza of Naco. Our excavations, although very incomplete, indicates that with adequate time a whole series of house floors could be easily cleared . . . we encountered two pieces of European glazed pottery. (1938:32)

Here the single-unit structures are not organized into *plazuela* groups but share large substructures. This may be a localized relationship between nucleation and trade facilities. However, the information on the San Juan region and the accounts reporting that traders from Acalan and other regions maintained factors and warehouses in Naco imply that it is a correlation of more general geographic distribution.

Although the information on substructures lacking masonry superstructures is generally scanty for northern Quintana Roo, there are indications that agglutinated substructures and massive low substructures are found elsewhere in the regions besides Cozumel. Sanders, in his survey of northern Quintana Roo, reports two settlements that sound very much like those on Cozumel. Monte Bravo is situated about 15km inland from the northern coast near Solfarino:

This site consists of half a dozen good-sized mounds of peculiar form . . . the mounds are scattered through the grassland. . . . There are no pyramids. Four large mounds, averaging 60-70m. long and 15-20m. wide, are low extensive platforms with curious hilly elevations on one end, a type I have not seen elsewhere in Yucatan but common in Vera Cruz. Half a dozen or so smaller platforms complete this group. (Sanders 1955:185)

Historically, several trading centers are reported in this region, including Conil with its market court (Roys 1957).

The second settlement, Vista Alegre, is identified by Sanders as a trading center. He states:

Named after a headland about 5 km. east of Chiquila on the south shore of the lagoon, the site begins some 50 m. behind a mangrove swamp, which borders a small inlet just east of the headland. . . . The largest [mound] is a pyramid, 12-15 m. high, which dominates the entire lagoon. . . . Scattered through the thicket were at least three smaller pyra-

mids, 3-5 m. high, and a very extensive low platform which may have served as the base of the cacique's palace. A dozen house mounds were counted and there were probably more, all of good size (one tested for sherds measured 12-18 m.). No intact buildings were seen, only platforms and pyramids. . . . Surface indications of pottery, like the house mounds, are fairly frequent, all pointing to the presence of a true town. The size of the house mounds suggests that it was not an agricultural or laboring class settlement but probably a merchant community. (Sanders 1955:188)

Vista Alegre was one of the few sites in northern Quintana Roo where Sanders found positive evidence of a Modified Florescent occupation. Sanders's low extensive mound may be an agglutinated or massive substructure comparable to those on Cozumel. Although the location of this settlement on a protected lagoon bordering the northern coast is reasonable for a community oriented to coastal trade, it does not fit the pattern of locating warehousing facilities away from the coast. In this respect we are undoubtedly working with the barest fragments of a wider locational range for such facilities at the time of the conquest.

This particular form of nucleation, agglutinated or massive low platforms in combination with dispersed smaller platforms, is distinct from the general trend toward compact, fortified settlements in the years just preceding the Spanish Conquest (Kurjack and Andrews 1976). It seems more than coincidental that this configuration is found in the Bay of Honduras region (Strong *et al.* 1938:Figure 3), in Vera Cruz near the coast (Escalona-Ramos 1946:563-567), and in Coastal Quintana Roo. Although some of the sites reported by Andrews (1943) in southwestern Campeche also seem to fit this pattern, they are not described in sufficient detail to be certain. It is, in short, a configuration that shows some promise of being associated with areas known to be actively involved in long-distance trade during the Postclassic.

Given the difficulties and uncertainties of long-distance transport, whether by land or by sea, both the collection-disbursement of goods and their transshipment would have required such facilities.

The peculiar combination of nucleated warehouses located in dispersed and otherwise unimposing communities is not so easily explained. Earlier, we took the attitude that the construction and maintenance of such facilities were carried out by families and communities and were not part of a master plan. In this sense, the dispersion of warehousing is analogous to the dispersion of religious foci in the Postclassic. These two features of Cozumel's settlement patterns were probably generated by the same factors. Just as the construction of religious buildings brought prestige to individual families and other social groupings within communities and yet contributed to the communities as defined and interrelated entities, so the development of warehousing facilities served to promote the well-being of individual families and the community as a whole by integrating them into a larger economic sphere. From this perspective, merchandizing was a family business not only in the Maya region but also within the Mexica empire below the level of the elite *pochteca*.

Thus, viewing merchandizing as an outgrowth of the domestic unit of production and consumption (a glorified cottage industry) presupposes a communication-transportation network of enormous complexity and the articulation of local economies into long-distance trade operating at a variety of levels simultaneously. This is precisely the type of complexity found in the modern marketing systems of Highland Guatemala (McBryde 1947), and there is no reason to think these modern traders are more adept or sophisticated than their forebears.

No doubt we have barely scratched the surface of the relevant historical literature pertaining to the institutions that maintained communication-transportation networks in the Decadent period. Given their close ties with Sahagun's elite Mexica informants, the *pochteca*, for example, may be only a particularly prominent example of merchant sodalities operating at a variety of social levels and in diverse regions within central Mexico. Although the organization of the Maya *ppolom* has yet to be elucidated, there are indications that these merchants may have had similarly complex social groupings. Some of the modern *cofradias* of Highland Guatemala may be analogous to such groupings because, in addition to

the religious festivals that they organize, they profit from the commercial fairs held in conjunction with them. Before we can proceed to formulate models of long-distance trade in the earlier periods of Mesoamerica with any confidence, we have much to learn about this rich and complex cultural phenomenon in the days of its final glory.

A Final Comment

Finally, we would like to return to the question of the relevance of our data and interpretations to the postulated rise in secularism during the Decadent period. It is commonplace for the Decadent period to be described as secular in comparison to earlier periods in Maya history. Thompson (1966:141) notes that "religion had lost its predominant place in the culture." Elsewhere, Thompson (1957:624) talks about "the rise of secular forces at the expense of sacerdotal control" at Mayapan. Sabloff and Rathje (1975a, 1975b; Rathje 1975) also have emphasized the growth of a materialistic mercantile ideology throughout the Postclassic period. Although there definitely is less emphasis on major religious architecture along with a decentralization of religious structures, the view that the Decadent period was more secular than earlier times is probably too simplistic. If we take *secular* to mean "of or pertaining to the temporal rather than to the spiritual" (also "secularize: to convert from ecclesiastical or religious to civil or lay use or ownership . . . to cause to draw away from religious orientation"; *The American Heritage Dictionary of the English Language*, Houghton Mifflin, 1976), then it is difficult to argue that the Decadent period was very much more secular than the Classic period. Clearly, "the age was materialistic" (Pollock 1962: 16), but it was not necessarily secular.

On Cozumel, we found community shrines, the possible use of ceremonial circuits to bind the island's population together, and the use of religion to legitimize, protect, and control trade on the island. As Freidel and Cliff (1978:204) have strongly argued:

> In brief, the ideology binding elites together on the Yucatan peninsula was manifestly religious in language and institutional organization as was the idology operative among the common people who

served them. It was at the interface between noble and commoner that the bond lacked strong religious sanctions and was, perforce, based on more pragmatic and materialistic values. This perspective would explain both the more modest architecture of elite centers and the general dispersion of energy invested in religious structures which marks the Decadent Period. On the one hand, the centralized structures were designed for small elite audiences; on the other, the social integration of the common-folk required a substantial, albeit diffused, investment in religious architecture and networks defined by such architecture. No doubt elites manipulated the ritual circulation of people and used it for political and economic ends, but it seems likely that they were unable to fully master the religious sentiments of their followers while remaining committed to a stance as foreigners.

The religious orientation of Decadent period Cozumel, and probably of the northern lowlands as a whole, was quite strong, although its expression was very different from earlier periods of Maya civilization. The attempt to understand religious and economic organization in the Decadent period and the nature of their development, as well as their integration, is just one of the factors which makes the relatively neglected archaeology of the Decadent period so fascinating and filled with potential. We can only hope that the recent rise in interest in the Maya just prior to the Spanish Conquest will prove to be an enduring development and that our understanding of this late phase of ancient Maya civilization will grow apace.

REFERENCES

Abrams, Ira R., and Pamela S. Webster
  n.d.   Toward a developmental process of domestic organization: An approach to the study of domestic change in Xaibe Village, a Maya Community in Northern Belize. Unpublished manuscript.

Adams, Richard E.W.
  1974   A trial estimation of Classic Maya Palace populations at Uaxactun. In *Mesoamerican archaeology: New approaches*, edited by Norman Hammond. London: Duckworth. Pp. 285-296.

Andrews, Anthony P.
  1980   The salt trade of the Maya. *Archaeology* 33(4):24-33.

Andrews, E. Wyllys, IV
  1943   *The archaeology of Southwestern Campeche.* Carnegie Institution of Washington Publication No. 546, Contribution 40, Washington, D.C.
  1965a   *Progress report on the 1960-1964 field season, National Geographic-Tulane University Dzibilchaltun Program.* Middle American Research Institute Publication No. 31. New Orleans: Tulane University. Pp. 23-67.
  1965b   Archaeology and prehistory in the Northern Maya Lowlands: An introduction. In *Handbook of Middle American Indians,* Vol. 2, edited by Gordon R. Willey. Austin: University of Texas Press. Pp. 288-330.

Andrews, E. Wyllys, IV, and Anthony P. Andrews
  1975   *A preliminary study of the ruins of Xcaret, Quintana Roo, Mexico.* Middle American Research Institute, Publication No. 40. New Orleans: Tulane University.

Andrews, E. Wyllys, IV, and George Stuart
  1968   *The ruins of Ikil, Yucatan, Mexico.* Middle American Research Institute Publication No. 31. New Orleans: Tulane University. Pp. 69-80.

Arnold, Channing, and F.J.T. Frost
  1909   *The American Egypt: A record of travel in Yucatan.* New York: Doubleday and Page.

Binford, Lewis R.
  1977   General introduction. In *For theory building in archaeology,* edited by L.R. Binford. New York: Academic Press. Pp. 1-10.

Bullard, William R., Jr.
  1952   Residential property walls at Mayapan. *Carnegie Institution of Washington, Current Report* No. 3, Cambridge.
  1953   Property walls at Mayapan. *Carnegie Institution of Washington, Year Book* 52:258-264.
  1954   Boundary walls and house lots at Mayapan. *Carnegie Institution of Washington,* Current Report No. 13, Cambridge.
  1960   Maya Settlement Patterns in Northeastern Peten, Guatemala. *American Antiquity* 25(3):355-372.

Carr, R.F., and J.E. Hazard
  1961   *Maps of the ruins of Tikal, El Peten, Guatemala.* University of Pennsylvania Museum Monographs, Tikal Report No. 11, Philadelphia.

Chamberlain, Robert S.
  1948   *The Conquest and Colonization of Yucatan 1517-1550.* Carnegie Institution of Washington Publication No. 582, Washington, D.C.

Chapman, Anne
  1957   Post of Trade Enclaves in Aztec and Maya Civilization. In *Trade and market in the early empires*, edited by Karl Polanyi, Conrad M. Arensberg, and H.W. Pearson. New York: Free Press. Pp. 114-153.

Coe, Michael
  1965   A model of ancient community structure in the Maya Lowlands. *Southwestern Journal of Anthropology* 21(2):97-114.

Connor, Judith G.
  1975   Ceramics and artifacts. In *A study of changing Pre-Columbian commercial systems: The 1972-1973 seasons at Cozumel, Mexico*, edited by Jeremy A. Sabloff and William Rathje. Monographs of the Peabody Museum No. 3.

Cambridge: Peabody Museum of Archaeology and Ethnology. Pp. 114-135.

Cowgill, Ursula M.
1962   An agricultural study of the Southern Maya Lowlands. *American Anthropologist* 64:273-286.

Davidson, William V.
1967   A study of settlement patterns, Cozumel Island, Quintana Roo, Mexico. Unpublished Masters Thesis, Department of Geography, Memphis State University.
1975   The geographical setting. In *A study of Pre-Columbian commercial systems: The 1972-1973 seasons at Cozumel, Mexico*, edited by Jeremy A. Sabloff and William Rathje. Monographs of the Peabody Museum No. 3. Cambridge: Peabody Museum of Archaeology and Ethnology. Pp. 47-59.

de Borhegyi, Stephen
1965   Archaeological synthesis of the Guatemalan Highlands. In *Handbook of Middle American Indians*, Vol. 2, Part I, edited by Gordon R. Willey. Austin: University of Texas Press. Pp. 3-58.

Documentos Ineditos
1885-   Relaciones de Yucatan. In *Collecion*
1900   *ineditos relativos al descubrimiento, conquista y organizacion de las Antiguas Posesiones Espanoles de Ultramar*, Second Series, Vols. 11 and 13. Madrid.

Duby, Gertrude, and Frans Blom
1969   The Lacandon. In *Handbook of Middle American Indians*, Vol. 7, edited by Evon Z. Vogt. Austin: University of Texas Press. Pp. 276-297.

Edwards, Clinton R.
1957   Quintana Roo: Mexico's empty quarter. Unpublished Master's Thesis, Department of Geography, University of California, Berkeley.

Escalona-Ramos, Alberto
1946   Algunas ruinas prehispanicas en Quintana Roo. *Boletin de la Sociedad Mexicana de Geographia y Estudistica* 61(3):513-628.

Fernandez, Miguel A.
1945   Exploraciones arqueologicas en la Isla Cozumel, Quintana Roo. *Annals of the Institution of Anthropology and History* I:107-120.

Flannery, Kent
1968   The Olmec and the Valley of Oaxaca: A model of inter-regional interaction in formative times. In *Dumbarton Oaks conference on the Olmec*, edited by Elizabeth P. Benson. Washington, D.C.: Dumbarton Oaks Research Library and Collection. Pp. 79-110.

Freidel, David A.
1975   The Ix Chel shrine and other temples of talking idols. In *A study of Pre-Columbian commercial systems: The 1972-1973 seasons at Cozumel, Mexico*, edited by Jeremy A. Sabloff and William Rathje. Monographs of the Peabody Museum No. 3. Cambridge: Peabody Museum of Archaeology and Ethnology. Pp. 107-113.
1976   Late Postclassic settlement systems on Cozumel Island, Quintana Roo, Mexico. Ph.D. Dissertation, Department of Anthropology, Harvard University.

Freidel, David A., and Maynard B. Cliff
1978   Energy investment in Late Postclassic Maya Masonry religious structures. In *Papers on the economy and architecture of the Ancient Maya*, edited by Raymond Sidrys. Monograph VIII. Los Angeles: Institute of Archaeology. Pp. 184-208.

Freidel, David A., and Richard M. Leventhal
1975   The settlement survey. In *A study of changing Pre-Columbian commercial systems: The 1972-1973 seasons at Cozumel, Mexico*, edited by Jeremy A. Sabloff and William L. Rathje. Monographs of the Peabody Museum No. 3. Cambridge: Peabody Museum of Archaeology and Ethnology. Pp. 60-76.

Garza T. de Gonzales, Silvia, and Edward B. Kurjack B.
1980   *Atlas Arqueológico del Estado de*

Yucatan. Instituto Nacional de Antropología e Historia. Mexico.

Gregory, David A.
1975   San Gervasio. In *A study of changing Pre-Columbian commercial systems: The 1972-1973 seasons at Cozumel, Mexico,* edited by Jeremy A. Sabloff and William L. Rathje. Monographs of the Peabody Museum No. 3. Cambridge: Peabody Museum of Archaeology and Ethnology. Pp. 88-106.

Hammond, Norman, editor
1973   *British Museum-Cambridge University Corozal Project, 1973 interim report.* Cambridge: Centre of Latin American Studies, University of Cambridge.

Harrison, Peter D.
1970   The Central Acropolis, Tikal, Guatemala: A preliminary study of the functions of the structural components during the Late Classic Period. Ph.D. Dissertation, Department of Anthropology, University of Pennsylvania. Ann Arbor: University Microfilms.
1975   Pre-Columbian settlement distributions and external relationships in Southern Quintana Roo Architecture, Part I: *Atti del XL Congresso Internazionale degli Americanists* 1:479-486.

Harrison, Peter D., and B.L. Turner, II, editors
1977   *Pre-Hispanic Maya agriculture.* Albuquerque: University of New Mexico Press.

Haselgrove, Colin
1976   Review of Ancient Civilization and Trade, edited by Jeremy A. Sabloff and C.C. Lamberg-Karlovsky. *Antiquity* 50:160-161.

Haviland, William A.
1963   Excavations of small structures in the Northeast Quadrant of Tikal, Guatemala. Ph.D. Dissertation, Department of Anthropology, University of Pennsylvania. Ann Arbor: University Microfilms.
1970   Principles of descent in 16th Century Yucatan. Unpublished manuscript on file, University of Vermont.

Henderson, John S., Ilene Sterns, Anthony Wonderly, and Patricia A. Urban
1979   Archaeological investigations in the Valle de Naco, Northwestern Honduras: A preliminary report. *Journal of Field Archaeology* 6:169-192.

Holmes, William H.
1895-   *Archaeological studies among the ancient cities of Mexico*, Parts 1 and 2.
1897   Field Museum of Natural History Anthropological Series 1, Chicago.

Jones, M.R.
1952   Map of the ruins of Mayapan, Yucatan, Mexico. *Carnegie Institution of Washington, Current Report* No. 1, Cambridge.

Kurjack, Edward B.
1974a   *Prehistoric Lowland Maya community and social organization, A case study at Dzibilchaltun, Yucatan, Mexico.* Middle American Research Institute Publication No. 31. New Orleans: Tulane University.
1974b   Distribution of Pre-Columbian architecture in Northwestern Yucatan, Mexico. Paper presented at the XLI International Congress of Americanists, Mexico, D.F., September 6.

Kurjack, Edward B., and E.Wyllys Andrews V
1976   Early boundary maintenance in Northwest Yucatan, Mexico. *American Antiquity* 41:318-325.

Leventhal, Richard M.
1974   Cozumel: A functional analysis of structures. Unpublished B.A. Thesis, Department of Anthropology, Harvard College, Cambridge, Massachusetts.

Lothrop, Samuel K.
1924   *Tulum: An archaeological study of the east coast of Yucatan.* Carnegie Institution of Washington Publication No. 335, Washington, D.C.

McBryde, Felix W.
1947   *Cultural and historical geography of Southwest Guatemala.* Smithsonian Institution, Institute of Social Anthropology, Publication No. 4, Washington, D.C.

MacNutt, Francis A.
  1912   *De Obre Novo: The eight decades of Peter Martyr d'Aughera*, Vol. 2. New York: Putnam.
Mason, Gregory R.
  1927   *Silver cities of Yucatan.* New York: Putnam.
  1940   *South of yesterday.* New York: Holt.
Maudslay, Alfred P.
  1908   *True history of the conquest of Mexico* by Bernal Diaz del Castillo, translated by A.P. Maudslay. London: Hakluyt Society, Vol. 1.
  1910   *True history of the conquest of Mexico* by Bernal Diaz del Castillo, translated by A.P. Maudslay. London: Hakluyt Society, Vol. 2.
Means, Philip A.
  1917   History of the Spanish conquest of Yucatan and the Itzas. *Papers of the Peabody Museum of American Archaeology and Ethnology*, Vol. 7. Cambridge: Peabody Museum of Archaeology and Ethnology.
Miles, Sarah W.
  1957   The Sixteenth Century Pokom Maya: A documentary analysis of social structures and archaeological setting. *Transactions of the American Philosophical Society* 47:731-781.
Miller, Arthur G.
  1977   The Maya and the sea: trade and cult at Tancah and Tulum, Quintana Roo, Mexico. In *The Sea in the Pre-Columbian World*, edited by Elizabeth P. Benson. Washington, D.C.: Dumbarton Oaks Research Library and Collection. Pp. 97-140.
Nuttal, Zelia
  1910   The island of sacrifice. *American Anthropologist* 12:257-295.
Pagden, A.R.
  1971   *Hernan Cortes: Letters from Mexico*, translated and edited by A.R. Pagden. New York: Orion Press, Grossman.
Parsons, Lee A.
  1967   *Bilbao, Guatemala: An archaeological study of the Pacific Coast, Cotzumalhuapa Region.* Publications in Anthropology 11. Milwaukee: Milwaukee Public Museum.
Pollock, Henry E.D.
  1936   *Round structures of aboriginal Middle America.* Carnegie Institution of Washington Publication No. 471, Washington, D.C.
  1962   Introduction. In *Mayapan, Yucatan, Mexico.* Carnegie Institution of Washington Publication No. 619, Washington D.C. Pp. 1-22.
  1965   Architecture of the Maya Lowlands. In *Handbook of Middle American Indians*, Vol. 2, edited by R. Wauchope and G.R. Willey. Austin: University of Texas Press. Pp. 378-440.
Pollock, Henry E.D.
  1970   Architectural notes on some Chenes Ruins. In *Monographs and papers in Maya archaeology*, edited by William R. Bullard, Jr. Papers of the Peabody Museum, Vol. 61. Cambridge: Peabody Museum of Archaeology and Ethnology. Pp. 1-87.
Pollock, Henry E.D., Ralph L. Roys, Tatiana Proskouriakoff, and A. Ledyard Smith
  1962   *Mayapan, Yucatan, Mexico.* Carnegie Institution of Washington Publication No. 619, Washington, D.C.
Proskouriakoff, Tatiana
  1962   Civic and religious structures of Mayapan. In *Mayapan, Yucatan, Mexico.* Carnegie Institution of Washington Publication No. 619, Washington, D.C. Pp. 87-164.
Proskouriakoff, Tatiana, and C.R. Temple
  1955   Excavations in a large residence at Mayapan. *Carnegie Institution of Washington, Year Book* 54:271-273.
Rapoport, Amos
  1969   House form and culture. *Foundations of Cultural Geography Series.* Englewood Cliffs, New Jersey: Prentice Hall.
Rathje, William L.
  1972   Praise the gods and pass the metates: A hypothesis of the development of lowland rain forest civilizations in

Middle America. In *Contemporary Archaeology*, edited by M.P. Leone. Carbondale: Southern Illinois University Press. Pp. 365-392.

1975   Last Tango at Mayapan: A tentative trajectory of production-distribution systems. In *Ancient civilization and trade*, edited by Jeremy A. Sabloff and C.C. Lamberg-Karlovsky. School of American Research Book. Albuquerque: University of New Mexico Press. Pp. 409-448.

Rathje, William L., and David A. Philips
1975   The Ruins of Buena Vista. In *A study of changing Pre-Columbian commercial systems: The 1972-1973 seasons at Cozumel, Mexico*, edited by Jeremy A. Sabloff and William Rathje. Monographs of the Peabody Museum No. 3. Cambridge: Peabody Museum of Archaeology and Ethnology. Pp. 77-86.

Rathje, William L., and Jeremy A. Sabloff
1973   Ancient Maya commercial systems: A research design for the Island of Cozumel, Mexico. *World Archaeology* 5:221-231.
1975   Theoretical background: General models and questions. In *A study of changing Pre-Columbian commercial systems: The 1972-1973 seasons at Cozumel, Mexico*, edited by Jeremy A. Sabloff and William L. Rathje. Monographs of the Peabody Museum No. 3. Cambridge: Peabody Museum of Archaeology and Ethnology. Pp. 6-20.

Rathje, William L., Jeremy A. Sabloff,
and David A. Gregory
1973   El descubrimiento de un jade Olmeca en la Isla de Cozumel. *Estudios de Cultura Maya* 9:85-92.

Redfield, Robert, and Alfonso Villa Rojas
1971   *Chan Kom: A Maya village*. Chicago: University of Chicago Press. (Reprint of 1934 publication.)

Roys, Ralph L.
1933   *The book of Chilam Balam of Chumayel*. Carnegie Institution of Washington Publication No. 438, Washington, D.C.
1939   *The titles of Ebtun*. Carnegie Institution of Washington Publication No. 505, Washington, D.C.
1943   *The Indian background of Colonial Yucatan*. Carnegie Institution of Washington Publication No. 548, Washington, D.C.
1957   *The political geography of the Yucatan Maya*. Carnegie Institution of Washington Publication No. 613, Washington, D.C.
1962   Literary sources for the history of Mayapan. In *Mayapan, Yucatan, Mexico*. Carnegie Institution of Washington Publication No. 619. Washington, D.C. Pp. 25-86.

Roys, Ralph L., Frances V. Scholes,
and Eleanor B. Adams
1940   *Report and census of the Indians of Cozumel 1570*. Carnegie Institution of Washington Publication No. 523, Contribution 30, Washington, D.C.

Sabloff, Jeremy A.
1978   Review of The Origins of Maya Civilization, edited by R.E.W. Adams. *Journal of Anthropological Research* 34:154:155.

Sabloff, Jeremy A., and David A. Freidel
1975   A model of a Pre-Columbian trading center. In *Ancient civilization and trade*, edited by Jeremy A. Sabloff and C.C. Lamberg-Karlovsky. A School of American Research Book. Albuquerque: University of New Mexico Press. Pp. 369-408.

Sabloff, Jeremy A., and William L. Rathje
1975a   The rise of a Maya merchant class. *Scientific American* 233(4):73-82.

Sabloff, Jeremy A., and William L. Rathje, editors
1975b   *A study of changing Pre-Columbian commercial systems: The 1972-1973 seasons at Cozumel, Mexico*. Monographs of the Peabody Museum No. 3. Cambridge: Peabody Museum of Archaeology and Ethnology.

Sabloff, Jeremy A., and Gordon R. Willey
1967   The collapse of Maya civilization in the Southern Lowlands: A consideration of history and process. *South-*

western Journal of Anthropology 23: 311-336.

Sabloff, Paula L.W.
1975   Changing patterns of dwelling distribution (1847-1972). In *A study of changing Pre-Columbian commercial systems: The 1972-1973 seasons at Cozumel, Mexico.* Monographs of the Peabody Museum No. 3. Cambridge: Peabody Museum of Archaeology and Ethnology. Pp. 29-46.

Sahlins, Marshall
1972   *Stone Age economics.* Chicago: Aldine.

Sanders, William T.
1955   An archaeological reconnaissance of Northern Quintana Roo. *Carnegie Institution of Washington Current Report* No. 24, Washington, D.C.

1960   *Prehistoric ceramics and settlement patterns in Quintana Roo, Mexico.* Carnegie Institution of Washington Publication 606, Contribution 60, Washington, D.C.

1963   Cultural ecology of the Maya Lowlands, Part 2. *Estudios de Cultura Maya* 3:203-241.

Scholes, Frances V., and Ralph L. Roys
1948   *The Maya Chontal Indians of Acalan-Tixchel.* Carnegie Institution of Washington Publication No. 560, Washington, D.C.

Seimans, A.A., and Dennis E. Puleston
1972   Ridged fields and associated features in Southern Campeche: New perspectives on the Lowland Maya. *American Antiquity* 37:228-239.

Simpson, L.B.
1966   *Cortes: The life of the conqueror by his secretary Francisco Lopez de Gomara,* translated and edited by L.B. Simpson. Berkeley: University of California Press.

Smith, A. Ledyard
1950   *Uaxactun, Guatemala: Excavations of 1931-1937.* Carnegie Institution of Washington Publication No. 588, Washington, D.C.

1962   Residential and associated structures at Mayapan. In *Mayapan, Yucatan,*

Mexico. Carnegie Institution of Washington Publication No. 619, Washington, D.C. Pp. 165-320.

Smith, R.E.
1971   *The pottery of Mayapan.* Papers of the Peabody Museum, Vol. 66. Cambridge: Peabody Museum of Archaeology and Ethnology.

Steggerda, M.
1941   *Maya Indians of Yucatan.* Carnegie Institution of Washington Publication No. 531, Washington, D.C.

Stephens, John L.
1843   *Incidents of travel in Yucatan.* New York: Murray.

Strong, W.D., Alfred V. Kidder, II, and A.J.D. Paul
1938   *Preliminary report on the Smithsonian Institution-Harvard University archaeological expedition to Northwestern Honduras, 1936.* Smithsonian Miscellaneous Collections Vol. 97, No. 1, Washington, D.C.

Thompson, J. Eric S.
1938   The Sixteenth and Seventeenth Century reports on the Chol Mayas. *American Anthropologist* 40:584-604.

1957   Deities portrayed on censers at Mayapan. *Carnegie Institution of Washington, Current Report* 40, Cambridge.

1966   *The rise and fall of Maya Civilization.* Norman: University of Oklahoma Press. (Revised edition.)

1970   *Maya history and religion.* Norman: University of Oklahoma Press.

Thompson, J. Eric S., Henry E.D. Pollock, and Jean Charlot
1932   *A preliminary study of the ruins of Coba, Quintana Roo, Mexico.* Carnegie Institution of Washington Publication No. 424, Washington, D.C.

Tozzer, Alfred M.
1928   Mexican and Toltec figures at Chichen Itza. *Proceedings of the 23rd International Congress of Americanists.* New York. Pp. 155-164.

1941   *Landa's Relacion de las Cosas de Yucatan,* edited by A.M. Tozzer. Papers of the Peabody Museum of Archaeology and Ethnology, Vol. 18.

Cambridge: Peabody Museum of Archaeology and Ethnology.

Trigger, Bruce G.
1973   The future of archaeology is the past. In *Research and current theory in archaeology*, edited by Charles Redman. New York: Wiley. Pp. 95-112.

Turner, B.L.
1974   Prehistoric intensive agriculture in the Maya Lowlands. *Science* 185: 118-124.

Turner, Victor
1974   *Fields, dramas and metaphors.* Ithaca: Cornell University Press.

Vance, James E., Jr.
1970   *The merchants world: The geography of wholesaling.* Foundations of Economic Geography Series. Englewood Cliffs, New Jersey: Prentice-Hall.

Villa Rojas, Alfonso
1934   *The Yaxuna-Coba causeway.* Carnegie Institution of Washington Publication No. 436, Contribution to American Archaeology No. 9, Washington, D.C.
1945   *The Maya of East Central Quintana Roo.* Carnegie Institution of Washington Publication No. 559, Washington, D.C.
1969   The Maya of Yucatan. In *Handbook of Middle American Indians*, Vol. 7, edited by Evon Z. Vogt. Austin: University of Texas Press. Pp. 244-275.

Vogt, Evon Z.
1968   *Some aspects of Zinacantan settlement patterns and ceremonial organization.* In *Settlement archaeology*, edited by K.C. Chang. Palo Alto, California: National Press Books. Pp. 154-175.

1969   *Zinacantan: A Maya community in the Highlands of Chiapas.* Cambridge: Belknap Press of Harvard University.

Wagner, Henry R.
1942a   *The discovery of New Spain in 1518 by Juan de Grijalva*, translated and edited by H.R. Wagner. Pasadena, California: Cortes Society, Val Treiz Press.
1942b   *The Discovery of Yucatan by Francisco Hernandez de Cordoba*, translated and edited by H.R. Wagner. Pasadena, California: Cortes Society, Val Treiz Press.

Wallace, Henry
1978   The strange case of the panucho plugs: Evidence of Pre-Columbian agriculture on Cozumel. Unpublished manuscript, Department of Anthropology, University of Arizona.

Wauchope, Robert
1938   *Modern Maya houses: A study of their archaeological significance.* Carnegie Institution of Washington Publication No. 502, Washington, D.C.
1940   Domestic architecture of the Maya. In *The Maya and their neighbors*, edited by C.L. Hay *et al.* New York: Appleton Century. Pp. 232-241.

Willey, Gordon R., William R. Bullard, Jr., John B. Glass, and James C. Gifford
1965   *Prehistoric Maya settlements in the Belize Valley.* Papers of the Peabody Museum of Archaeology and Ethnology, Vol. 54. Cambridge: Peabody Museum of Archaeology and Ethnology.

Wisdom, Charles
1940   *The Chorti Indians of Guatemala.* Chicago: University of Chicago Press.

Index

STUDIES IN ARCHAEOLOGY

Consulting Editor: Stuart Struever

Department of Anthropology
Northwestern University
Evanston, Illinois

Charles R. McGimsey III. **Public Archeology**

Lewis R. Binford. **An Archaeological Perspective**

Joseph W. Michels. **Dating Methods in Archaeology**

C. Garth Sampson. **The Stone Age Archaeology of Southern Africa**

Fred T. Plog. **The Study of Prehistoric Change**

Patty Jo Watson (Ed.). **Archaeology of the Mammoth Cave Area**

George C. Frison (Ed.). **The Casper Site: A Hell Gap Bison Kill on the High Plains**

W. Raymond Wood and R. Bruce McMillan (Eds.). **Prehistoric Man and His Environments: A Case Study in the Ozark Highland**

Kent V. Flannery (Ed.). **The Early Mesoamerican Village**

Charles E. Cleland (Ed.). **Cultural Change and Continuity: Essays in Honor of James Bennett Griffin**

Michael B. Schiffer. **Behavioral Archeology**

Fred Wendorf and Romuald Schild. **Prehistory of the Nile Valley**

Michael A. Jochim. **Hunter-Gatherer Subsistence and Settlement: A Predictive Model**

Stanley South. **Method and Theory in Historical Archeology**

Timothy K. Earle and Jonathon E. Ericson (Eds.). **Exchange System in Prehistory**

Stanley South (Ed.). **Research Strategies in Historical Archeology**

John E. Yellen. **Archaeological Approaches to the Present: Models for Reconstructing the Past**

Lewis R. Binford (Ed.). **For Theory Building in Archaeology: Essays on Faunal Remains, Aquatic Resources, Spatial Analysis, and Systemic Modeling**

James N. Hill and Joel Gunn (Eds.). **The Individual in Prehistory: Studies of Variability in Style in Prehistoric Technologies**

Michael B. Schiffer and George J. Gumerman (Eds.). **Conservation Archaeology: A Guide for Cultural Resource Management Studies**

Thomas F. King, Patricia Parker Hickman, and Gary Berg. **Anthropology in Historic Preservation: Caring for Culture's Clutter**

Richard E. Blanton. **Monte Albán: Settlement Patterns at the Ancient Zapotec Capital**

R. E. Taylor and Clement W. Meighan. **Chronologies in New World Archaeology**

Bruce D. Smith. **Prehistoric Patterns of Human Behavior: A Case Study in the Mississippi Valley**

Barbara L. Stark and Barbara Voorhies (Eds.). **Prehistoric Coastal Adaptations: The Economy and Ecology of Maritime Middle America**

Charles L. Redman, Mary Jane Berman, Edward V. Curtin, William T. Langhorne, Nina M. Versaggi, and Jeffery C. Wanser (Eds.). **Social Archeology: Beyond Subsistence and Dating**

Bruce D. Smith (Ed.). **Mississippian Settlement Patterns**

Lewis R. Binford. **Nunamiut Ethnoarchaeology**

J. Barto Arnold III and Robert Weddle. **The Nautical Archeology of Padre Island: The Spanish Shipwrecks of 1554**

Sarunas Milisauskas. **European Prehistory**

Brian Hayden (Ed.). **Lithic Use-Wear Analysis**

William T. Sanders, Jeffrey R. Parsons, and Robert S. Santley. **The Basin of Mexico: Ecological Processes in the Evolution of a Civilization**

David L. Clarke. **Analytical Archaeologist: Collected Papers of David L. Clarke. Edited and Introduced by His Colleagues**

Arthur E. Spiess. **Reindeer and Caribou Hunters: An Archaeological Study**

Elizabeth S. Wing and Antoinette B. Brown. **Paleonutrition: Method and Theory in Prehistoric Foodways**

John W. Rick. **Prehistoric Hunters of the High Andes**

Timothy K. Earle and Andrew L. Christenson (Eds.). **Modeling Change in Prehistoric Economics**

Thomas F. Lynch (Ed.). **Guitarrero Cave: Early Man in the Andes**

Fred Wendorf and Romuald Schild. **Prehistory of the Eastern Sahara**

Henri Laville, Jean-Philippe Rigaud, and James Sackett. **Rock Shelters of the Perigord: Stratigraphy and Archaeological Succession**

Duane C. Anderson and Holmes A. Semken, Jr. (Eds.). **The Cherokee Excavations: Holocene Ecology and Human Adaptations in Northwestern Iowa**

Anna Curtenius Roosevelt. **Parmana: Prehistoric Maize and Manioc Subsistence along the Amazon and Orinoco**

Fekri A. Hassan. **Demographic Archaeology**

G. Barker. **Landscape and Society: Prehistoric Central Italy**

Lewis R. Binford. **Bones: Ancient Men and Modern Myths**

Richard A. Gould and Michael B. Schiffer (Eds.). **Modern Material Culture: The Archaeology of Us**

Muriel Porter Weaver. **The Aztecs, Maya, and Their Predecessors: Archaeology of Mesoamerica, 2nd edition**

Arthur S. Keene. **Prehistoric Foraging in a Temperate Forest: A Linear Programming Model**

Ross H. Cordy. **A Study of Prehistoric Social Change: The Development of Complex Societies in the Hawaiian Islands**

C. Melvin Aikens and Takayasu Higuchi. **Prehistory of Japan**

Kent V. Flannery (Ed.). **Maya Subsistence: Studies in Memory of Dennis E. Puleston**

Dean R. Snow (Ed.). **Foundations of Northeast Archaeology**

Charles S. Spencer. **The Cuicatlán Cañada and Monte Albán: A Study of Primary State Formation**

Steadman Upham. **Polities and Power: An Economic and Political History of the Western Pueblo**

Carol Kramer. **Village Ethnoarchaeology: Rural Iran in Archaeological Perspective**

Michael J. O'Brien, Robert E. Warren, and Dennis E. Lewarch (Eds.). **The Cannon Reservoir Human Ecology Project: An Archaeological Study of Cultural Adaptations in the Southern Prairie Peninsula**

Jonathon E. Ericson and Timothy K. Earle (Eds.). **Contexts for Prehistoric Exchange**

Merrilee H. Salmon. **Philosophy and Archaeology**

Vincas P. Steponaitis. **Ceramics, Chronology, and Community Patterns: An Archaeological Study at Moundville**

George C. Frison and Dennis J. Stanford. **The Agate Basin Site: A Record of the Paleoindian Occupation of the Northwestern High Plains**

James A. Moore and Arthur S. Keene (Eds.). **Archaeological Hammers and Theories**

Lewis R. Binford. **Working at Archaeology**

William J. Folan, Ellen R. Kintz, and Laraine A. Fletcher. **Coba: A Classic Maya Metropolis**

David A. Freidel and Jeremy A. Sabloff. **Cozumel: Late Maya Settlement Patterns**

in preparation

Lewis R. Binford. **Faunal Remains From Klasies River Mouth**

John M. O'Shea. **Mortuary Variability: An Archaeological Investigation**

Robert I. Gilbert, Jr. and James H. Mielke (Eds.). **The Analysis of Prehistoric Diets**